# *Zen Wisdom*

Additional books by Chan Master Sheng-yen

Complete Enlightenment

Dharma Drum—The life and heart of
   Ch'an practice

Faith in Mind

Getting the Buddha Mind

Hoofprint of the Ox

Illuminating Silence

Infinite Mirror

The Poetry of Enlightenment—Poems by
   Ancient Ch'an Masters

Subtle Wisdom

The Sword of Wisdom

There Is No Suffering

# Zen Wisdom

## Chan Master Sheng-yen

North Atlantic Books
Berkeley, California

Dharma Drum Publications
Elmhurst, New York

Published by
Dharma Drum Publications
90-56 Corona Avenue
Elmhurst, New York 11373
    and
North Atlantic Books
P.O. Box 12327
Berkeley, California 94712

Cover design by Chih-Ching Lee
Text design by Trish Ing

Printed in the United States of America

*Zen Wisdom* is sponsored by the Society for the Study of Native Arts and Sciences, a non-profit educational corporation whose goals are to develop an educational and crosscultural perspective linking various scientific, social, and artistic fields; to nurture a holistic view of arts, sciences, humanities, and healing; and to publish and distribute literature on the relationship of mind, body, and nature.

Library of Congress Cataloging-in-Publication Data
Shengyan, 1930-
    Zen wisdom / by Master Sheng-yen.
            p.        cm.
ISBN 1-55643-386-7 (pbk.)
1. Spiritual life--Zen Buddhism.  I.  Title.

BQ9288 .S519 2001
294.3'927--dc21

                                           2001044748

# Contents

# *Introduction*

Shortly after I came to the United States from Taiwan and began guiding Westerners in the practice of Chan (Chinese Zen), students of mine decided to publish *Chan Magazine*, a quarterly journal of Buddhist ideas. Eventually, one of the regular features in the magazine became *Dharma View,* consisting of my extemporaneous answers to questions relating to Buddhism, posed by members of the Chan Center. The first question was "What is the Buddhist idea of self?" Perhaps I could have answered in one sentence, and if I had, *Dharma View* would have died right there, but I decided to answer in more detail. Since then, many questions have been asked on an array of topics. We have compiled these *Dharma View* articles into *Zen Wisdom*, whose aim is to help others who have similar questions, to find some answers and some guidance.

The ideas in *Zen Wisdom* are consistent with Buddhist tradition, as much of the Dharma (Buddhist 'law' or teaching) has been expounded for two millennia through dialogue between teacher and disciples. In the sutras the Buddha would respond to questions asked by disciples and bodhisattvas, for the sake of others. Chan masters have always opened themselves to disciples' probing questions regarding practice and understanding. Curiosity and skepticism are not exclusive to the modern era. Even during the Buddha's time, many people could not immediately and unquestioningly accept all of his teachings. It is normal for people to be skeptical. Moreover, some things are hard, or even impossible, to understand without direct experience.

Some of my students requested that I explain Buddhadharma (the Buddha's teaching of the Dharma) more fully. This was good, for to accept on faith everything I say can be problematical. Miscommunication can occur even when people share the same language, training, and culture. Imagine how much more room for error exists when a Chinese monk from Taiwan holds classes attended largely by English-speaking lay people! Therefore, if students do not question me, they may end up misinformed. Fortunately, my students did question me. Not being clear about some of my answers, they asked me for clarification, to give examples, and to not leave things so seemingly mystical or abstract. For this I am grateful to them because the more I am asked to clearly explain myself, the better it is for everyone.

Usually the questions and the discussions that followed were spontaneous. Class would begin with meditation. After the sitting period, the editor of *Dharma View* would begin the dialogue with a question on a specific topic. Sometimes a question would be asked on the spot. Other times I would be told in advance what the topic would be.

Appearing in *Chan Magazine* over several years, the articles have been organized into two sections—

*Buddhadharma* and *Practice and Daily Life.* Whereas the section on Buddhadharma more or less deals with questions about Buddhist concepts and teachings, the section on practice focuses more on application of the teachings to practice and daily life. These are not mutually exclusive groupings, and there is much overlapping. Each article is an entity unto itself, although some are related. The articles are not ordered chronologically, but according to editorial considerations. As such, this book need not be read straight through or in order.

We have not tried to address every subject germane to Buddhism, but I hope these dialogues will help answer some readers' questions. I am sure they will raise more questions, and that some will disagree with my answers. That is all to the good. To remain dynamic, Buddhism needs to be scrutinized. My ideas are not written in stone. I am a Buddhist monk humbly offering some of his insights to those who have questions. If this book answers some of your questions, or clarifies some confusion, or inspires you to practice Chan, my wishes have been met.

I am neither omniscient nor am I expert on Western culture. I am a Buddhist monk who has received transmission in two Chan lineages: Caodong (Jap. Soto) and Linji (Jap. Rinzai). 'Transmission' means that my masters have confirmed my practice experiences. I have a doctorate in Buddhist literature and have published on Buddhism in Chinese and English. I do not claim my answers are the ultimate truth. However, the principles of Chan transcend time and space. Thus, the answers to these questions were already in the West. While my answers derive from a lifetime of study and training, I am confident they do not contradict Buddhadharma.

The principles of Buddhadharma are universal, yet many outer aspects of Buddhism have changed as it has spread across the world. The Dharma has evolved along with humans and history, and this is fine and natural. The Dharma is not the enlightened state. The universal truths of Buddhism cannot be taught or intellectually learned. The Dharma's aim is to point the way to a better way of living, to enlightenment and liberation. But so often people attach to the words and manner in which the Dharma is expressed. It is like taking a finger pointing to the moon to be the moon itself!

Some people believe that Chan is somehow separate from Buddhism. Chan *is* Buddhism. It is one approach, among many, to the practice of Buddhadharma. Sometimes it may seem from the way I talk that Chan and Buddhism are different, and if this causes confusion, I apologize. There are many paths and many levels in Buddhism. However, the path of Chan is noted for its austere, direct approach. Free of adornment, perhaps Chan seems like something other than Buddhism, but it is not so. I hope this clears up any misunderstanding, if it existed.

I apologize if I mislead or offend anyone by my answers and opinions, but I do not apologize for the answers themselves. I said what I believe to be true. Also, a limitation of the English language stems from the fact that there is no neuter pronoun that adequately represents both males and females. The editors have tried to eliminate most gender-specific renderings; however, such manipulations can sometimes be awkward and cumbersome. When gender-specific pronouns do occur, our sincere intent is to include both genders.

Buddhism too has been accused of gender discrimination. I cannot speak for everyone in the long lineage of Buddhist teachers, but cultures and times are in a constant state of change. In the United States, Buddhism will become flavored and influenced by some of its values. I see this movement toward gender equality as being a long overdue, positive step, and it will be an improvement for Buddhism.

Finally, in these sessions, my answers are indicated as being spoken by "Shifu." This is simply the Chinese honorific for "teacher."

This second edition of *Zen Wisdom* differs from the first edition primarily in the ordering of the articles, and in some pruning of the articles to meet space constraints.

## *Acknowledgments*

Many people have helped to make this book a reality. Some wish to remain anonymous, so I will honor their wishes. First, I thank Ming Yee Wang and Guo-gu Bhikshu who very ably interpreted the dialogues as I spoke. Next are the transcribers who diligently converted the many taped discussions to digital format—primarily Dorothy Weiner and Echo Bonner. Ernest Heau and Chris Marano edited the trascriptions, first for *Chan Magazine*, and then for *Zen Wisdom*. They received editorial assistance from Alan Rubinstein, Harry Miller, and Linda Peer. Trish Ing did the book's typography, layout, and design. The cover was designed by Chih-Ching Lee. Iris Wang's efforts to bring this book to publication are much appreciated. I apologize

to anyone I have unintentionally left out. I thank my
students who asked all the questions, especially those who
were not satisfied with my replies.


Ven. Master Sheng-yen
New York, 2001

*Part One*

*Buddhadharma*

# *What Does it Mean to be a Buddhist?*

QUESTION   When people ask me what it means to be a Buddhist, I am usually at a loss for words. If I say that I am Buddhist, or that I believe in Buddhism, what does that mean?

SHIFU   A simple answer would be that Buddhism is what Shakyamuni Buddha taught his disciples. It includes philosophical concepts as well as methods of practice. Therefore, a Buddhist is one who practices according to the Buddha's teachings, the essence of which are the Four Noble Truths and the Noble Eightfold Path. People who sincerely follow these principles and who succeed in completing the Path will perfect their personalities and attain liberation. Generally, the practice includes three major endeavors: keeping the precepts, cultivating samadhi (meditative concentration), and realizing wisdom. A Buddhist should strive to master all three aspects.

The external form of Buddhism has three elements: the Buddha, the Dharma, and the Sangha. The Buddha is Shakyamuni, the historical Buddha for this Dharma age. The Dharma is the doctrine of the Buddha, his teachings and methods. The Sangha is the Buddhist community. The Sangha is not only the monks and nuns that make up the community of homeleavers; it also includes lay practitioners. Although Buddhism places monks and nuns at the core of the Sangha, with lay practitioners serving as an outer framework, the left-home community could not exist and perform its functions without the lay community. Without the structure created by these elements, Buddhism could not exist. For this reason, the Buddha, the Dharma, and the Sangha are called the Three Jewels.

A lay Buddhist, therefore, is a member of the Sangha. Lay practice of precepts, samadhi, and wisdom is part of the Dharma, and is included in the Noble Eightfold Path. The Noble Eightfold Path contains principles that all Buddhists, lay and monastic, aspire to follow, and include: right understanding, right thought, right speech, right action, right livelihood, right effort, right mindfulness, and right concentration.

If you adhere to the precepts, practice samadhi, and acquire wisdom, and you conduct your life according to the teachings and concepts of the Buddha, then you can call yourself a Buddhist. Even if you are not fully immersed in Buddhism, but you have the desire to follow Buddhadharma, you may consider yourself a Buddhist. It is difficult to embrace every facet of Buddhism completely, instantly, and with enthusiasm. It is a gradual process. But if you intend to walk the Buddha Path, and your intentions and desires are pure, then you can call yourself a Buddhist. On the other hand, if you do not understand even the basic teachings of Shakyamuni Buddha, and cannot practice the methods, or follow the precepts, you should not regard yourself as a Buddhist.

Let's talk in more detail about precepts, samadhi, and wisdom. The precepts are common moral principles. In Buddhism there are many precepts, but those that are shared by all members of the Sangha are five in number: not killing, not stealing, not engaging in sexual misconduct, not lying, and abstaining from alcohol and addictive drugs. I do not wish to explain them at this point [See chapter on The Five Precepts]. Suffice to say that a Buddhist should try to uphold the five precepts, especially the first—no killing.

Samadhi, in its most general sense, means mental discipline. There are many levels of samadhi, and there are even more methods of practice one can use to enter samadhi. A true Buddhist should practice at least one of these methods.

Wisdom, like samadhi, has many levels. One can gain wisdom through hearing the Dharma (from a monk, nun, master, or lay practitioner), reading sutras and sastras, practicing samadhi, or just by keeping the precepts. The simplest way of acquiring wisdom is through hearing the Dharma. An intellectual understanding of the Buddha's concepts and principles is important. A Buddhist should have begun at least this level of training.

It is not hard to be a Buddhist. If you are involved with all or even part of what I have just described, then you are a Buddhist. As long as you have a basic understanding of Buddhadharma and are willing to practice, that is sufficient. You do not have to be perfect. If you were, you would be a buddha. Probably everyone here, for instance, is a Buddhist. Otherwise, why would you travel to this Center, interrupt your daily schedule and listen to what I am saying?

The only other thing I will add is that one can explicitly make a commitment to follow the Buddhist path by taking refuge with a qualified teacher. Taking refuge consists of a short and simple ceremony in which one recites the following lines:

> I take refuge in the Buddha.
> I take refuge in the Dharma.
> I take refuge in the Sangha.

These lines simply declare your intention to follow the Buddha's teachings on the Dharma, and that you recognize the Sangha as your place of refuge in the teachings.

STUDENT   As a lay practitioner, I do not feel like a true Buddhist. I feel that only monks and nuns are truly Buddhists.

SHIFU   You should not feel that way. You should not think that left-home practitioners are true Buddhists and that you are a pseudo-Buddhist. You are all true Buddhists. In Shakyamuni's time, there were many left-home disciples, but there were many more lay practitioners. The same is true today.

In the Hinayana path, there are four levels of attainment of the arhat—stream enterer, once-returner, non-returner, and finally, arhat. I will not discuss these right now except to say that ordinary practitioners can attain the first three levels. After that, they will naturally lose their worldly desires, become monks, nuns, or full-time lay practitioners, and strive for arhatship, ultimately realizing nirvana. In the Mahayana path, bodhisattvas may manifest as any of these types, and there have been many famous lay Buddhists in the Mahayana tradition.

I think I know why you are puzzled. If both left-home practitioners and lay practitioners are true Buddhists, then what is the need for monks and nuns? It is a matter of commitment. Lay practitioners have the extra responsibility of family life. They are susceptible to all the distractions and problems that a family and society create. They are not able to devote their full energy and strength to the practice. A monk or nun, on the other hand, can concentrate fully on the practice, as well as spreading the Dharma.

STUDENT   At times you have said there is no difference between the Buddhist point of view and the Chan point of view. At other times you make a distinction between conventional Buddhism and Chan Buddhism. There are many different sects of Buddhism. Are there radical differences among the sects, or are they fundamentally the same?

SHIFU   Actually, more sects of Buddhism existed in the past than exist today. The seeds for the many sects were planted in Shakyamuni's time. The seeds were actually Shakyamuni's closest followers, who propagated his teachings. Each disciple approached the practice in his own special way, depending on his personality and talents. Ananda was interested in hearing the Buddha's teachings. Mahakasyapa was interested in ascetic practice. Upali's specialty was keeping the precepts. Others specialized in debating, or cultivating supernormal powers. Variations existed right from the start.

When various Dharma masters introduced Buddhism into China using certain sutras and sastras, different sects developed as a result. There were different forms of practice, each one appealing to a particular interest. Before the Tang dynasty (618-907), there were many Buddhist sects in China, but by the end of that dynasty, the methods of practice had reduced mainly to those taught by the Chan and Pure Land schools.

Is there a great difference between Chan and Pure Land? There is in Japan. Chan and Pure Land were transmitted to Japan from China just as Buddhism was transmitted to China from India. In the process, changes occurred, and the sects that emerged in Japan were flavored by the distinctive personalities of the particular Dharma masters who founded them. So, in Japan, Chan and Pure Land are distinctively different schools.

In Korea, Pure Land does not even exist. There are a few philosophical schools, such as Huayan and Tiantai Buddhism, but the only method of practice in Korea is Son (Chan). When Japanese and Korean Buddhists look at China, they wonder how Chan and Pure Land can coexist so harmoniously. Actually, Chan and Pure Land developed together in China. During the Tang dynasty they were distinct schools, but by the end of the Song dynasty, Chan and Pure land had blended together. Today, Pure Land Buddhists use Chan methods, just as Chan teachers are not opposed to Pure Land methods.

In fact, the term 'Pure Land' did not exist in Chan history until recently. It was borrowed, ironically, from Japan. Up until then, people who used Pure Land methods referred to themselves as the Lotus School. Since that school holds that every buddha sits on a lotus blossom, any buddha's name was acceptable in the practice. Since Amitabha is the only buddha whose name is recited as a practice, the method is called 'reciting Amitabha's name.' However, in the past the Chinese referred to it as the 'Dharma method of reciting the Buddha's name,' because they were not limited to Amitabha Buddha.

Some say today that Chan has disappeared from China. I do not agree. Buddhism remains there. Buddhist practice cannot be separated from Chan. If in practicing Pure Land you reach a level of one-mindedness, where there are no wandering thoughts, it is the same as attaining the concentrated mind of Chan.

In Chan there are sudden and gradual methods. After reaching one-mindedness, typically by a gradual method such as reciting Amitabha Buddha's name, a person can be given a question, or *huatou*, by the master, in order to raise the doubt sensation. At this point, practice shifts from the gradual to the sudden method.

In Chan, there is a saying: "Great doubt leads to great enlightenment, small doubt leads to small enlightenment, no doubt leads to no enlightenment." There is no guarantee of enlightenment, even if you practice diligently for a long time. Although the effort is never a waste of time, many people lack the faith and determination to pursue sudden methods. For these people, Pure Land Buddhism is very good. At least you have a chance of attaining the Pure Land. For this reason, Pure Land is a good expedient method for those who cannot practice with the vigor demanded by Chan.

This is not to say that Pure Land practitioners cannot reach deep levels, the most profound being to experience the Pure Land everywhere. This is the Pure Land of the mind, where practitioners realize that their nature is also Amitabha

Buddha's nature. This is not different from Chan enlightenment.

From the viewpoint of sentient beings, there are differences among the schools of Chan, just as there are differences between Chan and Pure Land. But from the Buddha's point of view, all Buddhist methods are the same. All paths lead to the same goal, so all methods are Buddhist practice, and all teachings which accord with the Dharma are Buddhist teachings.

# Sentient Beings

QUESTION   What is a sentient being?

SHIFU   The Chinese term for sentient being includes all forms of life, but Buddhism defines sentient beings as life forms that have sensation. Life forms can be sentient, such as human beings and animals, or non-sentient, such as grass and trees. However, because life forms include both sentient and non-sentient beings, people are confused. They may believe that humans can be reborn as plants or that the precept of not killing applies to plants as well as to animals.

Some traditions that believe in reincarnation do say that the transmigration of humans can include non-sentient beings, for instance, that a human being can be reborn as a tree. However, according to Buddhist philosophy, transmigration, or samsara, does not include non-sentient beings; that is to say, sentient beings are not reborn as non-sentient beings, and non-sentient beings do not become sentient.

Transmigration occurs in the human, animal and spirit realms only. Sentient beings continue in samsara, the cycle of birth and death, because of their attachment to the self.

I will explain 'sentient beings' from the perspectives of physical form and the presence of sensations. Living things can be classified according to four criteria of physical form. First, there are beings with a simple cellular structure. Second, there are beings having a nervous system comprised of living cells. Third, there are beings with memory. Fourth, there are beings capable of thought and reason. The highest level of animals, including humans, includes all four characteristics.

It is important to state that we can use different criteria to explain and categorize phenomena. For example, modern biology classifies humans as being members of the animal kingdom, using criteria grounded primarily in materiality (anatomy and physiology). Buddhism does not dispute this, but Buddhist philosophy uses criteria that also include spiritual principles such as karma. In this model, humans and animals are in separate realms.

The next level of animals possesses only three of the four characteristics—they lack the ability to think and reason. Thinking necessitates having symbols—one needs a language with which to think. Thinking also includes abstract reasoning, predicting future outcomes, solving problems, etc. At this point and on this planet, only human beings appear to have these capabilities in large measure.

Some animal species may have developed a crude symbolic language. The higher primates, dolphins, and dogs seem capable of understanding human language to certain degrees. These animals have developed an ability to think, but not nearly to the extent that humans can.

Having a memory means that an organism can store experiences for later use, as well as having the potential to retain and use symbols, a prerequisite for language. Memory, however, is not the only requirement for reasoning and language. One must also have the ability to recall experiences and string them together to form new abstract thoughts, such as discriminating between good and bad. Without reasoning, there is no foresight, or the ability to use experiences to create something useful in the future. Memory and reasoning are needed together for this to happen.

In addition to animals, there are spiritual sentient beings. They include spirits in the human realm and the heavenly realm, deities in the human realm and the heavenly realms, and also sages, buddhas, and bodhisattvas in the Pure Land.

STUDENT   Aren't the criteria for animals rather subjective? How do we really know how intelligent other animals are? How do we know if their languages are simple or complex?

SHIFU   It depends on what you mean by intelligent. In order to be placed alongside humans in thinking capacity, animals must be able to make moral judgments. Many animals have varying memory capacities, but no other animals use language to the extent and with the complexity that humans do. Some animals think on a rudimentary level. Chimpanzees, for example, are able to plan on a primitive level, and they exhibit other complex behavior. Again, however, their behavior is not nearly as complex as humans.

Furthermore, there are no sharp lines that separate one species from another. The borders that separate sentient beings according to the four criteria are gray and fuzzy.

Nonetheless, among all animals, humans are most evolved in the areas of memory and reasoning.

I read an interesting news story in Taiwan. An old woman owned a few dogs. There was a fire at her home and she died. One of her dogs had the opportunity to escape the fire, but it stayed behind with its master; it too died. At her funeral, one of her other dogs tried time and again to jump into the grave. Several people had to restrain it. Afterward, the dog refused to eat and it died as well. The old woman also had children. Soon after her death, they began quarreling over the property she left behind. The newspapers commented that the dogs were more dignified and remorseful than the humans were. From the human perspective, the dogs seemed to have more compassion than the people, and their behavior morally superior.

However, this is not the case; dogs do not think and act with the complexity that people do. These particular dogs remembered the old lady being nice to them and they experienced grief when she died. True, the woman's children did not act nobly, and one may think that the dogs were superior, but those are judgments based on a sense of morality and justice. Were the dogs making moral judgments and thinking logically? Dogs do not ponder what should or should not be done; they do what they do. If it is thinking, it is thinking governed by instinct and habit. Humans, on the other hand, make moral judgments. When humans display immoral behavior, we say it is bad. The fact that human beings can reason and make such judgments demonstrates that their mental functions are of a higher order than that of other animals.

Thus far we have spoken about higher life forms, those with memory at least, and others with the ability to think.

There are many more animals and life forms that do not have the capacity to think and remember. Some sentient organisms only have primitive nervous systems and living cells. Finally, there are life forms that have only cells. Such organisms are not sentient. These are the plants, fungi, and one-celled organisms.

Some argue that we are always killing; we kill plants to eat, and we kill numberless microscopic organisms that we cannot even see. Plants and bacteria are life forms, but not having nervous systems, or the ability to feel pain, they are not sentient. By Buddhist criteria, you cannot compare plants to sentient beings.

A sentient being with a nervous system can experience pain and pleasure, which are retributions for previous actions. A sentient being with memory can recall, anticipate, and enhance its experiences of pain and pleasure. This means that the experiences of suffering and pleasure are not limited to immediate physical responses. Memory allows organisms to respond to the environment with greater sophistication and complexity. Finally, if sentient beings can reason abstractly, speculate about the future, and rearrange memories to form new thoughts, they can also distinguish between the desirable and undesirable, the beneficial and harmful, and the moral and immoral. The ability to differentiate in this manner is the basis of all vexations.

To experience vexations means to further the creation of good and bad karma. These actions that create karma in turn lead to further consequences, or retributions. Only sentient beings with all four characteristics have the ability to reason, to ponder, to contemplate—to understand that they create karma.

Sentient beings that cannot reason and distinguish

between what is moral and immoral only receive retribution for their previous karma. In their present life form, they cannot create further karma. Their actions are natural and immediate responses to whatever situation arises. A lion that kills for food creates no karma by that act. Only human beings can generate karma because they reason and make judgments. Reasoning, then, is the basis of all vexations, and these vexations lead human beings to create new karma, which in turn creates further retribution.

On the other hand, only humans, among all sentient beings, are capable of practicing Buddhadharma. Buddhist sutras have talked about other animals that could practice, but the sutras explained that these animals were incarnations of buddhas and bodhisattvas and not just ordinary animals.

Once I observed one of my students watching a mosquito sucking blood from his wrist. He patiently watched until the mosquito was finished and bloated with blood. Then he thumped the mosquito with his finger and killed it. I asked him why he did that and he said, "That is the mosquito's retribution. It took my blood, and it paid for it with its life."

I said, "That wasn't equal retribution. The mosquito only took a little blood from you and you took its life. Furthermore, the mosquito doesn't know what it is doing. It has no idea that it is causing you discomfort." The mosquito that causes you pain is not doing wrong. It cannot reason or make judgments. You, on the other hand, can. The normal reaction would be to swat the mosquito. That is your choice, especially if you are concerned about being infected with disease, but if you do, realize that you have created karma.

STUDENT  Buddhism speaks of six forms or realms of

existence. Are beings in the non-human form sentient beings?

SHIFU   You are referring to the six forms that sentient beings may take, according to their karma. These are animals, hungry ghosts, hell beings, humans, titans (*asuras*), and heavenly beings (*devas*). Some people are aware of and believe in only those things they can observe. Buddhism, however, speaks of other forms of existence. It is not necessary to believe in the existence of these other forms in order to accept the Buddhist criteria for sentience and non-sentience. Deities and spirits are also sentient beings, but they have subtle bodies. They do not have nervous systems, per se, but they still receive the retribution for previous actions. They feel the retribution in the mind and not the body. Most cannot practice, but they can receive merit indirectly because some are protective of the Buddhadharma and some help other sentient beings.

STUDENT   Do spiritual beings have material bodies?

SHIFU   Sentient beings are sometimes said to reside in one of three realms: desire, form, and formlessness. Collectively, these realms are samsara. Sentient beings in the realms of form and formlessness are spirits that reside in the different levels of samadhi and dhyana. These beings will remain in these realms until their power of samadhi weakens. At that point, they will enter a lower realm.

Beings in the realm of desire have material bodies and can exist as animals, humans, or heavenly beings. The distinction is in the corporeal nature of their bodies. Humans and animals have solid bodies. Spirits in the human realm have subtle bodies. The bodies of spirits in the heavenly realms are even subtler in nature.

The bodies of spirits are material, but they are fine in comparison to the human body, having no definite form. When they wish to manifest their energy, they can usually make use of whatever matter is around, and take different forms Thus, they can work through wind, water, lifeless matter, and even living matter.

The difference in the corporeal nature of spirits residing in the human realm and heavenly realm is one of subtlety. Spirits in the human realm would be likely to manifest as a solid form or in a gaseous state. Spirits in the heavenly realm would manifest as light or energy. Whether or not you consider light and energy to be matter is not important for this discussion. Deities, spirits, and bodhisattvas can manifest in the human realm in one of two ways. They can manifest as a human by being born to human parents, or they may use their spiritual power to materialize in a human form for a time.

Arhats, Buddhist saints, have transcended the three realms of desire, form, and formlessness, and thus have liberated themselves from the wheel of samsara. This does not mean that these beings are literally and bodily outside of the three realms; rather, they are not being restrained or bound by these three realms. If these saints stay in the realm of form, then they will be like other beings in the realm of form. If they stay in the human realm, then they will be like human beings with human bodies. The difference is that they have dropped attachment to a self, and therefore do not experience the vexations of the three realms. We should understand that there is much more around us than we will ever be aware of, and many sentient beings around us that we cannot see.

STUDENT   Can beings from the realms of desire, form, and formlessness live side by side?

SHIFU   Yes. For example, if a person enters a deep level of samadhi, his or her mental body resides in the realm of form or formlessness, but the physical body still resides in the realm of desire. When the power of samadhi fades, the mental body will return to the realm of desire. The realms of form and formlessness are not necessarily places; they are states of mind. The realms of form and formlessness correspond to different levels of samadhi.

STUDENT   At what level of killing do humans begin to create karma?

SHIFU   Karma created from killing begins when you kill an organism at the second level, that with living cells and a nervous system. In other words, when you kill organisms that can feel pain.

STUDENT   Does bad karma increase as we kill animals with greater complexity?

SHIFU   Yes, as you kill creatures with greater complexity, your karma worsens. Killing sentient beings that possess memory creates worse karma than killing sentient beings that only possess nervous systems. Killing a sentient being that can reason creates worse karma than killing a sentient being that cannot. Killing another human being creates the worst karma.

STUDENT   If animals cannot create karma but only receive

retribution of previous karma, were they not previously human, because humans are the only creatures that can create karma?

SHIFU   This is a common question. People are always trying to find a beginning. Where does it all begin? It is not that simple. First, there are beings on other worlds. Second, there are other realms besides the human realm. In all worlds and all realms of sentient beings, karma is without beginning and without end.

If there is a beginning, then we must answer the question, "Where did these sentient beings come from and why did they arrive in the form they did?" There have always been innumerable sentient beings and there always will be innumerable sentient beings. Animals are sentient beings that are receiving the retribution for previous karma; therefore they must have been, at one point, sentient beings that could create karma. But it does not mean they had to be human beings living on planet Earth. There are other sentient beings that can create karma and there are other worlds. Also, these animals can become human in another lifetime. They can also become the same animal, a different animal, or a being in another world. Who is to say?

There are very few hard and fast rules in Buddhadharma. Buddhism says that only humans can practice, but certain individual animals, deities, and spirits can practice too. They know something that enables them to practice. There are also certain heavenly realms where beings can practice. For the most part, however, it is humans that can practice Buddhadharma.

STUDENT   How does all this tie in with evolution?

SHIFU   According to the sutras, when conditions on this planet became suitable, sentient beings appeared. Where did they come from? From anywhere and everywhere. Earth is not the only place where life exists. The cosmos is vast. Sentient beings are here because their karma led them here. Therefore, we share a certain collective karma with all earthly sentient beings. It does not matter where sentient beings came from; we are here. We could have come from any realm and any world.

As sentient beings create karma, the world changes. We can see this directly. The world will change as more karma is created, and the karma is not limited to those beings on Earth. Earth does not float in a vacuum. All the karma of all sentient beings has an influence on the condition of Earth. Likewise, our actions here on Earth influence all realms and all worlds everywhere.

People ask, "What will happen to sentient beings if humans destroy the world, or when the world perishes?" When that happens, sentient beings will go somewhere else. Where you go depends on your individual karma and the collective karma you share with innumerable other sentient beings.

STUDENT   Scientists cannot explain all the different phenomena that Buddhism describes. Can you elaborate further on this point?

SHIFU   As I have said, to practice Buddhism, it is not necessary to believe in the existence of all the various types of beings and states. There are certain basic truths in Buddhism we accept, but from these truths we can elaborate and speculate. In Buddhism, the Twelve Links of Conditioned Arising, the Five Skandhas, and the Eighteen Realms are basic truths that we cannot dissect or dispute. From these concepts, we can only elaborate.

Scientists cannot explain all phenomena. They can explain only as far as they can measure or predict. Scientists only study phenomena that they can empirically observe. This is a limitation. Buddhism does not dispute the findings of science, either its proven facts or its well-established theories. When scientists speculate and elaborate from the known facts, their ideas become debatable.

Furthermore, Buddhism does not emphasize questions such as where we come from and why we are here. Buddhism is concerned with what sentient beings, particularly humans, can do about their suffering and vexations. It teaches people how to recognize, work with and eventually put an end to vexations and liberate themselves from suffering. Buddhism does not need to elaborate on anything beyond this concern. Buddhism, for the most part, is pragmatic.

We can also discuss sentience from the point of view of feelings. Sentience means that a being has emotions. If a sentient being did not have self-centered emotions and attachment to ideas, then it would be liberated from samsara. It would be liberated from all vexations and from the law of cause and consequence. However, if a being still has any attachment to ideas and emotions, then it is still in the realm of samsara. It is still an ordinary sentient being.

Buddhism distinguishes between various levels of feelings. The most basic level of feeling includes arbitrary moods and emotions that come and go from moment to moment. These free-ranging emotions and arbitrary moods result from deeply embedded vexations. At this level also exist feelings of greed, hatred, and ignorance.

A higher level includes feelings that contribute to stability, such as love for one's family, spouse, friends, and Sangha. If people feel anger or hatred while on the second level, then they drop back to the first level again.

A third and still higher level includes those feelings described as noble, such as divine love. These feelings are a kind of selfless love or selfless involvement in a noble cause. Noble feelings can include one's natural appreciation for art. This can be considered only slightly higher than affections and feelings of the second level. Higher than this are philosophical aspirations—feelings involved with abstractions, ideas, and conceptions. Higher still is religious aspiration—'selfless' dedication to religion, God, or spirituality.

All of these feelings, however, are vexations. In all cases, attachment and self are present still. Even the highest level, that of so-called selfless love and noble aspiration, involves a self and attachment. Sentient beings are sentient because they have feelings. All beings in the three realms of samsara are called sentient beings. If you transcend samsara, it does not mean that you become non-sentient. It means you have transcended attachment, birth, and death. You have been liberated from samsara. It is the condition of the enlightened sentient being. You are still a sentient being, with all the faculties of a sentient being. Remember that buddhas are also sentient beings.

# The Self

QUESTION  Buddhism teaches that people suffer because of attachment to the self, but in the West the discovery and strengthening of one's 'identity,' or self, is considered the path to success and happiness. How do we reconcile these views? What is the Buddhist idea of self?

SHIFU  In Buddhism we can think of the self in three ways: small self, universal self, and no-self. Most people look upon their everyday selves as being their true selves, but if that were truly the case, then there would be no reason to practice. What we commonly think of as our self, is what Buddhism calls the small self—a name and idea we fabricate in response to the external environment. The small self emerges from the constant process of evaluating our perceptions and making judgments: "This is my town, my friends, my spouse, my situation, my views, my feelings." Our ideas of existence arise from our interaction with the external environment, the people and things around us, as well as the internal environment, our bodies, feelings and thoughts. Moment to moment, we string together evaluations of ourselves: "This morning I felt refreshed and went to work. This afternoon I came home tired, but did chores. This evening I desired company, so I went to a party, and before I go to sleep tonight I will think about tomorrow's plans." From constant evaluations like these, we create an illusory small self.

Successful and accomplished individuals have a strong sense of existence and power, and if their success persist, they will continue to believe strongly in their own existence. But no matter how strong this sense of self may be, it is only the small self. Even to have a strong sense of self is unusual. Most people do not always feel that they have a firm and focused existence and character. Their perception of self is not strong and cohesive. Meditation can help people to cultivate calmness, clarity, and inner resolve so that they may develop a stronger sense of small self.

'Discovering oneself' usually means cultivating a strong sense of small self. This is not exclusively a Western way of thinking. It is common to all of humanity. Without the will power that comes from a strong sense of self, one would accomplish little. Chan practice begins with methods to establish a strong sense of small self. It is small because there is nothing genuine or enduring that we can lay our hands on. The small self comes from our moment-to-moment judgments, but we are not always aware that our evaluations, and therefore our ideas of self, change from moment to moment.

Ideas of the large or universal self posit an unchanging, eternal nature. In Chinese philosophy, this is called *li*.

Another idea of large self comes from spiritual experience. In dhyana and samadhi, as well as in other spiritual practices, one can have a sense of experiencing an absolute and unchanging spiritual self. At such times it seems as though all of existence moves while one's true nature remains still, as if one's own essence is the basis for, or, indeed, is everything else.

The concept of no-self is harder to grasp. Buddhism does not say that small self and large self are bad or unworthy things. However, in either case there is attachment, and as long as there are attachments, one cannot be truly liberated. With no-self, there are no attachments. It does not mean that everything ceases to exist once you attain liberation. After liberation, wisdom and merit continue to exist. Likewise, after a no-self experience, life goes on and there are still things to do. However, in order to get to no-self, one must start from the beginning, and that means developing a strong sense of small self.

STUDENT   Does self-evaluation continue after liberation?

SHIFU   It is not evaluation in the ordinary sense. It is more what we would describe as a natural response. An enlightened being responds to the world spontaneously, without judging.

STUDENT   You said that meditation can help to strengthen one's sense of small self. Wouldn't it make it that much harder to let go of later on in practice?

SHIFU   Before you practice, you have a scattered mind, and so you do not even know what a self is. Meditation helps to concentrate the mind and build a focused, strong sense of self. Only when the small self is concentrated can one move beyond it. In *gong'an* (koan) practice, one's self must be concentrated in order to break through it.

First I teach people how to concentrate and strengthen their small sense of self. If they do not experience enlightenment, at least they will have improved their self-esteem and confidence; and they will not be as scattered as they were before. In the course of practice, the levels of self one experiences are as follows: first scattered small self, then concentrated small self, then large (universal) self, and finally no-self.

STUDENT    What would one who has reached the level of large self think about and feel?

SHIFU    Large self is an experience that comes and goes, like a spiritual revelation. At such a time you feel at one with the universe—as if you *were* the universe. After the experience leaves, you would again be normal, but the feeling would endure, and you would feel more expansive, more settled, more compassionate, and more confident.

STUDENT    Is it possible for this experience to last for a long time?

SHIFU    The feeling can endure, but the experience will not.

STUDENT    You said that after liberation, wisdom and merit continue to exist, and that this is no-self. Can you expand on this?

SHIFU    A fully enlightened person would have wisdom and

merit, but would not perceive it as such. If they thought, "I have wisdom and merit," they are still attached to an idea of self, and are not truly liberated. It is others who perceive their wisdom and merit, and who come to them for guidance.

STUDENT   Why would someone want to go beyond universal self to no-self?

SHIFU   Remember, these terms are invented so that we may talk about the experiences of practitioners. If there were actually a 'no-self' to attain, it would just be another kind of self. The same is true for large self. Practitioners would spend all their time chasing after attractive false selves.

Who would want to go beyond universal self? People who want to experience Buddhist enlightenment. However, once they reach that stage, they will not feel that they are enlightened or liberated. In fact, they will return to their everyday world and their lives will continue, but with a major difference: they will no longer have attachments.

# Causes and Conditions

❦

QUESTION   Please explain the Buddhist concept of causes and conditions, and its relationship to dependent origination, to self and illusion, and to causes and consequences.

SHIFU   The principle of causes and conditions and its corollary, causes and consequences, are fundamental to Buddhism, and distinguish it from other philosophies and spiritual disciplines. These principles explain the relationship between events happening at different moments in time, and different points of space.

Before going further, I should introduce the term dharma, which can refer to any event, phenomenon, or object of consciousness. All dharmas, whether they are worldly or transcendental, are part of, and influenced by causes and conditions. Also, let me make a distinction between Dharma and dharma. 'Dharma' in upper case refers to Buddhadharma, or the teachings of the Buddha, the methods of practice, and the principles that underlie practice. The lower case 'dharma' refers to any phenomenon. Of course, in Sanskrit, there is no upper or lower case; this is just a convention we use in English, depending on the context. Even the teachings of the Buddha and the methods of practice are themselves phenomena, or dharmas.

Simply put, causes and conditions come into play when something happens in one moment, and later something else happens that would not have, if the previous event had not taken place. The relationships and interactions of these two events we call the conditions.

It might be easy to confuse causes and conditions with causes and consequences. In fact, the two principles are intimately connected, and it is difficult to talk about one without mentioning the other. From the standpoint of causes and conditions, we have said that one event happens now and another related event happens later. From the standpoint of causes and consequences, we can say that the earlier event is the cause and the later event is the consequence.

Conversely, when no event occurs, then no succeeding event will take place. For example, parents lead to children. Parents are the cause and children, the consequence. When there are children, there must be parents, but when there are no parents, there can be no children. In other words, having parents is a necessary condition for children to be born, at least in the conventional manner.

A cause, however, cannot turn into or lead to a consequence by itself. Something else must occur, must come together with the cause, so that it may lead to a consequence. The coming together of events and factors is referred to as causes and conditions. A man and woman together do not automatically lead to children. Other factors must come together in order for the cause (parents) to lead to the consequence (children). Parents, children, and the other factors involved are all considered causes and conditions.

Hypothetically, if there were a cause standing alone, and no other condition came along to interact with it, then there would be no consequence. If a cause could remain static and not lead to a consequence, it could not even be considered a cause, since 'cause' implies movement toward something else. In such a case, there is no relationship of causes and conditions. Therefore, one can say that causes and consequences are dependent upon the coming together of causes and conditions.

Furthermore, the condition (one dharma) that interacts with a cause (another dharma) must have itself been caused by something else, and so on and so on, infinitely in all directions throughout space and time. All phenomena arise because of causes and conditions. Any phenomenon that arises is itself a consequence of a previous cause, and arose because of the coming together of causes and conditions. This leads to the concept of conditioned arising, also known as dependent origination, which means that all phenomena, or dharmas, arise from causes and conditions. Dharmas do not arise out of nothing; they are dependent on causes and conditions. Ultimately, all dharmas, no matter when or where they occur, are interconnected.

Since all dharmas are the consequences of causes and conditions, their arising is conditional. This includes not only arising and appearing, but also perishing and disappearing. A person being born is a phenomenon, and a person dying is a phenomenon; a bubble forming is a phenomenon, a bubble bursting is a phenomenon; a thought appearing is a phenomenon, and a thought disappearing is a phenomenon. All dharmas arise and perish because of causes and conditions.

Dharmas include all phenomena, whether physiological, psychological, social, internal, or external. Some may think that dharmas only include physical (external) and physiological phenomena. They would not consider psychological phenomena, such as thoughts, to be dharmas. Buddhism considers all phenomena, physical or mental, to be dharmas. The six sense organs interact with the six kinds of sense objects—eyes see forms, ears hear sounds, etc. These are all dharmas. The sixth sense organ, consciousness, has thought as its object. The object of consciousness also includes the symbols, words, and language that people use in thinking, reasoning, remembering, and communicating. All of these symbols and thoughts are dharmas from the standpoint of Buddhadharma.

The Yogacara School classifies dharmas into three types. The first type includes all physical objects and is sometimes called the dharma of form. The second type includes mental dharmas, for example thoughts, moods, and feelings. There are also dharmas that are neither physical nor mental. These are the symbols we use in conceptualizing, and include names, numbers, and abstract ideas such as space and time. Though these symbols are absolutely necessary when one is thinking and remembering, they are not the thoughts themselves. Therefore, they are not considered to be mental dharmas.

All three kinds of dharmas described above are called *samskrita*, or dharmas with outflows—that is, they are dharmas arising from attachment. All phenomena that are part of the world of ordinary sentient beings are considered dharmas with outflows. On the other hand, all phenomena that arise in connection with enlightened beings are dharmas without outflows, and are called *asamskrita*. Such dharmas include nirvana, true suchness, and emptiness.

The principles of causes and conditions and conditioned arising definitely hold true for *samskrita*, but what about *asamskrita*? Here, a subtle distinction must be made. Take, for example, nirvana. From the perspective of ordinary sentient beings, nirvana does arise from causes and conditions. A person practices the path; if the causes and conditions are right, then a consequence of practice will be ultimate nirvana. However, one who has already attained liberation makes no distinction between nirvana and samsara. An enlightened person, even though he or she can still function in the world, perceives that the world and phenomena have no true existence. In this sense, *asamskrita* are not dharmas that arise from causes and conditions, and there is no such thing as causes and conditions and causes and consequences.

What I have just said may seem to contradict the Buddhist concept of impermanence, which states that nothing remains unchanged. This concept, however, is from the perspective of ordinary sentient beings. Liberated beings do not perceive a world, sentient beings, or dharmas arising and perishing. For liberated beings, there is no change to speak of.

Ordinary sentient beings are not enlightened. They perceive themselves as having a self, and they interact with and give rise to physical and mental phenomena. What is this self? Previously we said that physiological, mental, and psychological phenomena arise because of causes and conditions. With sentient beings, the aggregate of these phenomena is perceived as the 'self.' Even though we may intellectually accept that the self is illusory, we still cling dearly to our illusions and perceive the self to be real. If, however, we accept the premise that the self is an illusion and recognize that we have many attachments, then we will at least have a solid foundation on which to build our practice and experience emptiness.

The self exists as a consequence of causes and conditions both in a temporal sense (the continuum of past, present, and future) and a spatial sense. A cause cannot turn into a consequence unless it interacts with causes and conditions. These causes and conditions interact in a spatial sense. Therefore, we must intellectually grasp that the self is the consequence of causes and conditions, and we must practice so that we can experience it arising from causes and conditions in a temporal as well as a spatial sense.

To say that the self is an illusion is not to say that the self is a hallucination. The self is not a mirage. We say that the self is illusory because it is forever changing due to causes and conditions, and to causes and consequences. It never stays the same. Therefore, we say that the self is an illusion. For the same reason, all phenomena are considered illusions. All things change from moment to moment, evolve, and transform into something else. The self, therefore, is an illusory existence ceaselessly interacting and changing amidst an illusory environment.

To intellectually understand this is not enough. One must experience it directly; yet it is difficult to do so, because we are emotionally attached to our perception of self. This is vexation, and the only way to loosen the bonds of attachment and vexation is to practice. Through practice one can experience, in varying degrees, that time and space have no existence, and that self is an illusion. One might experience time passing very quickly, or one might experience the boundaries of the body merging with the universe. An ancient Chan master composed a short verse:

One is empty-handed, yet holds a hoe.
One is walking, yet riding a buffalo.
One stands on a bridge—the bridge is flowing,
and the water is still.

This master uses the concepts of ordinary sentient beings to describe his own perceptions. To him, holding a hoe and being empty-handed are the same; walking and riding a buffalo are the same; bridges and water are the same. The descriptions he uses are the activities and phenomena of ordinary people; they are things that are in motion. Yet, this master uses the movement of phenomena to describe the experience of non-motion. The experience of non-motion is free from causes and conditions. This master perceives reality, not illusion. It is we who perceive the illusion.

STUDENT   Is cause and consequence similar to karma?

SHIFU   Karma means force or action. Karma is definitely related to causes and consequences, because actions have a force that leads to consequences. In fact, the Twelve Links of Conditioned Arising (*nidanas*) are sometimes referred to as the Twelve Links of Conditioned Arising from Karma.

STUDENT   What about physical phenomena? Purely physical phenomena, such as clouds crossing the sky, are products of causes and conditions and causes and consequences, yet they do not seem to have anything to do with karma. Karma seems to refer only to those actions connected with sentient beings.

SHIFU   The fact that this world exists, or the fact that we think that this world exists, is because of the karma of sentient beings. Everything occurs because of sentient beings' karma. There are no purely physical phenomena.

STUDENT   This reminds me of relativity, both in the Einsteinian sense, and also in a more general sense. In other words, this is this because that is that. Nothing exists, or can come into existence, by itself. All phenomena are dependent upon causes and conditions, causes and consequences, and the force of karma of sentient beings. Is this correct?

SHIFU   That is correct. Causes and conditions work in both a temporal and spatial sense. Einstein's theory of relativity says that things move only in relation to other things. Buddhism has no problem with this statement. If something is moving, it is because it has been influenced by other phenomena, both in a temporal sense and in a spatial sense. And it in turn affects other things, both in a temporal sense and in a spatial sense.

STUDENT   I believe I heard you once say that causes and conditions are empty, but causes and consequences are not. What does this mean?

SHIFU   All causes and conditions arise because of other causes and conditions. They are impermanent and forever changing, so we say that they are empty. With causes and consequences, it is all a matter of before and after. For sentient beings, there are causes and consequences. For buddhas, there are not. There are no longer causes and consequences for buddhas because they have no self-centeredness. Buddhas do not look upon anything from the standpoint of an ego. Things still happen to buddhas, but buddhas do not perceive things as happening to themselves. They see all things as being empty. Sentient beings, on the other hand, are incapable of seeing the world in this way, so they still perceive the effects on themselves of their previous karma.

Shakyamuni Buddha lived in the world and interacted with people and the environment. Sentient beings saw it their way and said that the Buddha performed good deeds, taught Buddhadharma and helped save sentient beings. But the Buddha did not see it this way. He just acted spontaneously. The source of his action was wisdom, not self-centeredness.

The Buddha still experienced bodily pains after he was enlightened. Sentient beings would say that the Buddha was suffering from causes and conditions and previous karma, but because the Buddha no longer perceived a self, he did not suffer mentally. Only his physical body experienced pain.

STUDENT    Are causes and conditions controllable? Can I manipulate them to directly control my life?

SHIFU    The *Avatamsaka Sutra* states that all dharmas are created by the mind. If our minds change, then causes and conditions also change. Whichever direction our minds move, so do causes and conditions. If our attitudes change, then what we perceive also changes. If we do not make an effort to change our lives and minds, then we will be influenced by the course of events we have already set into motion. If we adopt Buddhadharma into our worldview, then causes and conditions will shift direction, and events in our lives will change.

STUDENT   It seems, however, that there are times in our lives when our karma is so bad that we cannot alleviate the suffering in our lives. Is there anything we can do to alleviate the bad karma and change the causes and conditions that influence our lives?

SHIFU   It is true, there are times when your karma is so overpowering that you cannot control yourself or free yourself from the vexations in which you are trapped. This can result from a build-up of many previous actions, and now the causes and conditions have ripened such that the cumulative force of this karma manifests all at once. It might also mean that you created deep, heavy, bad karma in one instant, and now the causes and conditions have ripened and the consequence of this bad action manifests. When it happens, it is like a great flood that swamps you. There is not much you can do other than ride it out.

The only way you can avoid or alleviate this bad karma is to somehow catch the consequence before it manifests, before the causes and conditions have fully ripened. To use the same analogy, if you see the flood coming, then you can move to higher ground, so that it will not affect you as much. You can do this by practicing with diligence, by repenting past actions and by performing virtuous deeds—making offerings, giving donations, helping others. The accumulated merit from these virtuous deeds and the power of your practice can help to alleviate or offset bad karma.

Of course, if you are a true practitioner of Chan, then you know that vexation is vexation, whether it is good or bad. A true practitioner would strive to maintain his or her equanimity in all situations—good, bad, or neutral. However, as anyone here who has been caught in a flood knows, maintaining one's practice and equanimity at such times can be challenging.

# The Five Skandhas
## and Consciousness



QUESTION   The diverse uses of the word 'consciousness' in Buddhist philosophy tend to confuse me. Buddhism speaks of consciousness as one of the Five Skandhas; there are also the sixth, seventh, and eighth consciousnesses. The Five Skandhas are a fundamental teaching of Buddhism, but I still have problems distinguishing between sensation, perception, volition, and consciousness.

SHIFU   I will answer your questions about the Five Skandhas and the levels of consciousness together, since they are related. The teaching of the Five Skandhas—form, sensation, perception, volition, and consciousness—is among the most fundamental of the Buddha's teachings. In essence, one can say that the Five Skandhas make sentient beings what they are. Without the Five Skandhas, there would be no way to sense and interact with the environment. In fact, there would be neither beings nor environment.

The first skandha is form, and it refers to the material realm: our body and the environment. Thus it encompasses both physiological and physical aspects. The five sense organs (eyes, ears, nose, tongue, and touch) and the nervous system (brain, spinal cord, and nerves) make up the physiological aspect of form. Everything in the environment, as well as the symbols we use to understand the environment, make up the physical aspect of form.

Now I would like to skip to the fifth skandha, or consciousness. It is important not to confuse the consciousness described by the fifth skandha with the eight consciousnesses of the Mind-Only, or Yogacara, School. This school developed long after the Buddha expounded Buddhadharma, and it expands upon the ideas underlying the Five Skandhas.

The first five consciousnesses of the Yogacara School arise from the five sense organs: sight, sound, smell, taste, and touch. The sixth consciousness refers to the discriminating mind. These six consciousnesses roughly correspond to the middle three skandhas—sensation, perception, and volition. Whereas form falls within the physical realm, sensation, perception, and volition fall within the mental realm. Likewise, the first six consciousnesses of Yogacara fall within the mental realm.

The second through fourth skandhas—sensation, perception, and volition—are mental activities. Fitting them into the framework of Yogacara, one can say that they are the result of the five senses coming into contact with the environment.

The fifth skandha, consciousness, refers to more than the discriminating mind; it includes the other four skandhas, which encompass both the material and mental realms. The fifth skandha thus also includes both material and mental aspects. Seen this way, the fifth skandha is simultaneously the cause and the consequence. This means that the fifth skandha is the cause because the physical world, including our bodies and the environment, exists as a result of the content of our consciousness. Remember, the consciousness of the fifth skandha is much more than the discriminating mind; it holds within itself the karmic seeds of all past actions. It is our karmic storehouse, our karmic force. Our bodies and the environment are manifestations of our karma. Therefore, from this perspective, form (the first skandha) is a consequence of consciousness (the fifth skandha). Consciousness is also the consequence, because when the three mental skandhas interact with form—the environment—this generates new karma, which then enters our karmic storehouse, the consciousness of the fifth skandha.

STUDENT   So you are saying that the material world—body and environment—exists in the first place because of karma, and that is why consciousness is the cause. At the same time, consciousness is a consequence because, as our bodies encounter the environment, our six sense consciousnesses perceive the experience and we respond, thereby generating new karma, which is in fact the consciousness of the fifth skandha.

What you are saying, really, is that the environment, in fact the entire universe, exists because sentient beings exist. The karma of all sentient beings creates the universe?

SHIFU   Yes, you can say it that way. Your physical body is also called the body of retribution. The environment is also called the environment of retribution. They exist because of the effects of sentient beings' past karma. Dependent origination (conditioned arising) is a principle of Buddhadharma that holds that all phenomena are interconnected, and arise and perish because of karma. The environment and our bodies are manifestations of both individual and collective karma.

Everything that we are, experience, and encounter is the consequence of our previous actions. The previous actions generate the karmic force that is stored in our consciousness (fifth skandha). Eventually the karmic seeds within our consciousness manifest, becoming what we encounter and experience. And as we experience and act upon the effects of previous karma, we create more karma, which in turn gets stored in this consciousness.

Now let's go back and compare the framework of the Five Skandhas to that of the Yogacara School. Sensation, perception, and volition (second, third, and fourth skandhas) roughly correspond to the first six consciousnesses (sight, sound, smell, taste, touch, and thought) of the Yogacara School. The fifth skandha (consciousness) refers to the seventh and eighth consciousnesses of the Yogacara School.

The fifth skandha is also known as the karmic retribution consciousness. When the Five Skandhas were originally taught, there were no fine distinctions made between a sixth, seventh, and eighth consciousness. Eventually, Yogacara expanded upon the Five Skandhas and made finer distinctions between the functions of this karmic retribution consciousness, and so they speak of a sixth, seventh, and eighth consciousness.

As I said earlier, sensation, perception, and volition fall within the mental realm. Basically, there are three stages of any mental function. First, one's senses come into contact with the environment; this is sensation. Second, one discerns whether the sensation is pleasant, unpleasant, or neutral; this is perception. Third, one is motivated to react to the experience; this is volition. For example: I hear a loud irritating noise. The sensation is whatever is impressed upon me, in this case the sound impressed upon my ears. My perception might be: "What a harsh sound! I don't like it!" Volition is my decision to do something about it: I frown or I put my hands over my ears. Whenever a person acts upon a perception that arises because of a sensation, they generate karma, which is planted in the fifth skandha—consciousness. I hope you are now clear about the distinction between the consciousness of the Five Skandhas and the different levels of consciousness of the Yogacara School.

STUDENT    Inanimate objects do not have consciousness, but they are reflections of our minds. That microphone you are speaking into is there because of our individual and collective karma. Is this what is meant by the Buddhist prayer: "To know all the buddhas of the past, present and future, perceive that *dharmadhatu* nature is all created by the mind"?

SHIFU    Yes and no. Any lifeless, inanimate object exists because of the past karmic power of sentient beings. Whatever we encounter enters through the five sense organs and is perceived by the discriminating mind. Without the discriminating mind (the sixth consciousness of the Yogacara School), we would not be able to perceive anything. When someone's sixth consciousness does not function, the outside world ceases to exist for that individual. The world still exists for other sentient beings, but not for the person without a discriminating consciousness.

However, it is not the sixth consciousness alone that creates the world. The environment arises from the inter-action of all Five Skandhas. With our senses and discriminating mind we experience the world. Whenever we make decisions, think, say, or do something, we are creating karma, and karma in turn helps to create and shape the environment. The world is the way it is because of everyone's karma. The world changes as you live your life and create new karma. Therefore, it is important to be aware of your actions and speech. Your karma is shaping not only your future, but also the world's.

On the other hand, only the enlightened can see *dharmadhatu* nature, the nature of emptiness. Emptiness means that all dharmas, or phenomena, are in constant change—nothing is permanent. Furthermore, every dharma interconnects with all other dharmas; nothing stands on its own, in isolation from everything else. If one attains buddha-hood, one perceives this nature of emptiness. Enlightened beings perceive the world with pure minds, and they deal with the world through their wisdom. Ordinary people perceive the world with vexed minds, and they deal with the world through their discrimination. This in turn, creates the environment. Pure mind is wisdom; it creates *dharmadhatu* nature, and *dharmadhatu* nature makes pure mind possible.

STUDENT Buddhadharma also speaks of the Eighteen Realms, which include the six consciousnesses. Three components must come together whenever a sentient being comes into contact with the environment: a sense organ, a sense object, and a sense consciousness. For instance, the eye is a sense organ; form, shape, and color are sense objects; and seeing is the sense consciousness. The same is true for sound, smell, taste, and touch. This is clear. But I am still not sure what the three components of the sixth consciousness are.

SHIFU    The six sense organs, the six sense objects, and the six sense consciousnesses make up what we call the Eighteen Realms. The six sense objects are also called the six kinds of sense dust. The objects of the sixth (mental) consciousness are the symbols we use to think, reason, and remember. These symbols make up the sense dust of the sixth consciousness. Thinking, reasoning, remembering make up the consciousness component of the sixth consciousness.

The symbols come from the five other kinds of sense dust. We conceptualize with images and language. Language consists of the combination of varying sounds that present themselves as symbols to the sixth consciousness. When the mental consciousness uses these symbols, it can reason, remember, and make judgments. The mental consciousness cannot function without symbols.

The sense organ of the sixth consciousness includes a mental component and a physical component. The mental component is the retribution consciousness. It arises from the eighth consciousness where the karmic seeds reside. However, without the physical component, the karmic seeds cannot manifest. The physical component functions like a doorway, allowing the retribution consciousness (past karma) to leave the karmic storehouse and allowing newly created karma to enter the karmic storehouse. The physical component is one's nervous system.

STUDENT    Then the mental function of the sixth consciousness incorporates the other five sense organs? Don't the brain and nervous system sense, perceive, and process all information?

SHIFU   Yes, but when I speak of the sixth consciousness I am talking about that part of the brain associated with thinking, reasoning, and memory. The nervous system also includes the other sense consciousnesses and the life functions, but they are not part of the sense organ of the sixth consciousness. The brain and nervous system have more than one function.

In order for a sentient being to reason or have memory, it must make use of symbols. As long as an organism has a nervous system, then it still has the first four skandhas: form, sensation, perception, and volition. Without the first four skandhas, a sentient being would not be able to function; but only sentient beings with memory and reasoning power have all Five Skandhas.

STUDENT   What about plants and vegetables? They seem to respond to things. They grow toward light.

SHIFU   Plants are alive but they do not have nervous systems. They can react in certain ways and exhibit primitive behavior because they have cells, and chemical reactions take place in their bodies. But their reactions to the environment cannot be called sensation because sensation comes with a nervous system. Activities like photosynthesis and growth are purely chemical reactions.

STUDENT   Isn't the sixth consciousness really part of the first five consciousnesses? When I look at something, don't I use my reasoning power to discern what I see?

SHIFU    One can say that the sixth consciousness (discriminating mind) incorporates the first five consciousnesses: seeing, hearing, smelling, tasting, and touching. But the sixth consciousness refers specifically to the functions of reasoning and remembering. At the moment of sensation, the sixth consciousness is considered to be whatever sense consciousness is operating at that time. Immediately following that moment, one begins to remember, reason, and make judgments. These are functions of the sixth consciousness.

STUDENT    Can there be pure awareness that is there before language and symbols, before what one would call the sense objects of the sixth consciousness?

SHIFU    Impossible. Without symbols and other sense objects of the sixth consciousness, the discriminating mind cannot function. You would either be dead or brain dead. When someone has pure awareness, then symbols, memory, and reasoning are still in the sixth consciousness, but the individual has no attachment to them. The individual has reached equanimity. Nothing moves in the mind, but the functions of the mind are still present.

Enlightened beings and buddhas are like ordinary sentient beings in that they still have and use a sixth consciousness. They remember, reason, think, and learn. The difference is that fully enlightened beings are not attached to selves. They are free from desire, ignorance, arrogance, and doubt. They are not self-centered. Their discriminating mind has been transformed from vexation into wisdom.

STUDENT    So one can say that I have a sixth consciousness, but I am attached to it. I believe that the sixth consciousness is what I am. But an enlightened being just uses the sixth consciousness like a tool.

SHIFU   Yes, a buddha still uses the sixth consciousness. A buddha still talks in terms of "I and you, I and it." A buddha can still distinguish between subject and object, but is not attached to any such discriminations. An ordinary sentient being says, "I am I and you are you," and believes it to be true. An ordinary sentient being identifies with his or her thoughts and body. Buddhas are not attached to their bodies and thoughts, but they still use them expediently. If buddhas did not make use of their bodies and minds, they would not be able teach ordinary sentient beings.

STUDENT   What, then, is in the mind when it reaches a level of no-thought?

SHIFU   I think you are confusing no-thought with no-self. It is possible to reach a point in meditation when the mind is still. At this point there seem to be no thoughts, but there is in fact one thought. The person continues steadily on one thought. The mind does not move. No thinking is going on. This is samadhi. One does not have to be enlightened to experience this; or to put it another way, experiencing samadhi is not automatically enlightenment.

On the other hand, if a person experiences true enlightenment, then the idea of a self disappears. There is no self. But thoughts continue, just as they would in an ordinary person's mind. An enlightened person can function, reason, and make judgments. The difference is that the enlightened person does not attribute these mental functions to a self.

STUDENT   The first few lines of the *Heart Sutra* read: "While coursing through deep *prajnaparamita* (perfect wisdom), the bodhisattva Avalokitesvara perceived that all Five Skandhas are empty, thereby transcending all suffering." If Avalokitesvara perceived that all Five Skandhas are empty, how did he know there were any skandhas to begin with?

SHIFU   In the *Heart Sutra*, the Buddha tells us what Avalokitesvara has done. Bodhisattva Avalokitesvara is not saying it. Avalokitesvara is not pointing to the Five Skandhas and saying, "These are empty."

The Buddha spoke the *Heart Sutra* for the sake of sentient beings. He was trying to make things understandable for people who have not experienced enlightenment. Ordinary sentient beings still believe in and perceive the Five Skandhas. The Buddha is saying, "If, like Avalokitesvara, you can perceive that the Five Skandhas are empty, then you will transcend all suffering." Buddhas and bodhisattvas have perceived that the Five Skandhas do not exist, but enlightened beings can still see things from an ordinary sentient being's point of view. They know that sentient beings identify with the Five Skandhas.

The *Heart Sutra* contains other seemingly contradictory statements. Further on it says that there is no such thing as wisdom or any attainment, and then immediately afterwards it says that because of this, buddhas attain *anuttara-samyak-sambodhi*: complete, supreme wisdom. If there is no attainment, how can buddhas attain wisdom? The point is that the sutra is spoken for the benefit of sentient beings. Ultimately, there is no wisdom and no attainment, but because of their attachments, sentient beings perceive such things as attainments, so a buddha speaks of wisdom and attainment. In fact, *anuttara-samyak-sambodhi*, the complete, supreme wisdom, is 'no wisdom,' 'no attainment.'

# Karma

QUESTION   How does karma relate to the actions of an individual, both in reference to past and future?

SHIFU   Karma in Sanskrit means 'action.' When we have carried out an action, that action is over. It is something of the past. What remains can be called karmic force. It is this karmic force that leads to a particular consequence in the future, either in the present life or in a future life. In all cases, what exists is a cause and consequence relationship. Therefore, what people generally refer to as karma is more correctly described as karmic force.

Many people think: "If I do something now, I will suffer or enjoy the fruit of that action at some time in the future." This is not quite correct. It is true that we will experience the consequences of our actions later on, but those consequences are not fixed. Karmic force relates to us as a shadow relates to a person. Although the shadow always follows, it changes shape and intensity with changes in light and position. In the same way, karmic force will always follow an individual, but the karmic effects of a particular action are not fixed.

Why is this so? The continual performance of new actions modifies the karmic force accordingly. So, if you generate virtuous karma, then the force of previous non-virtuous karma will lessen. Of course, the opposite is also true: evil actions will magnify the force of already-existing bad karma. In some cases, where particular actions have been performed for a long time, the karmic force of all these separate actions can come together in one gigantic conse-quence. If the bulk of that karmic force were bad, the consequence could be terrible.

STUDENT   How does karmic force govern rebirth?

SHIFU   For people with virtuous karma the best rebirth is in the heavenly realm of the *devas*. One is not born into the heavens through parents; rather, these heavens are attained through one's self-consciousness. Also, in the heavenly realms, one's body, however subtle, does not die; it will expire only when the consequences of its karma are exhausted.

For people with evil karma, the worst rebirth would be in the hell of the *avici* realm. As with the heavens, the body emerges from one's self-consciousness, but whereas in heaven the sentient being enjoys a free and pleasurable existence, in hell the being is bound and experiences great suffering.

STUDENT   You say that the best consequence for a person with good karma is to be reborn in the heavens. Isn't it better for a practitioner to be reborn in human form to continue to practice?

SHIFU   There is a difference between karma related to practice and virtuous karma. Sentient beings aspiring to liberation from samsara generate karma related to practice. They will be reborn in worlds where it is possible to continue to practice. Virtuous karma does not necessarily include karma related to practice. If a person practices with both wisdom and virtuous merit in mind, then he or she may be reborn in certain heavens of form where practice is still possible.

STUDENT   When I experience the consequence of a previous action, does that karmic force disappear?

SHIFU   The force of karma remains with you until you transcend the three realms of desire, form, and formlessness. When you experience the consequence of an action, karmic force does not disappear, but changes. Karmic force is like water rushing down a mountain; it will alter its course around rocks and terrain, and continue to flow until it reaches the ocean. Likewise, when you experience the consequence of a previous action, your karmic force will change direction.

STUDENT   If this is the case, is it then wrong to say that I have burned off some of my previous bad karma whenever I experience suffering in my life?

SHIFU   No, you can still say that. After you have suffered, your karmic force remains, but in an altered form. In other words, your karma does not exist as individual packets of good and bad actions waiting to manifest. It is all one karmic force. Therefore, if you experience something bad, it is the consequence of previous actions, and your karma changes accordingly. The same is true for experiencing something good.

STUDENT   Where does the karmic force reside?

SHIFU   In the teaching of the Yogacara School, the eighth consciousness (*alaya*) is known as the storehouse consciousness. It stores the consequences of our actions. Karmic force resides there. Mahayana Buddhism describes the eighth consciousness as containing the seeds of all our karma, but we should not think of these seeds as separate units of karmic force. The eighth consciousness is not comparable to a computer memory disk, where data increases or decreases. The eighth consciousness does not become larger or smaller as individuals create karma and experience consequences. Although it consists of many different karmic seeds, the eighth consciousness is one, ever-changing karmic force.

STUDENT   To a large degree, karma depends on the intention behind the words or actions. Is it possible, without attaining enlightenment, to control our intentions and volition to the point where no karma is created?

SHIFU   It is possible, but very difficult. I suppose you would never be able to interact with others. Words spoken and actions performed without volition do not create karma. How can you speak and act without wanting to speak and act?

STUDENT   What if I kill a sentient being without knowing it? Suppose I am driving down a dark street at night and a cat runs under the car before I can react. Is karma created then?

SHIFU   First, you were riding the car by choice. Second, that situation came about because of causes and conditions and because of your karma and the cat's karma. Therefore, karma is created; but the karma is lighter than if you had purposely killed the cat.

STUDENT   Do random thoughts create karma?

SHIFU   No. Thoughts that come and go of their own accord do not create karma. Only thoughts that arise with volition create karma. Such karma is also lighter than karma created by words and actions.

STUDENT   What about the willful choice to think about my method of practice, or to think about the welfare of sentient beings? Does that create karma?

SHIFU   Yes. That creates good karma.

STUDENT   If a bomb falls on this city, it cannot be my personal retribution. Is there collective karma?

SHIFU   Collective karma exists. If a bomb were to fall on this city, and we all suffered, we should understand it as retribution from collective karma. All of us, at different times and in different places, created similar karma, and at this time, the karma for all of us ripened simultaneously. We do not share the karma of other people. Every person suffers the consequence of his or her own actions. However, one consequence may take care of many people's karma.

STUDENT   Is it the action, the intent behind the action, or a combination of intent and action that brings about a consequence?

SHIFU   If an action is carried out without any awareness of it, there will be no karmic consequence for that action. Karmic force corresponds to the type of awareness that the individual has at the time of his or her action. If I kill a man in a drunken stupor but have absolutely no awareness of doing so, I will take the consequence that corresponds to being drunk, not to the consequence of taking someone's life. However, it is extremely rare to do or say something that drastic without being aware of it, so the chances are, some karma is created.

STUDENT   If a person breaks the law, will that draw a negative karmic consequence, or will it be the guilt the person feels that draws the karmic consequence?

SHIFU   In terms of karma, there will be a consequence whether you feel guilty for your action or not. If a bodhisattva feels it is necessary to kill someone, though in his or her mind it may have been the best thing to do under the circumstances, he or she must still take the karmic consequence.

STUDENT   Who determined what actions create good and bad karma?

SHIFU   The principles of Buddhism come from Shakyamuni Buddha. His principles are not commands telling us what to do and what not to do. They are not a moral code. Rather, they are based on observation. With his wisdom, Shakyamuni was able to tell his disciples what consequences followed certain kinds of action, and he advised them to avoid actions that generated bad consequences and perform actions that generated good consequences.

In society, laws are necessary in order to maintain structure and stability. For this reason, laws are relatively rigid. Karma, on the other hand, is flexible. Suppose I have done something bad, but because causes and conditions are not ripe, I have not yet taken the consequence for that action. If I then do something good, the karmic force may change. However, if instead I do something else which is bad, it may lead more quickly to that consequence. There are people who have never taken the consequence for a bad action because they constantly generate good karma. With this in mind, it should be an encouragement to practice more diligently.

# The Five Precepts

QUESTION At the end of every retreat we take the Five Precepts. What do these precepts encompass? To what level should practitioners embrace the precepts? During one's practice, does the depth to which one accepts the precepts change?

SHIFU The Five Precepts are a basic part of Buddhism and are: no killing, no stealing, no sexual misconduct, no lying, and no using alcohol or drugs. The Five Precepts are a protecting mechanism for practitioners. They help to ensure the purity of their lives and minds so that they can safely and steadily continue to practice. For this reason, precepts are necessary for the serious practitioner.

In taking the precepts, you check yourself in regard to actions and speech. If your bodily karma and verbal karma are relatively undefiled, then your mind will tend to be more stable and pure. A stable mind leads to better practice, which in turn can lead to samadhi. Thus, the attainment of samadhi is dependent on the practice of the precepts. Taking the precepts must be voluntary. You must be willing to curb your actions and speech. Being forced to take the precepts will only create frustration and anger. This will not help someone attain samadhi, or harmonize daily life.

It is not only for attaining samadhi that you should take the Five Precepts; it also signifies that you accept the teachings of the Buddha. In addition to taking the Three Refuges, the precepts are basic requirement for being a Buddhist. When you follow these precepts, your behavior will likely be different from an ordinary person's. Either people will recognize that your actions and speech are different because you are a Buddhist, or, conversely, they will surmise that you are a Buddhist by your actions and speech. At this point, whether you practice to attain samadhi is another issue. Therefore, even if you wish to practice Buddhism without practicing meditation, you should take the Five Precepts.

STUDENT   Do people's attitudes towards and relationship to the Five Precepts change as they journey deeper into practice?

SHIFU   Yes, definitely. We can view the precepts at three levels. At the level of the ordinary practitioner, there are the 'precepts of individual liberation.' Here, we hold the precepts one by one, from one period of time to the next. Each precept is taken and followed separately. If you are sincere in keeping a particular precept, then you will acquire the benefits of that precept. It does not mean that you will, or can, hold all Five Precepts simultaneously.

At the second level are the 'precepts in conjunction with

samadhi.' When people progress sufficiently deeply into samadhi, they will no longer have any desire to break any of the precepts, and will naturally refrain from breaking them. If people claim to have attained deep samadhi, yet break the precepts, then the samadhi they speak of is not genuine.

At the third level are the 'precepts in conjunction with wisdom.' From the time people first see their true nature to the time they achieve buddhahood, their wisdom will progressively deepen. During this time, they will not have to remind themselves to keep the precepts. At this point precepts are a natural part of the practice.

STUDENT   What is the difference between the second and third levels?

SHIFU   At the second, or samadhi level, it is possible to regress. While in samadhi you cannot and will not break the precepts, but when the power of the samadhi experience fades, you have the potential to break the precepts. However, as samadhi power increases, wisdom often deepens. Although it is possible for such people to break a precept, their breaches will not be serious ones. People who have experienced deep, genuine samadhi are not very likely to indulge in sexual misconduct.

Now let's talk about the different levels within each precept. The depth to which you value a precept depends on you and your practice. The worst infraction of the first precept is to kill another human being. If you intentionally kill another person, then you have permanently broken the precept for this lifetime. Even if you repent your action you cannot take the first precept again. Other than this extreme infraction, the first precept can vary from individual to individual. Killing any animal, whether a cow, a dog, or a cockroach, goes against the first precept, but humans have a lot of anger and desire stemming from deep-rooted habits. Being in samsara, we are vulnerable to countless vexations. Even serious Buddhists will kill ants and mosquitoes if they interfere with daily life. If you value the precept, on one level, you may not kill a cockroach, but on another level you might. It depends on you and your commitment to the precept.

In regard to animals, if you kill them and are aware of your actions, and later repent your actions, then the first precept remains intact. If someone were to take an extreme position and say all types of killing are equal and beyond redemption, then nobody would take the precept and people would drift away from Buddhadharma. Precepts must be adaptable to situations.

As I said, only if you kill another person is the precept broken. Otherwise, precepts can be forsaken, but not broken. If you know that you may kill someone, such as during war, then you should officially return the precept. Afterward, you can take the precept again. This is permissible, because during the time that you killed, you were not a Buddhist. And, if you violate the precept to a lesser degree, you can repent and continue to keep it.

STUDENT   Wait a second. Returning the first precept when you are going to kill someone is premeditated murder. How do you explain that? Also, what happens if you kill someone accidentally after taking the precept?

SHIFU   Let me clarify what I just said. If you are angry with someone, you do not hand in your precept, kill that person, and then take the precept again. That would be ridiculous.

The point of the precept is not to harm or kill anything, especially human beings. But if you know you will be in a situation where you may have to kill someone, such as in war, then you can officially return the precept. When you return from war, then you can take the precept again.

What about killing someone accidentally? There are a few criteria regarding the first precept. In order for the precept to be violated, the killing must be premeditated. You must intend to kill someone, and you must succeed in doing so. And when you are killing the person, you must be aware of your actions. These elements must be present before it is clear that you have irrevocably broken the precept. However, regardless of the precept, if you kill accidentally or intentionally, it still affects your karma.

STUDENT    What is the consequence of mentally killing someone?

SHIFU    Just wishing someone dead is confined to your own mind. If you have not physically killed someone, then you have not broken the precept.

STUDENT    In reference to killing, are all Buddhist monks and nuns vegetarians? Don't certain sects permit eating meat?

SHIFU    Yes, other than Chan, some sects of Buddhism permit monastics to eat meat under some conditions. Although some monks and nuns eat meat, they do not kill the animals themselves. Furthermore, the animals must not have been killed specifically for them. The reason they eat meat is because of the environment in which they live, where perhaps other foods are scarce.

STUDENT    Enlightened people will keep the precepts naturally. Does that mean that if their house is infested with roaches, ants, and rats, will they not do anything about it?

SHIFU    Enlightened people will not kill these animals. The more compassionate thing to do is to create the conditions in one's home where it would be difficult to become infested. However, if one does take steps to eliminate pests, one must be aware of the suffering and karma that is created.

The second precept is not to steal. The precept of not stealing was based on the legal system of ancient India. If the crime was punishable by death, then the precept was permanently broken. In ancient India, you did not have to steal much to be executed. In the United States, the legal system does not execute people for stealing, no matter what the amount. Some people might take this as a green light to go out and rob the nearest bank, but stealing is wrong, no matter how small or large the amount stolen. It violates the second precept, but you can repent your action.

The third precept, no sexual misconduct, is important. People who do not uphold this precept can create a lot of grief and turmoil in families and society. I urge all Buddhist lay practitioners to take this precept. According to ancient Indian standards, the following actions constituted an extreme infraction of the precept: sex between unmarried couples, adultery, and unnatural sex acts. According to custom sex had to be performed at night in the privacy of the bedroom, and anything other than genital sex was considered unnatural.

Again, times have changed, and the Western moral code is different. Many couples live together without being married. In today's society, this behavior is not always considered sexual misconduct. Even so, I encourage these people to marry. If you are unmarried and have children, it can create problems for the children. And even if you do not have children, it is better to be married because it shows that you are committed to your partner. Marriage is a sign of responsibility and maturity.

If you are not married and you are not living with someone, you should try to curb your sexual urge and not change partners all the time. Adultery would be a serious violation for this day and age. But passions are strong. If you think you cannot control your sexual urge at this point in your life, perhaps it would be best to return the precept, and take it when you think you have more control over your desires. However, this is only a last resort, and I do not advise it.

The worst violation of the fourth precept, no lying, would be to tell someone that you are a buddha or bodhisattva, or to falsely claim enlightenment to gain wealth, respect, or social power. You must be aware that you are lying. This is the extreme violation of this precept and repentance will do no good. If, on the other hand, you really believe that you are enlightened, then it is not an infraction of the precept. It is a consequence of arrogance and pride, and not a lie.

If a person lies in order to gain money, then it is lying and stealing. Lying in order to have sex is both lying and sexual misconduct. If in lying you are directly responsible for the death of another, then it is lying and killing.

In itself, the fifth precept against taking alcohol and drugs is not that important. If broken, it can be repented. Most religions have precepts or moral commandments. With minor differences, most of the precepts among the many religions are similar. No religion will say that it is permissible to kill, steal, lie, or commit sexual misconduct, but only a few sects of some religions, and Buddhism, emphasize abstention from alcohol and drugs. The purpose of the fifth precept is to protect the previous four precepts. When you are intoxicated you are likely to break one or more of the other precepts. Furthermore, Buddhism emphasizes wisdom and maintaining a rational attitude toward life. Since alcohol and drugs lead to a loss of judgment and rationality, they are directly opposed to Buddhist principles.

Because it is difficult for many people to take the precepts, I allow for an expedient method. During the precept ceremony, those who feel that they would be unable to uphold a particular precept can refrain from taking it. The precepts are not written in stone. They are guidelines for behavior.

Over the years I have explained the Five Precepts many times. How I explain them depends on the audience and the situation. If I do not think the audience is capable of strong conviction, then I only point out the extreme situations: do not kill people, do not rob banks, do not be promiscuous, do not tell people you are a buddha or a master. If people are more stable, then I will expect more, and I will explain the precepts in more depth. I do not change the meaning of the precepts arbitrarily.

# Precepts and Karma

QUESTION    Shifu, I thought I once heard you say that speech and action create karma, but that thoughts by themselves do not; rather, thoughts can lead to speech and action that create karma. Previously I had understood thoughts to be dharmas, just like speech and action. As such they have a certain force, and therefore they can affect things. You have also said that mental power can help, hurt, or even kill. This is neither action nor speech. It is purely mental. For instance, at the end of retreat we silently transfer merit with the intention of helping sentient beings. Lastly, the Mahayana tradition says that thoughts alone can break precepts. Can you clear up the confusion?

SHIFU    Of the three activities—actions, speech, and thought—thought is most important. If an apparently conscious person acts or speaks without mental awareness, the person is being directed by an outside force, or is insane.

Therefore, if the mind is not involved when the body acts or speech occurs, then no karma is created.

What if the mind is active but neither speech nor actions manifest? In this case one must distinguish between precepts and karma. The Hinayana tradition says that precepts are broken only when actions and speech are involved. Hinayana takes the perspective of ordinary sentient beings. When we speak or act we influence others, perhaps conspicuously. On the other hand, if only the mind moves, the influence is much lighter and much less conspicuous. Thinking about stealing is not a crime. You have to follow through with actions to break the law. Therefore the Hinayana tradition does not consider bad thoughts as breaking precepts.

Mahayana recognizes the mind as the most important component, so the mind alone can break the precepts. That is to say, intention is paramount. Furthermore, bad thoughts can create bad karma, but the karma created is much lighter than that created by speech or action.

Remember, also, that you are thinking constantly. Some thoughts are good, some are bad, and some are neutral. They all create light karma. If you focus only on the bad thoughts and condemn yourself for them, then you are doing yourself an injustice. You are thinking good thoughts throughout the day, too, and these create good karma. So there is a balance. For instance, you are here learning Buddhadharma. This is good. You are creating good karma. Hopefully, during the course of our lives we will think more good thoughts than bad.

Even if you take the approach that evil thoughts do not break precepts, be aware that when one has evil thoughts that persist and persist, eventually they may lead to questionable speech and action. It is better to deal with evil thoughts right from the start and try to maintain a mind of purity.

STUDENT   What about the question of free will versus predestination in terms of karma? The Buddha once related a story about how he, after becoming the Buddha, still experienced retribution for a mild, boyish prank he played lifetimes before. This posits a tit-for-tat, fatalistic interpretation of karmic retribution that I find difficult to accept.

SHIFU   I think there is a bit of confusion in your understanding of this story. Yes, the Buddha did experience the consequence of an action he performed lifetimes before. However, he did not experience it as retribution. There may have been pain, but there was no suffering such as we would experience. To enlightened beings, receiving retribution is the same as not receiving retribution. If there is no self, how can there be retribution? Only beings that have an idea of self can experience retribution.

STUDENT   If you break the precepts in your dreams, have you still broken Mahayana precepts?

SHIFU   If you have taken the bodhisattva precepts, then whether you have bad thoughts while awake or dreaming, you still break the precepts. However, if in a dream you steal something or kill someone, you have not truly done so, so you should not concern yourself with it, and you should not punish yourself. If a person is completely enlightened, then it is impossible to break precepts, even in dreams. If you are on the bodhisattva path, you can always repent your bad actions, speech, and thoughts and still practice the precepts.

Precepts are guidelines for behavior, not commandments.

The bodhisattva precepts alert us to what we should or should not do. We should not break precepts, but if we do, what is done is done. We should then repent and continue with our practice. Nevertheless, we are still responsible for the karmic consequences.

Precepts in Buddhism should not be thought of as commandments that are either kept or broken. You should think of precepts more as clear bodies of water. If you break a precept, then you pollute the waters. The precept is still there, but it is not pure anymore. By repenting and vowing to try harder, you help to purify the precept once again.

STUDENT    Can thoughts alone cause harm to others?

SHIFU    If you think bad thoughts about someone all the time, day after day, the cumulative effect of those thoughts can grow very strong. Eventually you may be led to say or do something that will harm that person. If you have bad thoughts about someone for a day, it is doubtful that something bad will immediately happen to that person.

On the other hand, there are people who cultivate mind power in order to harm someone directly with their thoughts. This is extremely rare and not relevant to what we are talking about. For most of us, thoughts remain within the mental realm. You must speak or act in order for things to happen.

We should not think of the precepts as something mysterious or mystical; rather, we should try to understand them from a common sense, humanistic point of view. Think of what is reasonable and normal. If you just sit there and think of giving someone gifts, but never do it, and then later tell them, "I've done good things for you," does that work?

STUDENT   Then what about transferring merit at the end of retreats?

SHIFU   At the end of a retreat you have earned personal merit. In transferring merit you are saying that you wish to give it to others in hopes of helping sentient beings. This is the way of a bodhisattva. You do this with your mind. You can transfer merit only when you have such merit. If you do not have such merit, then you can think and imagine all you want, but no merit will be transferred. Likewise, if you have done bad things, you cannot transfer the bad thoughts to someone else thinking that you will then be free and clear of them.

When you transfer merit you should do so with a mind of generosity and compassion. In other words, you should give it all away without your own benefit in mind. If you are thinking that by transferring merit you will gain even more merit, then you have not transferred any merit.

STUDENT   What accumulates merit? Does saving a puppy from drowning earn merit, or does merit come only with deep cultivation of Buddhadharma?

SHIFU   If you have done something good, in the future you will receive good karmic effects. Good speech and actions accumulate merit. Some speech and actions create more merit than others. In your mind, you should say that you do not really want this good effect. You wish to give it others so that they can benefit. This is transferring merit. It is like giving money to someone. If they try to pay you back, you tell them to give it to someone else instead.

The less people dwell on themselves, the greater their

cultivation will be. Transferring merit should not be done with the idea of gaining more merit. The first of the Six Paramitas (Perfections) of the bodhisattva path is *dana*, or giving. People on this path simply give because they are on the path. As a result, egocentrism may be reduced, but that is not the purpose. Transferring merit is just another way to practice this paramita.

STUDENT   In the past you have said that your karma is your karma. You cannot take other people's karma and you cannot give yours away. But if you are giving your good karma to others when you transfer merit, isn't that precisely what you are doing? And if it is possible to give it away, then why shouldn't I get rid of my bad karma as well? I'll give it to Harry over there.

SHIFU   The difference is that good karma is like money earned. You have a right to do with it what you want. But bad karma is like owing money. When you owe money you do not have a say in the matter.

STUDENT   When you talk about karma in this way, it sounds too neat and structured. It sounds like a man-made invention. Is karma really set up like a banking system? I think of words like principal and interest and it seems a bit too pat. It also makes it seem like there is some standard of measurement for the severity of actions committed. It all sounds a bit contrived to me.

SHIFU   The Buddha taught that there were certain questions that were inexplicable and unfathomable; and if people contemplated these concepts in hopes of coming up with answers they could become deluded or confused. One of these is to try to understand what the Buddha's mind is capable of. Another is to try to understand the workings of karma. Karma is difficult, and in fact, impossible to fully and clearly explain. Yet, people insist on knowing more about it. They want crystal-clear, concrete descriptions to help them understand their existence and experience.

The point is, while karma is inconceivable, we have to come up with analogies to try to explain its facets. None of them does justice to the actual thing. This time around I used a banking analogy. If you do not like that analogy, I will try and come up with another one. But all of them will be analogies, and will therefore fall short of the real thing. As Buddhists, the main thing for us to understand is that our thoughts, speech, and actions have consequences that we will receive, in this life and in future lives.

# Is Chan a Religion?

QUESTION   Is Chan a religion?

SHIFU   Shakyamuni Buddha attained enlightenment and taught Buddhadharma in India, at a time when its culture was spiritually and religiously oriented. He began his teachings by questioning some of the prevailing beliefs, such as the existence of individual souls, but for the sake of inducing followers of other faiths to follow the Dharma, he incorporated elements from other spiritual traditions. Also, as Buddhadharma spread, it absorbed some ideas and beliefs of other cultures. In the process, Buddhism became a religion. However, Buddhism is different from all other religions, and its fundamental principles are not necessarily of a religious nature.

Shakyamuni Buddha did not teach his disciples to pray to a deity, or even to himself for help or salvation. He encouraged sentient beings to help themselves as well as others. By studying and practicing Buddhadharma, sentient beings can relieve themselves of life's vexations, and eventually free themselves from the cycle of birth and death.

Inevitably, however, people asked: "Where do we come from? And if we do not get enlightened, what will happen after death, where will we go?" In answering these questions, Shakyamuni Buddha relied on a modified version of the teaching of reincarnation, which already existed in Indian religions. Shakyamuni perceived that sentient beings have past and future lives, were imprisoned in the seemingly endless cycle of samsara, and would remain that way unless they began to practice Buddhadharma. If sentient beings practice until they were fully enlightened, then they would be free from vexation—from desire, aversion, and ignorance—which keeps them imprisoned in samsara.

People then asked, "If anyone can practice and attain buddhahood, is Shakyamuni the only buddha? If not, where are others who have attained buddhahood?" Shakyamuni Buddha said that the scope of ordinary sentient beings' perceptions and power is limited. This world is tiny and the universe vast. There are innumerable buddhas who have attained ultimate enlightenment, and when causes and conditions ripen, ordinary sentient beings will also attain buddhahood. Again, the Buddha's answer encouraged people to practice.

But people are rarely satisfied, so they asked, "How long will it take to attain buddhahood?" Shakyamuni Buddha explained the path and process of practice, describing the levels of attainment, which culminate in complete enlightenment. He spoke about the bodhisattvas, those exemplars of practice who attained saintly status. Yet, Shakyamuni did not exhort people to pray to bodhisattvas, but to emulate them.

Shakyamuni spoke of the wisdom and compassion of the bodhisattvas and their eternal vows to help sentient beings attain liberation. He spoke of Avalokitesvara, the bodhisattva of compassion, Manjusri, the bodhisattva of wisdom, and many others. At first, practitioners looked to the bodhisattvas as role models, but later, many who lacked determination and faith in themselves stopped practicing and began to pray to one or another of the bodhisattvas. They prayed for the fulfillment of their needs and the appeasement of their suffering. Such practices continue to this day. In this latter sense, yes, Buddhism is a religion.

It is not bad that Buddhism has developed this religious aspect. When people sincerely pray to deities, bodhisattvas, or even God, they will be helped or appeased. But the response to the prayers does not come from the deities, bodhisattvas or God. It comes in part from the mental power of the person seeking help, and it also comes from the collective power of all the people seeking help from a particular deity or bodhisattva. When a sufficient number of people sincerely seek help from a bodhisattva or deity, power will manifest, whether or not the bodhisattva or deity exists. It happens. People seek help and their prayers are answered. It is common in every religion. In this respect, Buddhism is like other religions.

Chan Buddhism, however, is different; it penetrates directly to the original essence of Buddhadharma and encourages practitioners to rely on themselves, to solve their own problems. In fact, Chan describes people who seek the Dharma outside of their own minds as following outer-path teachings—teachings outside the Dharma. Since Chan espouses self-initiative, it can do without the religious, supplicating aspects of other Buddhist sects.

Chan practitioners do not deny the existence of bodhisattvas. They believe strongly in bodhisattvas, buddhas and patriarchs, but they do not pray to them as people would pray to a deity. They recognize that patriarchs and bodhisattvas are beings at different levels of practice. They revere bodhisattvas and seek to emulate them, but they do not typically ask for their help. In a humble, sober manner, Chan followers practice on their own, or under the guidance of a master.

If Chan practitioners should ask the Buddha or bodhisattvas for anything, it is for the Dharma. They seek the Dharma through the help of the Sangha, and through the study of the sutras and sastras. They do not ask for power, spiritual experiences, or enlightenment. Likewise, if they burn incense and prostrate to images of the Buddha and bodhisattvas, it is not worship. Rather, they are expressing their gratitude, because without buddhas, bodhisattvas, and the Sangha, there would be no Buddha-dharma in the world. For Chan practitioners, buddhas and bodhisattvas are role models, not idols to be worshipped, or guardian angels that protect their lives. For them, bodhisattvas are not crutches.

I, as well as other Chan masters, teach people to recite Amitabha Buddha's name or Avalokitesvara Bodhisattva's name, but not for religious purposes. Some Buddhists recite Amitabha's name in order to be reborn in the Pure Land. They recite Avalokitesvara's name to fulfill their wishes and needs. These are religious practices. I ask you to recite their names solely as a method of meditation. The recitation focuses your mind. In reciting a buddha's or bodhisattva's name, either aloud or silently, your body, speech and thoughts are focused on a great, enlightened being. It is a good method to discipline and purify the mind. Through this method, you can even experience samadhi and cultivate wisdom.

Sometimes, people ask me to pray for them. From a religious point of view, these people might think that I kneel down and pray to a deity or bodhisattva to help them. Perhaps they think I have a hot line to the Buddha. I do not have any special connections and I do not pray. Then why do I agree to pray for these people? Two reasons. First, if I say I will pray for them, they will feel better. Usually, that is all people need. Second, I can transfer merit to these people through the power of my practice. People who practice can transfer merit to others. In fact, even without practice, people who are sincere in their intentions can bring about a good effect on others. The opposite is also true. If many people wish someone harm, then that person will likely suffer. It is not magical. It is merely the power of the mind.

I recite Avalokitesvara's name, with the idea that my merit will be transferred to others. I do not care if he exists or not. Why do I bother? First, Shakyamuni Buddha praised Avalokitesvara and his power, and I trust the Buddha's words. Second, precisely because so many people believe in and pray to Avalokitesvara, his power exists. For these reasons, I recite his name and use him to transfer merit.

Avalokitesvara serves as a giant reflector, upon which thousands of people direct their thoughts. If these individuals direct their thoughts to different objects, it is like thousands of weak flashlights shining with limited power. But if people concentrate their thoughts on a single entity, it is like shining all of the flashlights' beams onto a giant mirror, increasing tremendously the illumination. Avalokitesvara is such a mirror. Externally, this may seem similar to the practices of many other religions, but the perspective is different. Other religions say that power comes from the deity one prays to. Buddhism maintains that power comes from the person or people who pray.

Some Buddhists who do not practice well, or do not have strong faith in themselves and their methods, will seek the help of bodhisattvas, or ask that a master transfer spiritual power to them. Chan masters, as well as serious practitioners, do not seek anything from buddhas and bodhisattvas except the Dharma. They are willing to help and give to others, but they will not seek supernatural power or spiritual benefits. It is all right for beginning practitioners to seek external help, as long as they realize that, eventually, they must not seek at all, and that they must rely solely on themselves. Help that comes from outside can only temporarily relieve your problems. It will not penetrate to the root and solve your problems. The basic approach, in fact, the only thing that works, is to rely on yourself, and to solve your own problems through practice.

# Practicing Buddhism and
## Other Religions

❦

QUESTION   Is it possible to practice Buddhism and still maintain faith in another religion?

SHIFU   Buddhism can be practiced at five levels of aspiration. The first level corresponds to the human realm, the second to the heavenly realms. The three other levels are unique to Buddhism, and these are the levels of the arhat, the bodhisattvas, and the buddhas. I will restrict my answers mostly to the first two levels. At these levels, the human and heavenly, there are appropriate ways to practice according to Buddhadharma. Most religions do not venture past the human and heavenly realms. Some, perhaps, are not even concerned with the heavens, but only with human life. In the sutras, the appropriate actions and practices necessary for sentient beings at the first two levels, or for those beings in the human realm who wish to enter the heavenly realms, are explicitly taught in accordance with Buddhadharma. In this sense, Buddhism is not opposed to people seeking to be reborn in the heavens, and therefore, is not opposed to other religions that teach the same.

Buddhism wants to help everyone, and welcomes people of any faith to use Buddhist methods of practice. People of other religions who are newcomers to Buddhism need not give up their previous faiths. If you wish to hold on to your original faith, it is not a problem.

In most societies, families usually pass on their faiths from generation to generation. If you had to give up your original faith in order to practice Buddhism, you would separate yourself in many ways from family and society because a large part of any religion is social and cultural interaction. There is no need for people to abandon all of this. When I came to the United States, I believed that people who espoused Buddhadharma should be very flexible and accepting of all people, no matter what their beliefs.

How does Buddhism respond to Western religions? Throughout their history, Christianity, Judaism, and Islam have done much good and have helped many people. Had these religions not existed, some of the civilizations of Europe might have been deprived of moral and ethical teachings. Nevertheless, accepting the teachings of Christianity would not be the same as accepting the teachings of Buddhadharma. The fact is that certain aspects of Jesus' teachings do not accord with Buddhadharma, and vice versa. As Buddhists, we should only consider those aspects of Jesus' teachings that are in accordance with those of the Dharma, and we can only consider the teachings of Christianity at the level of the human and heavenly realms.

I doubt that in the future the numerous religions will fuse into one. The world is not that simple. It is important for the major religions to recognize and support those parts of their faiths that are the same, as well as understand and respect those parts that are different. For Buddhists to claim their way is superior would cause unnecessary dispute and tension. We can only explain our teachings so others may understand. It is not our right to judge whether another religion is good or bad, correct, or incorrect.

STUDENT   Can we think of Buddhism and in particular the Chan sect, as a religion?

SHIFU   This is a very important question. On one hand, the teachings of the Dharma, and especially the teachings of Chan, are methods of practice. Shakyamuni Buddha taught methods. He did not tell people to believe in anything or to accept anything on faith. From the point of view of strict practice, there seems to be no need for religious ritual, for performance of rites of adoration toward the buddhas. In this sense, Buddhism need not be classified as a religion.

On the other hand, if the teachings of the Dharma encourage one to follow the methods taught by the Buddha and the patriarchs, one must have the highest faith in the buddhas and bodhisattvas to benefit from the practice. Without faith, one would not practice for very long. With half-hearted faith, the benefits of practice would be superficial. In this sense, then, faith in the buddhas and bodhisattvas is necessary, and if we are to speak of a religion as a tradition involving faith, then Buddhism can be classified as a religion. On the other hand, if a religion is limited to ritual alone, then Buddhism does not have to be considered a religion.

STUDENT  No religion would admit that it is purely ritual. All religions claim more.

SHIFU  This is true. In that case, Buddhism is definitely a religion. We must ask ourselves if these rituals are necessary or useful to the religion. In the spreading of the Dharma throughout the Orient, people started by observing the ritual aspects. When I came to this country, I incorporated a minimal amount of ritual in my teachings. However, after practicing for a while, people here naturally developed great respect, faith and gratitude towards buddhas, bodhisattvas, and patriarchs, and the normal way to express such feelings is through ritual.

What, then, do we mean by religion? Religion is faith in the existence, power, or authority of a charismatic entity or entities, whether human or divine. This includes teachers, prophets, gods, or a god. The objects of this faith often are founding teachers, such as the Buddha, Jesus, Abraham, or Mohammed. The teachings of a religion are of greatest importance, for that is what we have to work with, to learn from, to practice.

STUDENT  This question concerns people of other faiths who practice Buddhism. Is it possible to intellectually understand the concepts of the Dharma and benefit from the practice without incorporating the teachings into your religious belief system?

SHIFU  Is it possible to ignore the teachings, the concepts

and theories, and just practice? It may be possible, but only in the beginning stages. When I teach meditation to a newcomer, I can ignore such teachings, but after a while I have to introduce ideas like karma, rebirth, and causes and conditions.

Can one understand these teachings and yet not accept them? Perhaps, but only if you are content with gaining only a small amount of benefit from the practice. But if you want to enter deeper and deeper into the practice of the Dharma, then you must accept the teachings.

STUDENT   Then the earlier question returns. One can gain much from meditation and Buddhist principles without abandoning one's original faith. However, if a person from another faith wants to practice Buddhism on a deep level, eventually must that person give up at least some of the beliefs of the original religion?

SHIFU   That is correct. On a shallow level, you can hold onto your previous religion's doctrine. If you wish to practice Buddhism seriously, then inevitably you should relinquish other beliefs. It would be impossible to have absolute faith in two sets of teachings. To say that one does not have to give up the original religion pertains to the social and cultural aspects of that religion. But, even if one gives up the beliefs of the other religion, it does not mean that one is then opposed to that faith.

STUDENT   Isn't it possible to go one step beyond this, and say it is all in the mind? They are just beliefs and concepts and therefore I can believe anything I want to? I can even hold contradictory beliefs in my mind at the same time?

SHIFU   It is difficult to hold contradictory beliefs. It is hard to get rid of one's ideas of one's religion. Many people of other religions would like to benefit from Buddhadharma. They are intrigued by the philosophy, but they interpret it in terms of their own beliefs. They try Buddhist meditation in order to reach higher levels of their own religions, to experience their God. Buddhist methods can be used for these purposes. It can be said, also, that people who have reached higher levels of their religions have had enlightenment experiences, but they are not true Buddhist enlightenment experiences. They have not left all conceptualization behind. They have not left behind their beliefs. They have not let go of their selves. People who hear this may interpret it as though Buddhists feel their beliefs are superior to other beliefs, that their levels of enlightenment are above all other types of enlightenment. This is also not true. It is the manner in which Buddhists describe their experiences. Other religions have their points of view. To speak of higher and lower or better and worse is irrelevant, non-productive, and even dangerous.

STUDENT   Earlier you spoke about whether other religious figures, such as Jesus Christ, are bodhisattvas. Can you elaborate?

SHIFU   Religions generally have three basic elements: someone who started the religion, the teachings of the religion, and ritual. In the case of Christianity, I do not want to say that its originator, Jesus, was a bodhisattva, nor do I want to oppose that view. By his teachings alone you or I cannot determine whether Jesus was a bodhisattva. Only bodhisattvas would be able to tell if Jesus was a bodhisattva, since they would be able to see his Dharma body. Since I cannot do this, I do not want to take a definite position for or against this view. Really, the issue is irrelevant, unimportant. What are important are the teachings and the example of the founder's life. That is what people should be concerned with.

STUDENT   We were raised as Catholics. When our child is born, our parents expect that we will have the baby baptized. We, however, do not follow that religion, so we would rather not have this ritual performed. We feel to do so would be hypocritical.

SHIFU   If your parents are not strongly opposed to your wishes, then it is not necessary to go through with the ritual. If it really upsets them, then it is all right to go through with the baptism as a favor to your parents. There is another point. Buddhism recognizes the power of the mind. If someone gives a sincere blessing, such as through baptism, then the receiver of the blessing will benefit. The blessing comes from the power of the mind of the person giving the blessing as well as from the power of the deity that the person believes in. Buddhism does not deny the existence of deities. Buddhism accepts that deities of other faiths do exist, and that they do have certain power.  In the case of your child, if a Catholic priest baptizes your child, that is good for the child. If you want me also to bless your child, I would be happy to do so. Your child will be doubly blessed.

# Buddha Images



QUESTION   Why do Buddhists use and revere images and statues of the Buddha?

SHIFU   When Shakyamuni, the historical Buddha, was still alive, there were no such things as statues or images of the Buddha. It was not until one hundred years or so after the Buddha entered nirvana that people started to use things to symbolize the Buddha. Some of these symbols are the Dharma Wheel representing the Buddha's first setting in motion of the teaching of the Dharma, two trees representing the spot where Shakyamuni entered nirvana, and the bodhi tree, under which Shakyamuni attained complete enlightenment. At this time, there also began a worship of the Buddha's relics. These symbols and relics probably represent the origin of all later Buddhist images, such as Buddha statues.

During the earlier periods after Shakyamuni's departure, people used places and things that helped them to remember the Buddha. Eventually, people built stupas—shrines that contained relics of the Buddha. Soon, however, shrines outnumbered relics, so Buddha statues were placed in stupas instead. This is the origin and general history of the emergence of Buddha statues in Buddhism.

STUDENT   The idea of worship is a key issue. In the minds of some people, the images and statues of the Buddha can take on supernatural powers. It seems that many people view the statues as an extension of a deity.

SHIFU   This belief does exist among people who do not have a deep understanding of the Buddha's teachings. They view the statues as an extension of a deity, and they worship these statues in order to derive responses and gain benefit from the Buddhas. In this sense, the Buddha statues do function as deities for many people.

From the standpoint of Buddhism, it is acceptable for people to worship statues and buddhas as if they were deities, because buddhas exist everywhere, and their purpose is to help sentient beings. So, if there are requests from sentient beings, then buddhas will respond. However, this is only one viewpoint.

Sentient beings asking the Buddha for responses receive benefit not only from the Buddha, but also from the making of the requests themselves. If people have a desire to fulfill or attain something, they can accomplish it because of their own desire, just as your own voice, because it projects inward as well as outward, can cause you yourself to respond. It is a product of your own effort.

For serious practitioners, who have a deep understanding of the Buddha's teachings, Buddha images are just a tool for practice. When they want to express gratitude, or practice concentration, the Buddha statue serves as a focus for their attention.

In addition, in paintings and sculptures, the Buddha image appears serene and splendid. When practitioners and others see this, they are inclined to conduct themselves similarly, to emulate the Buddha—one who possesses infinite merit and wisdom. In this way, too, the image of the Buddha helps people.

STUDENT    It was said that Shakyamuni would alter the content of his Dharma talks to match the audience he was addressing. What you are saying about Buddha statues seems to parallel this aspect of the Buddha, that Buddhism has many levels of entry, and that the Buddha image can be used by people in different ways.

SHIFU    Exactly. For example, there is an old Buddhist anecdote of Chan Master Tianran (739-824), who burned a wooden statue of the Buddha in order to keep warm on a cold winter day. People were alarmed. "You are burning the Buddha statue! You are a master! How could you, of all people, do that?" Tianran replied, "That which can be burned cannot be the Buddha." For Tianran, the Buddha exists everywhere, but it is not something that can be grasped or attained, much less burned.

Master Baizhang (720-814), who started the monastery system in China, did not build Buddha Halls with statues and images, only Dharma Halls, where people practiced and listened to lectures. According to Baizhang, Buddhadharma is the representation of the Buddha. As long as Buddhadharma is present, Buddha statues are unnecessary.

Even before the Tang dynasty (618-907), Chan monasteries incorporated Buddha statues. We can see how important Buddha statues are from the Yungang and the Longmen, two famous Buddhist sites that have many Buddha images carved in the walls. These sites were built in the third and fourth centuries. Statues were important for general practitioners after the Tang dynasty as well.

STUDENT    I assume that Tianran burned the wooden Buddha statue in order to teach a lesson to his disciples. If I, on the other hand, burned a Buddha statue in order to demonstrate my understanding of Buddhism, would it make a great deal of difference? In other words, would burning a Buddha statue be an act of desecration if the right understanding were not there?

SHIFU    You must understand that the story of Tianran is a *gong'an*. Every *gong'an* that is described only happens once. Such occurrences are not repeated. If someone repeats or imitates a *gong'an* later on, it is false, and definitely not an indication of enlightenment. If anybody hears a *gong'an* and then tries to recreate the scene, it would be an act that would create bad karma.

STUDENT    But what if an individual truly believes that something that can be burned cannot be the Buddha? What if the person truly believes that he or she is burning this wooden statue to get warmth? It is not showing disrespect. Why would this be creating bad karma?

SHIFU    If you had to burn a Buddha statue to survive, would your actions be justifiable, knowing that you acted not out of true realization, but with the intellectual understanding that this is only a piece of wood? No, you cannot do this, without creating karma. Tianran did this to help his disciples cut off their attachments. He did it for the sake of others. He did not do it because he was freezing. If you were to follow his example and repeat the scene, it would be for your own sake, not for the sake of others. In other words, since your action is self-motivated, some bad karma would result.

To an enlightened person, the Buddha statue is still a Buddha statue. An ordinary piece of wood is still just a piece of wood. The two are different in his or her mind. Another person may think that the two objects are the same, but that person is confused and not enlightened. It is not wise to recreate a *gong'an*. They cannot be imitated. If you purposely imitate them, it can lead to trouble.

STUDENT    I still do not understand. If all things have buddha-nature, then why would an enlightened person see a Buddha statue and an ordinary piece of wood as being different?

SHIFU    In terms of buddha-nature, there is no difference between a block of wood, a Buddha statue, or anything else for that matter. But, there is a difference in terms of phenomena in the world. In terms of phenomena, everything is different, but in the enlightened person's mind, there is no discrimination. If Chan masters do not even have the common sense to see ordinary phenomena as being different, they would be considered lunatics.

STUDENT   Earlier, you said that the serious practitioner uses the Buddha statue as a tool, a focus towards which to direct his or her gratitude. Some Westerners misunderstand the practice of prostrating before the Buddha statue as worshipping idols.

SHIFU   As I said before, there are two types of worshipping. First, ordinary people worship the Buddha statue in order to get some type of response or benefit from the buddhas. Second, serious practitioners use the Buddha statue as a tool. This does not mean that serious practitioners do not derive benefit. There is a response, but it comes from the actions of the individual. Serious practitioners should not have the thought or wish that the buddhas should do their work for them.

If there is any benefit to be gained from the buddhas at all, whether it be by paying respect to the Buddha, or by using the statue as a tool, that benefit comes from the Dharma that the Buddha taught. The act of paying respect to the Buddha helps to incorporate more Buddhadharma into our practice. Thus, what may appear to be worshipping becomes, in fact, a kind of practice, cultivation. Prostrating to the Buddha becomes a meditative exercise. However, this is a Chan point of view. Other forms of Buddhism, such as esoteric Buddhism, teach differently.

STUDENT   From the Chan point of view, it would seem that prostrating to a Buddha statue is the same as prostrating to Shifu. It is a momentary act of giving up the self.

SHIFU   Yes.

STUDENT   Coinciding with Buddha statues or images is the concept of 'opening the light,' which manifests itself in a ritual called the 'Opening the Eye Ceremony.' Can you provide more information on this topic?

SHIFU   In such a ritual, people initiate a statue for the benefit of the general religious practitioner. The procedure may vary, but usually the initiator invokes the name or the mantra of the buddha or bodhisattva that the statue represents. They use their own mind energy to create a channel for the energy and responses of a buddha or bodhisattva. Of course, if the initiated statue is placed in a museum, no response will come from it. On the other hand, if the statue resides in a temple where people use it, it is more likely that responses will come. The 'eye-opening' ceremony transforms the Buddha statue from an ordinary piece of art into a religious piece of art. For the people who perform the ceremony, and for the general practitioner, the ritual makes a difference. Also, the statue itself differs before and after the ceremony.

For Chan practitioners, however, it is not necessary to use a statue that has undergone an 'eye-opening' procedure. They can use any statue, because it is not their purpose to get any response from the Buddha.

# Merit and Virtue
## in Buddhism

🍃

QUESTION   You often speak of compassion and meritorious deeds, but for ordinary sentient beings it is impossible to be compassionate in the ultimate sense that is expounded by Buddhist teachings. For instance, when the Emperor Wu asked Bodhidharma how much merit he would receive for all the temples he had built, Bodhidharma said "None," because the Emperor was doing it with attachment. Unless we are enlightened, it is impossible to act and be compassionate without attachment. It is disheartening, and if what Bodhidharma said is true, then it implies that there really is no such thing as merit. If that is the case, what is the point of transferring merit?

SHIFU   In the story of Emperor Wu and Bodhidharma, it is important to understand the meaning behind Bodhidharma's words, which was to break up the emperor's attachment. Bodhidharma did not literally mean that the emperor had earned no merit. He was trying to point out that the emperor had an attachment to the idea of merit. If people perform actions with merit in mind, then their egocentrism will grow and become stronger. For this reason, Chan masters often make such comments.

There are two vantage points from which to view Buddhadharma. One is the view of ordinary sentient beings, which takes the perspective of phenomena and looks forward. This is also known as the causal position. Whenever you say or do something, karma is created, and of course afterwards there will be some effect stemming from that karma. Therefore, when your good deeds accumulate merit, later there will be good effects. This is the principle of cause and consequence. For ordinary sentient beings, cause and consequence work in the worldly, or phenomenal, realm. Causes and consequences in the worldly realm have outflows (karmic results); that is, they are part of and influenced by self-attachment. These causes and consequences include good karma, bad karma, virtue, and merit.

The second view is that of enlightened beings. There are causes and consequences that transcend the worldly, or phenomenal, realm. These causes and consequences have no outflows, and likewise, the effects of these causes and consequences have no outflows. Such phenomena are bodhi, nirvana, and buddhahood. These completely enlightened beings are at the consequential position, looking backward at the causes.

People with the first perspective are sentient beings who exist in samsara. If they think there will be no retribution, no bad karma for bad deeds, and no merit for good deeds, then they have an incorrect view. Such people would likely not practice Buddhism because they would feel there is nothing to gain. Worse, they might do or say things they would not, if they believed in retribution.

Completely enlightened beings, however, perceive and understand that there really is no merit or virtue of which to speak. Merit and virtue only exist in relation to a perceived self. Enlightened beings have realized the nature of emptiness. Their merit and virtue have been transformed into wisdom. Enlightened beings would also say that there is no such thing as wisdom or attainment. One does not attain enlightenment through wisdom and merit because those are concepts relative to a self. So from the enlightened position it is correct for Bodhidharma to say that there is no merit or virtue.

We must not confuse the enlightened position with the unenlightened position. If enlightened beings still claim that merit and virtue exist, then they are not fully enlightened. If unenlightened people claim there is no such thing as virtue and merit, they are talking out of ignorance. People who hold this belief would not practice, and without practice, they would never have the opportunity to achieve realization. It is important to understand the difference between the causal (unenlightened) position and the consequential (enlightened) position.

We can interpret the story of Emperor Wu and Bodhidharma from two positions. From the causal position, the emperor did in fact accumulate merit and virtue because he performed worthy deeds. But Bodhidharma answered from the consequential position. He did this to shock the emperor, to help him wake up from his attachment and see into the emptiness of phenomena. He was trying to get the emperor to realize that in any situation, the action, the agent of the action and the result of the action are all empty. Unfortunately, Bodhidharma's method did not work on the emperor.

We should not disparage Emperor Wu for his views. He was a dedicated Buddhist and a loyal supporter of the Sangha. His life and deeds were exemplary and he deserves praise. He was not, however, receptive to the shockingly direct approach of Chan methods. Historically, this exchange between Bodhidharma and the emperor probably never took place. Nonetheless it is famous because of its relevance to the teachings of the Buddha.

This story has generated much confusion through the centuries, so in order to help people, another story was told to help clarify things. The story involves Master Baizhang (720-814), who lived a few hundred years after Bodhidharma. After one of Baizhang's talks, an old man in the assembly lingered behind and said: "I am not really a human being, but in fact the spirit of a fox. In ancient times I was a monk. A student asked me if an enlightened person was still subject to cause and consequence. I told him that an enlightened person was not so bound. For this reason I have been reborn as a fox for five hundred lifetimes. Now I am asking you to enlighten me on this matter."

Baizhang said, "An enlightened person is not ignorant of cause and consequence."

The old man became enlightened by these words. Happily, he prostrated to Baizhang and said, "Tomorrow, please go behind the mountain where you will find a dead fox, and perform the ceremony appropriate for a dead monk." The next day Baizhang obeyed the old man's wishes and went behind the mountain. In a cave he found the body of a fox, which he cremated.

This story is also probably legendary, but it serves a good purpose. Many people misunderstood the story of Bodhidharma and the emperor, and both suffered and caused suffering because of their misconception. Hence, the story of Master Baizhang and the fox was created.

Chan does not speak of process or progress. It does not take the causal position. It speaks only from the result, or consequential, position, so it always uses the negative approach instead of the affirmative approach; that is, it aims to break up any and all attachments. Chan does not want the individual to rely on or embrace anything.

Master Linji (d. 866/67) once commented that all the buddhas of the past, present, and future were simple fools, and he had similar comments for bodhisattvas and arhats. What he meant was that beings called buddhas, bodhisattvas, or arhats do not really exist. However, this is the standpoint of an enlightened being. For ordinary sentient beings, there truly are buddhas, bodhisattvas, and arhats. If people take Linji's words at face value, they may believe that the Buddha did not exist, that all of his teachings are garbage, and that there is no purpose in practicing. If it is your idea that it is okay to remain a sentient being without attempting to practice, you deserve rebuke. On the other hand, if you are over-awed and intimidated by the teachings of Buddhadharma, then you also deserve a scolding. As I said, Chan often speaks from the ultimate position. These are the realizations and attainments of completely enlightened beings. They are aspirations to admire, not fear.

The Chan approach is like a sharp, double-edged sword. It can both help and hurt. People who have good karmic roots can be helped by the methods of Chan, and they can use the methods to attain realization. On the other hand, people with serious karmic obstructions may interpret the teachings incorrectly and then suffer because of their erroneous understanding. That is why it is necessary to study Buddhadharma and practice with a good teacher, so that you do not stray down the wrong path.

Many people misunderstand the Chan approach. Someone once said to me, "Shifu, I just read a couple of *gong'ans*. They are mystifying. A monk asked a master if he should repeat the Buddha's name, and the master replied that if he repeated the Buddha's name even once he should wash his mouth for three days. In another story a monk asked what the Buddha was. The master replied that he had never heard of such a thing. So the monk asked him about Shakyamuni, and the master said that if he had run into him he would have beaten him to death and thrown his body to the dogs. It sounds like we are listening to the words of crazy people!"

Buddhist teachings say that cursing the Buddha creates one of the five worst kinds of karma, and these masters would have incurred heavy retribution; but these stories are in the same vein as that of Bodhidharma and the emperor. They are meant to shock practitioners into awakening, and are usually spoken to someone very close to realization. In Chan these statements are sometimes called 'turning words.' Chan masters use such methods to break up people's attachments. In such situations, Chan masters are not being arrogant. They make these statements to help practitioners. The same Chan masters who made these comments would likely have been seen prostrating to a Buddha statue later on. People who hear their masters' words and later witness their actions might think the masters were hypocritical or insane. But in fact it is simply those masters' ways to help sentient beings transcend discriminations such as self and other, nirvana and samsara, buddhas and ordinary sentient beings. They try to shatter a person's reliance on polarities and relativity.

On one retreat a long while ago in Taiwan, someone asked me if he could recite a buddha's name as a method instead of counting breaths. I asked, "Which buddha?"

"Amitabha Buddha."

"Here we don't have Amitabha Buddha, so you can't recite his name," I replied.

The person returned to his cushion, looked around and noticed a statue of Amitabha Buddha. He returned and said, "How come you said that? There's a statue right over there."

"I didn't put that statue there," I said. "My master did."

Later on the practitioner saw me prostrating to that very statue, so he asked, "How come you can prostrate to Amitabha?"

I said, "If my master prostrated to Amitabha, how dare I not do the same? All the same, you can't recite Amitabha Buddha's name."

But the person was persistent and said, "Shifu, I'd really like to use that method because I don't feel there is any virtue or merit in counting breaths."

Eventually I let him do what he wanted to do, and it was from that point on that I allowed people to use the method of reciting a buddha's name.

STUDENT    Speaking from causal position, which is where all of us are, what is compassionate behavior and what is not? If someone performs an action of charity or goodness, but has ulterior motives—not harmful but selfish—and another person performs a similar action out of altruism, is the compassion different and is different merit accrued? From the point of view of the recipient of the action, it is the same, but in one case the person gets a big tax exemption and his name in the press, and the other person does so anonymously and with no strings attached. Is there a difference?

SHIFU  If someone does something good, then there is merit involved, and the person is being, to a greater or lesser degree, compassionate. The question is how compassionate is the person really? It depends on the motive or intention behind the action. If a person is acting altruistically, then that is more compassionate than a person who is merely looking for a tax break. But they both receive merit because they both performed virtuous deeds. The general rule is, the more selfish the mind, the less the compassion, and therefore, the less merit accrued.

STUDENT  But, everything we think, say, and do stems from a selfish mind. It is impossible for ordinary people to do things devoid of a self. I suppose I could do something good automatically, without thinking about the consequences of my actions, but later, in hindsight, I might give myself a pat on the back. Does that change the merit of my action?

SHIFU  It is normal to feel good about yourself if you do something good. As long as you are attached to a self, then it is impossible not to be self-centered. If you could do something without being self-centered, then there would be no merit or virtue involved. You would be a buddha or bodhisattva. There is merit and virtue only if there is a self. If you do good deeds, then of course you are creating good karma, and you will receive merit for your actions. As I said earlier, it depends on your state of mind. Your actions might be based on greed or they might be based on love. One is more virtuous than the other, but in each case, the actions and motives stem from a self.

STUDENT   Is it possible to be less attached to things, or is it an all-or-nothing proposition?

SHIFU   Yes, there are different levels and degrees of attachment. Some people are obsessive about everything; some people are excessively greedy; some people are very attached to some things and not at all to others; some people's desires are light across the board. It all depends on the person, the level of his or her practice, his or her state of mind, and the situation. If you are concerned with the motives behind your thoughts, words and actions, the best thing is to practice so that you develop clearer self-awareness.

STUDENT   In Buddhism, what is the relationship between compassion and wisdom? It seems they always go together, like two sides of a coin. Are they necessarily a pair? Can you have one without the other? Are they the same?

SHIFU   Wisdom can be described in two ways. One way refers to your own self. The other refers to how you relate to other sentient beings. When you use wisdom to interact with others, that is compassion. Compassion only exists in relation to others. True compassion does not exist without wisdom, and ultimate compassion only exists when there is no self and no attachments.

# Bodhisattvas and Arhats

QUESTION   What are the similarities and differences between arhats and bodhisattvas? When someone attains arhatship, what reason is there to do anything but remain in that state? If bodhisattvas have no more desire, what causes them to progress further?

SHIFU   What is gained and what is lost when a person attains arhatship? Is an arhat necessarily a Hinayana practitioner? Could a bodhisattva also be an arhat? Under what circumstances can an arhat change to the bodhisattva path? Will he or she remain an arhat indefinitely? Finally, if a bodhisattva extinguishes desire, what motivates him or her to practice further?

People do not become arhats because they want to become arhats; rather, when vexations have ceased or have been eradicated through long cultivation, people naturally become arhats. Some people, having heard a phrase or sutra from the Buddha, instantly eradicated all vexations, including greed, anger, and ignorance, and immediately attained arhatship. Such people were very rare, but we do read about them in the sutras. Others practice in a gradual manner to cut off all vexations.

There are four stages of arhatship. The first stage is to eliminate the view of the self and eradicate doubt. The second stage is to cut off greed, anger, and ignorance. The third stage is to completely cut off greed and anger in the realm of desire. The fourth stage is true arhatship—when greed, anger, and ignorance in the three realms (desire, form, and formlessness) are eradicated. At this point all vexations are cut off. People who practice gradually differ from those who attain arhatship instantly; nonetheless, gradual practitioners do not have the intention or desire to become arhats. Their goal is to terminate vexation.

There is a correspondence between the Hinayana arhat and the Mahayana bodhisattva insofar as how much vexation has been eradicated. For example, the first stage of Hinayana attainment is reached when one has dissolved one's view of the self and has also eradicated all doubt. Doubt here means doubting the Three Jewels as well as doubting whether one can transcend samsara and eradicate vexation. This is the first *bhumi* level of bodhisattvahood. *Bhumi* means ground, and can be considered the fertile ground of practice from which wisdom sprouts. There are ten *bhumis*, of which the tenth is at the threshold of buddhahood. The fourth stage of arhatship corresponds to the end of the seventh *bhumi*.

You must realize that these stages in the Hinayana and Mahayana traditions are extremely advanced. The difference between the two paths is that bodhisattvas place greater emphasis on compassion; their foremost thought is how to help sentient beings. Because they are constantly interacting with sentient beings, it is more difficult for them to eradicate vexation. That is, they may have already gotten to the first *bhumi* and they may not have any view of the self or any doubt, but they will still have many vexations. These vexations are there because bodhisattvas manifest in the world of sentient beings and must continue to deal with them. Therefore it takes much less time for Hinayana practitioners to attain arhatship then it does for Mahayana practitioners to become advanced bodhisattvas.

Bodhisattvas do not have as their objective the termination of vexations. Their goal is to cultivate merit and virtue for the sake of sentient beings. Merit and virtue are still incomplete at the eighth *bhumi*, so bodhisattvas must continue cultivating the path through the tenth *bhumi*, at which point all vexations and attachments are eradicated, merit and virtue are perfected, and buddhahood is attained.

As the sutras tell us, most of the Buddha's famous disciples became arhats. It is also obvious from the sutras that they were concerned with the welfare of sentient beings. The First Patriarch Mahakasyapa, Ananda, and Sariputra asked the Buddha many important questions for the sake of sentient beings. Hence, although they were considered arhats, their compassionate nature indicates that they also embodied bodhisattva ideals and were not solely concerned with their own welfare.

Furthermore, the Buddha exhorted all of his arhat disciples to spread the Dharma. For example, he told the original five bhikshus (monks) who studied with him and became arhats to disperse in different directions so that they could help more people. Therefore, there were many arhats who exhibited bodhisattva attitudes. How many we do not know. Among the 1250 disciples who became arhats under the Buddha's guidance, we only know details about a few dozen.

There are reasons why arhats might not pursue the bodhisattva path. Perhaps they may not have the confidence to help others; or perhaps they feel they have already attained the ultimate. There exist four lines in the scriptures that read:

> My birth and death are over,
> My purity has been established;
> All that needs to be done has been done,
> There will be no more retribution.

Some of the original arhats, knowing these lines, may have felt they had attained the ultimate goal. They felt confident that their practice was complete. After all, the Buddha had ascertained that they had attained liberation. If they thought there was nothing higher, then there was no need to return to the human realm.

Perhaps some arhats felt that the human realm is filled with too much suffering. They may have helped others for the remainder of their lives, but felt that their duties to others had been fulfilled. Some arhats changed their attitudes before they died and started following the bodhisattva path, but others entered nirvana. From a buddha's point of view, these arhats may have attained liberation, but they do not have sufficient merit and virtue. Therefore, the sutras state that these arhats who feel they are liberated are in fact only taking a temporary rest in nirvana. Ultimately they will return. From this perspective, then, there are no permanent arhats. Eventually, all arhats who enter nirvana will return and follow the bodhisattva path.

Beginning bodhisattvas have strong self-centers, but they have learned that to make progress and attain buddhahood they must help sentient beings. Not doing so would be truly selfish; their self-centeredness would never diminish. That is why the first of the Four Great Vows is to help sentient beings. Through this process, we diminish self-centeredness.

There are also bodhisattvas between the first and eighth *bhumi* levels who have terminated the view of the self. For them, however, the goal is still to help others. On the other hand, the goal for Hinayana practitioners is to end vexations. For this reason Hinayana practitioners can attain their goal much more quickly than do bodhisattvas.

Finally, there are bodhisattvas at the eighth *bhumi* level or above. These are called the stages of non-functioning. At this point bodhisattvas are already spontaneously helping sentient beings. It is like riding a bicycle downhill; no more effort is needed to keep the bike moving. One can also use the analogy of the law of inertia. Once a body is set in motion, it will continue to move unless it meets resistance. Prior to the eighth *bhumi*, bodhisattvas have accumulated power, momentum, and direction, so when they reach the eighth level, they no longer have any intention of helping sentient beings, yet they continue to do so. So long as sentient beings exist, bodhisattvas will continue to help.

STUDENT   You say that at a certain point arhats and bodhisattvas no longer have a view of a self, yet they still have vexation. How can there be vexation without a sense of self? What is there to vex?

SHIFU   Here is an analogy. The view of the self is like the root of a big tree. A person who has terminated the view of self is like a tree that has had its roots cut off. The roots are gone but the tree is big. There is still a lot of sap in it. The tree can still live for some time. Some parts may still grow and flowers may still bloom, but the tree's days are definitely numbered. All of the activities that continue in the tree after the roots are cut off are like the vexations that linger after the view of self goes away.

# Buddhism and Death

QUESTION    How does Buddhism explain death? What happens between death and the next life? What carries over from one life to the next? How should one practice in the face of death?

SHIFU    For most human beings, death is very frightening, yet it is an inevitable event all of us must come to grips with. However, the ways ordinary sentient beings and enlightened beings view death are different. Furthermore, conventional Buddhism and Chan have different perspectives on death.

Conventional Buddhism speaks of two types of death—that for ordinary sentient beings and that for saints. Accumulated karma determines to what life an ordinary sentient being will be reborn. If the sentient being is overwhelmingly dominated by bad karma, they will likely be reborn either in a hell, ghost, or animal realm. If good karma overwhelmingly predominates, the being will be reborn in a heavenly realm. If good and bad karma are relatively balanced, then the being will be reborn in the human realm.

The period between one death and the next life is called the bardo in Tibetan Buddhism. Chan Buddhism calls it the intermediate body stage. After death, human beings do not necessarily go through an intermediate body stage. If one's karma is overwhelmingly good, one will go directly to a heavenly realm; and if one's karma is overwhelmingly bad, one will go directly to a hellish realm. Karma that is relatively balanced will go through the intermediate body stage; where and how it will be reborn, no one knows. There are many types of parents creating new life. Depending on causes and conditions, an intermediate body could be born in the animal realm, the human realm, or in certain heavenly realms.

For these reasons, it is helpful for the living to perform services to help alleviate the karma of the intermediate body. If people perform services—chant, recite sutras, make offerings—and transfer merit to the intermediate body, this will help the departed being. For example, if the being was destined to be reborn in a lower realm, performing services may cause it to be reborn in the human realm. If it was to be reborn in poor conditions, then the transfer of merit may help it to be reborn in better conditions. The intermediate body can do nothing on its own behalf; it cannot practice and it cannot create new karma. It can only receive merit from living beings.

According to Chinese Buddhism, the intermediate body stage lasts forty-nine days at most. According to the *Tibetan Book of the Dead*, it can be longer. The time varies for different beings and depends upon causes and conditions. When causes and conditions ripen, a being will be reborn. According to Chinese Buddhism, if, after forty-nine days, the intermediate body does not proceed to the next life, then it will immediately become a hungry ghost or a deity.

If a being that does not proceed to the next life has weak karma, then its activity will be limited. It will appear only at certain times and in certain places. Such a being is called a hungry ghost (*preta*). If the being's karma is stronger, then its activity will span a larger area and longer time. Such a being is called a deity (*deva*). However, nothing is eternal, and eventually these beings will be reborn in other realms. While they are ghosts or deities, these beings cannot practice. Like beings in the intermediate body stage, they can only receive the merits of living beings through services.

The second type of death involves saints. I sometimes speak of saints and sages. Sages are sentient beings whose practice is much deeper than that of ordinary practitioners, but who have not yet attained liberation. Some of the patriarchs were sages. In the Hinayana tradition, a saint has reached at least the first of four levels, or fruits, of arhatship. After reaching the first level, the being will be reborn no more than seven additional times, before being forever liberated as an arhat. For such an arhat, the stage after death is known as non-lingering nirvana. There is no lingering karma attached to the being, so it enters nirvana.

According to Mahayana Buddhism, a being who is above the first *bhumi* level is a bodhisattva saint. For a bodhisattva, there is no such thing as birth and death. A great bodhisattva with supernatural powers can manifest in more than one place or form.

Chan Buddhism accepts Buddhist scripture but does not depend on it. Chan stresses that a practitioner must come to realize that there is no life or death, no good or bad, no internal or external, no future or past. Chan does away with dualities, and adopts the attitude of non-discrimination. With such an attitude you can face death with equanimity, and without clinging to life.

STUDENT   If you practice for your entire life and do not get enlightened, will it have been a waste of time, or will something carry over into the next life?

SHIFU   If you have the attitude I just described and practice diligently, whether you become enlightened in this life does not matter. But I am sure you are not satisfied with this answer. The best answer is that serious practitioners should avoid creating bad karma, which will help to ensure a good rebirth, wherein they can continue their practice. When they commit misdeeds they should know it immediately and repent. This will soften the karmic consequences of their actions.

Chan practitioners who have mastered their fear of death do not care if they go through the intermediate body stage. It does not matter in what realm or world they are born. If the causes and conditions are conducive for practice, then they will practice in their next lives.

What carries over from one life to the next? Obviously it is not the physical body, but Buddhism holds that there is also no true or eternal self. What determines the next life and what carries over to the next life is karma, of which there are two types: karma with outflows and karma without outflows.

Karma with outflows—whether good, bad, or neutral—is created by sentient beings attached to an illusory self; its course is conditioned by the three poisons of desire, anger, and ignorance. In fact, the illusory self *is* the power of karma.

Therefore, one can say that the power of karma carries over from one life to the next, or one can say that the attachment to an illusory self carries over from one life to the next. In either case, sentient beings will continuously experience karmic effects, life after life. Karmic seeds reside in the eighth (*alaya* or storehouse) consciousness. After death, karmic seeds continue to ripen, and the most powerful karmic seeds will influence where and how one is reborn. The being will be drawn to a set of parents like a magnet.

Karma without outflows is created by saints and enlightened sages, who have no attachment to self. Not attached to self, the consequences of this karma are without outflows, free from the wheel of samsara. Such karma does not reside in the storehouse consciousness. What carries over from one life to the next is just the power of wisdom. Such beings are only reborn because they respond to the needs of sentient beings.

STUDENT  What mental attitude should you maintain on your deathbed? If possible, should you meditate or recite Guanyin's (Avalokitesvara's) name, or recite sutras? You said that a Chan practitioner should realize that there is no life or death, but what about people who have not attained such realization? What mental attitude should they have?

SHIFU  Many of these questions arise because one encounters different Buddhist traditions, and one is therefore lead to ask many questions relating to death. What I said earlier still holds. Chan practitioners should not be preoccupied with the question of death. It is not necessary to be enlightened in order to be fearless. Furthermore, there are no special preparations one needs to make before death.

The important thing is to maintain a regular practice while alive.

If you want to do something for yourself on your deathbed, meditating or repeating Guanyin's name will be of some use, but its effect will not be significant. The important influence comes from your practice while alive, and the kinds of vows you made as well as the sincerity with which you made them. If you are afraid of death or concerned about where you are going after death and think there is something you should do, it is not true Chan spirit. The Chan way is to cultivate a fearless attitude toward life and death regardless of your attainment, an attitude that can only come from diligent practice.

People often ask what attitude a Chan practitioner should have in various situations because it seems that Chan is different from other Buddhist traditions. As always, I must stress that, with one exception, Chan methods do not diverge from fundamental Buddhist concepts. The exception is that the conventional Buddhist approach speaks of different levels of experience and a gradual process, whereas the Chan approach is direct and always emphasizes practice. Other than this, the attitude and beliefs of the Chan practitioner accord with traditional Buddhadharma.

From the Song Dynasty (960-1279) onward, Chan Buddhism absorbed some elements from other Buddhist traditions, especially the Pure Land sect. It was then that people became preoccupied with questions about death: "If you practice your whole life and die without getting enlightened, what happens?" Perhaps people preoccupied with such questions should practice Pure Land Buddhism so that Amitabha Buddha will take them to the Western Paradise, but such an attitude is not in the true Chan spirit because it is driven by desire.

STUDENT   Is it important to recite prayers or sutras for the deceased? What about the Chinese practice described in the *Ulabana Sutra?*

SHIFU   There really is no need to do anything for relations or friends after they pass away. Services are useful, but not that significant. Besides, to depend only on the help of other beings after death, whether they are relatives, bodhisattvas or buddhas, is not in accordance with Buddhadharma. What is important is the power of one's own karma and vows.

The customary Chinese services are not really Chan practices. They are considered expedient methods. The dead person may not have practiced much while alive, so his or her relations perform services and make offerings in order to transfer merit to his or her spirit. Is this useful? Of course, but for whom? Many people need such ideas because they feel helpless, great sorrow, and regret in the face of death. To believe that some service can be of benefit to the deceased makes them feel better.

Such beliefs are not exclusively Chan. Once I asked a Hindu practitioner, "Do Hindus believe that friends and relatives can perform a service that will send a deceased person's spirit to a better place?"

The Hindu replied, "In general we do believe such things, but it is not really in accordance with the principles of karma."

I asked, "If your father or mother passed away, would you perform a service for them?"

He replied, "Yes, definitely. I choose to believe that it is useful."

STUDENT   It seems the services are more for the living than for the dead.

SHIFU   To an extent you are right, but one cannot say that these service are completely useless. The power of the mind is indeed capable of helping the deceased. As I said earlier, if the people who perform services are sincere and their practice is strong, they may be able to improve the dead person's rebirth. Also, when people chant or read sutras, deities, spirits, and other beings will gather to listen and are benefited by the service. If they benefit, then the deceased will benefit indirectly. An analogy would be if someone were locked up in prison and his family did charitable work in his name. The person would not be freed, but he might be treated better.

STUDENT   Thank you, Shifu. You always answer from the standpoint that Chan is absolutely self-reliant. It's clean, it's pure, and it's not affixed to the supernatural. But at the same time, we are intelligent creatures, and if we direct our compassionate and well-intentioned minds and energies toward someone or something, it cannot harm but only help, and create good karma.

SHIFU   Yes, you are right. Buddhists, including Chan Buddhists, should perform such services for relatives and friends who have died. I recite sutras for my parents, and I do it seriously, with sincerity.

STUDENT   Suppose a Chan practitioner goes through a 'near-death' experience, such as going 'through a tunnel,' or moving 'toward a light,' or having an out-of-body experience.

What should a practitioner do in such a situation? Should he or she be attracted to images of buddhas, bodhisattvas, or dead relatives, or should they be ignored?

SHIFU    People who have had a near-death experience should not rely on or put total faith in anything they may have experienced during that time. To begin with, a person who 'comes back to life' never really died in the first place. Some bodily functions may have temporarily ceased, but the brain did not die. If it were a case of brain death, the person would not be able to return to life.

As long as the brain is alive, the person still retains memories. Perhaps the individual did interact with other beings, perhaps he or she did meet dead relatives, perhaps he or she did visit another realm, or perhaps it was a vivid fantasy. Such experiences can be extremely powerful, but who is to say what they were really were? For this reason, Chan says that such experiences are unreliable and practitioners should not put much stock in them.

On the other hand, as religious experiences they are useful and powerful and should not be negated. Even when healthy and meditating deeply, you may feel that you have traveled to an extremely beautiful place—heaven or the Pure Land—and you may be certain that the experience was real. These are your personal religious experiences. Nonetheless, Chan maintains that they are unreliable, and practitioners should not put too much faith in them or in their interpretations of them.

STUDENT    What do you mean by religious experiences?

SHIFU    Religious experiences can be any number of things:

profound, sudden insights, revelatory experiences, feelings of unification with others, the world, or the universe. They are of great importance to one who experiences them and they help to build faith and confidence. Religious experiences are usually spontaneous and not necessarily a result of practice, which makes them seem all the more powerful. Such experiences can change people's lives, or, at the very least, help people to become more settled and peaceful. As such they are good experiences, but Chan considers them illusions like everything else. Chan practice emphasizes seeing one's own nature, illuminating one's own mind, and leaving illusions behind.

STUDENT   Could you elaborate further on what you mean by 'unreliable?'

SHIFU   Any experience you have, no matter how vivid, may or may not be real. A dead relative you meet during a near-death experience, or even in a dream, might be your dead relative, but it might also be a deity, a ghost, or your own imagination. How can you be sure? One thing is clear: experiences like these are powerful and fall under the category of religious experience. But if you put too much faith in such things, you might spend all your time waiting for it to happen again. Yes, the phenomenon might be as you experienced it, but it might also be something that arose from your own mind.

When one dies, the first five sense consciousnesses stop working and the person loses sensation and perception. But the sixth consciousness still exists and works. The sixth consciousness might experience the bliss of being free from the burden of body and its pains, and from the consciousness might rise beautiful images, sounds, and smells. On the other hand, the sixth consciousness might cling to the suffering and pain the body experienced, and from the consciousness might rise something terrible or nightmarish. Are these experiences real or illusory? The explanation I have just given describes these phenomena as products of the sixth consciousness. I am not saying that this is the explanation for all near-death experiences, but it is one possible explanation. The fact that there are numerous interpretations makes such experiences unreliable.

STUDENT    Sometimes Chan teachings seem schizoid. Chan is very practical. It says you should not rely on anything, but in the next breath it talks about ghosts and deities, heavens, and hells. Bodhisattvas are the hardest of all to believe. Supposedly, they are beings who can incarnate in innumerable forms in innumerable places in the same instant. It takes a stretch of the imagination to accept this. Then, after all of this, Chan says everything is illusion.

SHIFU    Everything you say is true. And you do not have to 'die' and come back to life to experience the supernatural. Even when one meditates one can experience things that are beyond the ordinary. For example, suppose you are meditating deeply and in your mind you see a beautiful picture. Then you enter the picture and experience this new world. Did it really happen? Was it your imagination? Is what you imagine any less real or more real than what you experience with your senses during those times you say you are awake and conscious?

Experiences can be objectively real, but they have to filter through the sixth consciousness. Therefore they are subjective and not entirely reliable. Indeed, the sixth consciousness itself is unreliable. Buddhism does not deny the existence of ghosts, deities, heavens, hells and bodhisattvas. However, as long as you perceive and interpret the world through the sixth consciousness, everything you experience will be illusory. This right now is illusory. If you want to experience the world clearly, directly, practice Chan.

# The Dharma Ending Age

QUESTION  What is the meaning of the Dharma Ending Age? Does it mean the world is getting worse? Are there realms where there are no buddhas at all? If bodhisattvas return to help sentient beings, how can there ever be a Dharma Ending Age? Are there people who cannot be enlightened?

SHIFU  Everything, including our world, goes through a process of creation, abiding, decay, and destruction. All that comes into being eventually disappears. Furthermore, we must admit that in many ways the world is not as good as it used to be. Yes, people today live longer and there is better technology, but people today seem to have more vexations than did people in the past; and obviously, the environment is in bad shape.

Beings are born in worlds according to their karma. Beings with good karma will be born in worlds that are better. Our world was better in the past, so the beings that came into the world then had better karma. Likewise, the beings who were around Shakyamuni Buddha also had good karma. But as time goes on and the world becomes less wholesome, fewer beings with meritorious karma or who practice and penetrate the Dharma reside here. These days it is very difficult to practice Buddhadharma and attain sainthood.

The idea of the Dharma Ending Age can be found in all of the ancient sutras—the *agamas*. It means that people have always had a sense that Buddhadharma would not remain in this world forever. They knew that as time passed after the Buddha entered nirvana, the number of people who would be enthusiastic about the Dharma and practice wholeheartedly would diminish. It does seem that the number of people in the world attaining high levels of practice is scant these days. In the past, it was possible for large numbers of people to devote their entire lives and energies to practice, to leave society and practice in monasteries. These days it is difficult to find isolated environments in which to practice, and there is a lot more temptation to cope with.

On the other hand, some might say that as long as someone practices diligently and has profound attainment, then it is the right Dharma age for that person. That is correct: it is the right Dharma period for that individual.

Of course, there are innumerable realms in the universe, and many of them do not have the presence of the Dharma and buddhas. Even during the time of Shakyamuni, only a small percentage of the world knew of him, and fewer still understood and practiced the Dharma. For such people there was no buddha and no Dharma. The percentage of the world population today that accepts and practices the Dharma is negligible. Not everyone has a karmic connection with the Dharma.

Bodhisattvas may manifest in any place in order to help sentient beings. They may be here right now, but people without the right karmic roots would not be aware of them. Furthermore, bodhisattvas are not limited to planet Earth and the human realm. There are many other worlds and realms where bodhisattvas appear.

STUDENT   All of this is perplexing. It would seem that the number of good practitioners should increase as the years go on. As Buddhism spread in the early years and more and more people experienced high levels of attainment, one would assume that would increase the amount of overall exposure to the Dharma. There should be thousands of saints today and they should be more recognizable. It seems, instead, that the power cannot sustain itself, and that it is going to end.

SHIFU   Some practitioners consider themselves seekers, but that does not mean that they have deep enough karmic roots to meet and interact with a bodhisattva. Also, as I said before, this is not the only world. People who lived here once do not have to be reborn here again. Bodhisattvas do not come only to this world. If bodhisattvas manifest in this world and see that the karma of sentient beings is such that they are not ready to practice the Dharma, they may plant a few seeds for future generations and then leave.

I am not sure if the Buddha himself ever spoke of a Dharma Ending Age, but the idea definitely exists in all of the sutras and sastras, so the compilers and authors obviously noticed that interest in Buddhadharma waned as time passed.

To have an idea of a Dharma Ending Age is, in fact, good. It makes us vigilant. It keeps us alert to the fact that, unless we are serious and dedicated, our attainment will be small or nonexistent. And if we do not practice diligently, the next time we are born we may find ourselves in an environment with no Dharma.

STUDENT   What about the *icchanti*, or beings who cannot get enlightened? I thought Buddhism stated that all sentient beings can become enlightened.

SHIFU   *Icchanti* are people who have not planted any seeds in Buddhadharma. If they have not done so yet, then their chance of doing so later, when the Dharma Ending Age is further along, is highly unlikely. On the other hand, if you look into the infinite future and acknowledge the infinite number of worlds, then I suppose anything is possible. Since all things change, then perhaps all beings do have a chance to attain buddhahood.

In the *Mahaparanirvana Sutra*, it is said that all sentient beings can attain buddhahood. In some earlier sutras, it is written that there are some beings that are incapable of becoming enlightened. Some beings have certain characteristics that make it impossible for them to learn and practice Buddhadharma successfully. Even though the sutra says that all beings can attain buddhahood, I believe this was spoken by the Buddha more out of compassion than anything else—to encourage every sentient being to study and practice Buddhadharma. The Buddha's words were meant for practitioners as well as for teachers and the Sangha. If the Sangha believed in *icchanti*, they might begin to prejudge people as to whether they were worthy of being taught Buddhadharma.

STUDENT   I thought that according to Buddhadharma, all things were mutually interacting and penetrating. If that is true, then the Dharma will always be with us and there will always be the possibility of attainment.

SHIFU   What you say comes from the *Avatamsaka Sutra*. But you can only experience that truth once you attain high levels of practice. It is said that all things are mutually related, mutually connected, mutually penetrating; but if you are just an ordinary sentient being, you cannot experience that condition. Your body is yours, not mine. Your home is yours, not someone else's. If we as unenlightened people tried to incorporate this ultimate principle into our daily lives, society would fall into chaos. Although all phenomena interpenetrate, we as ordinary sentient beings do not experience it that way.

STUDENT   I suppose the best attitude to take is to make a vow to practice now and do the best possible, regardless of what age it is said to be. Perhaps I should vow to be reborn where Buddhadharma flourishes, so that I may continue to practice in the future.

SHIFU   Chan says there is no coming or going, so it does not matter where you are reborn. What matters is now, this life. What matters is your practice in the present moment. Do not worry about Dharma Ending Ages and other worlds. Just practice and cultivate Buddhadharma.

# Part Two

*Practice and Daily Life*

# The Importance
of Having a Teacher

QUESTION    How important is it to have a teacher in Buddhist practice? Would problems arise in practicing the Buddhist precepts and principles without guidance from a teacher?

SHIFU   It would be difficult to practice Buddhism seriously without the guidance of a good teacher. Deriving guidance solely from books is only superficially adequate, and in some cases, can be unsafe. Books, this one included, can talk about the principles but, by themselves, they cannot convey the intricacies and subtleties of practice; they cannot observe a practitioner and offer guidance for a unique situation. Each practitioner is unique, and there are constant changes and fluctuations of physiology, mentality, mood, and *chi*, the vital energy. People react to situations in different ways, so there must be different methods for the teacher to use in response to a practitioner's situation. Furthermore, responses and situations, though they may appear similar or even identical to the casual observer, must be treated each time as unique events. Only a qualified teacher can observe and interpret this complex and ever-changing array of phenomena, and offer proper guidance.

Would you trust doctors or surgeons if the totality of their experience came from reading books? Every patient is different; conditions and illnesses change. Doctors do not rely only on book knowledge, but also draw upon their direct experience of practice, and what they learn from others. Doctors utilize all of their resources in order to help their patients. It is the same with practice. As you cultivate, you will undoubtedly face challenges and circumstances— responses in body, speech, and mind—that will be unfamiliar to you. It would be foolhardy and risky to rely completely on books to answer all of your questions and concerns. First, because books do not contain all the answers; second, because the answers in books may not apply to your specific condition; and third, because you may interpret the book's advice incorrectly. Therefore, it is vital that serious Buddhists—whether their path is Tibetan, Zen, Chan, or Pure Land—have a qualified teacher near at hand for guidance, advice, and encouragement. On the other hand, occasional practitioners do not need to study and practice with a teacher, although it is still encouraged.

STUDENT   What is the teacher's role for students following the three paths of practice—precepts, samadhi, and wisdom?

SHIFU   First all Buddhists should take the Five Precepts as fundamental guides for behavior: no killing, no stealing, no sexual misconduct, no lying, and no use of intoxicants. On the surface—and perhaps for the merely curious or the 'window shopping' practitioner—precepts may appear to be straightforward and simple; but for the serious practitioner, the principles and subtleties of precepts can become complex, and questions undoubtedly arise.

Because many beginning practitioners, some long-time practitioners, and those unfamiliar with the cultural milieu from which Buddhism evolved, are unclear about precepts, many people are afraid to take them. They may misunderstand them to be strict commandments rather than guidelines for behavior. They may be unsure as to how they are to keep the precepts pure, or if they have broken one or not, and if so, how to deal with such an actuality. Good teachers, especially those who specialize in studying and keeping precepts, are clear and experienced about the details and intricacies of precepts. They know the difference between keeping and breaking a precept in a variety of circumstances. For example, two individuals might appear to be doing or saying the same thing, but one might be breaking a precept while the other is not.

Similarly, most people do not have a clear understanding of samadhi—meditative concentration—the second aspect of practice. In many cases, practitioners erroneously mistake shallow quietude or calm clear-headedness to be samadhi, or even enlightenment. This is because they have had no direct experience of samadhi and enlightenment. All they know is what they have read in books, or what they have imagined. A qualified teacher is needed to verify the genuineness, type, and level of an experience. A qualified teacher who has experienced samadhi and enlightenment can determine a student's state of mind by observing their reactions to everyday activities, their speech, and their moods. Such observations enable a teacher to assess a student's levels of practice and attainment.

Over the years, many of my students have approached me, convinced that they had experienced samadhi or en-lightenment. In almost all cases, they had not. It did not grow into anything serious because I was there to correct their understanding and guide them in the right direction. It becomes dangerous when practitioners fall into demonic states. A demonic state can mean any number of things, but in this case I am referring to those situations when students delusively think that they have achieved enlightenment, or have developed supernormal powers. If they become strongly attached to such delusions, their attachment will become a major obstacle on the path of cultivation. Such demonic obstructions can arise from physical or psychological re-sponses to their practice, and it is not always a simple, obvious matter. On the surface, those who have fallen into a demonic state may appear the same as other practitioners, and may not even know that they are in a demonic state; but while they are deluded, they can potentially do damage, both to themselves and to others. In the worst case, where people truly believe that they are fully enlightened beings, it may be impossible for a teacher to help them return to the correct path.

STUDENT   How can such people be helped?

SHIFU   Much depends on their karma. If they have good karmic roots, they will eventually recognize that they are not enlightened, or that they do not have supernormal powers. Genuine wisdom is non-attachment. It is not knowledge, nor one's point of view, nor quick thinking and spontaneous reacting.

The right view that is described in the Eightfold Noble Path is not the same wisdom as that which is described by genuine wisdom. The wisdom of right view would be better described as stubborn wisdom, that is, wisdom that enables one to stay clearly and persistently on the correct path marked by the principles of Buddhadharma. Genuine wisdom derives from the direct experience of what Buddhism calls 'emptiness.' People who have not yet experienced enlight-enment must therefore rely on the wisdom of the Buddha for guidance and direction. Listening to Buddhadharma is the first step in cultivating wisdom. Buddhism describes know-ledge that comes from listening to Buddhadharma as 'wisdom that derives from hearing.' Further cultivation leads to 'wisdom which derives from thinking.' Finally, if one diligently practices Buddhadharma, one may attain 'wisdom which derives from practice.' Genuine wisdom is of this last category, and can come only from the experience of emptiness.

STUDENT    Can you elaborate further on the differences between wisdom from hearing, from thinking, and from practice?

SHIFU    One who has listened to and accepts the Buddha's fundamental teachings—the Four Noble Truths, the Twelve Links of Conditioned Arising, and the Eightfold Noble Path—has attained wisdom that derives from hearing. As one absorbs and assimilates these principles through analysis and contemplation, one begins to cultivate wisdom that derives from thinking. Initially, such wisdom is the product of discrimination and reasoning. Eventually, however, one tastes this wisdom through direct contemplation. To the beginning practitioner, what I have just said probably makes no sense, but there is a difference between intellectual thinking and direct contemplation. It is a difference that can only be recognized and understood through practice. Finally, there is the wisdom that one gains directly from practice, the highest of which is genuine wisdom, or the experience of emptiness. Though it is clear that genuine wisdom arises almost exclusively from practice, it is important to understand that such attainment builds upon wisdom cultivated from hearing and thinking. Furthermore, all of these levels require a teacher's guidance and experience. One can begin by reading books, but, if one wishes to practice seriously, a teacher's help will be necessary.

STUDENT    How should one go about choosing a teacher? Are there specific guidelines that will help one decide whether someone is qualified to teach?

SHIFU    A qualified teacher should demonstrate right knowledge and the right view, keep pure precepts, have the ability to guide others, and emanate compassion. With such qualifications, one can at least teach beginners. However, serious practitioners should find a teacher with 'bright eyes'- —someone who has experienced genuine wisdom. Only teachers who have experienced enlightenment can discern whether or not others have experienced emptiness. Without such experience, a teacher might mistake clear mindedness and samadhi for enlightenment.

Teachers who have not experienced enlightenment cannot guide others to deep practice. Even if their samadhi power is strong, they can only teach to the level they have reached; and their attainment is analogous to a stone sitting in cold water, or a ghost sitting in a dark mountain cave. How can teachers guide others to experience something that they themselves have not experienced? Even if practitioners somehow did experience enlightenment, such teachers would not have the personal, direct experience to discern such attainment.

STUDENT    Why would people change their Dharma teacher?

SHIFU    If it happens at all, it usually occurs when adepts are not satisfied with their practice. Perhaps it is because they feel they are stuck somewhere or somehow, and they do not know how to proceed through this bottleneck. To resolve their predicament, they may travel to other places looking for help. During their journey, it may happen that a particular teacher helps to clear their path or change their direction. This might signal that at least for now, that teacher is qualified to teach them.

STUDENT    Are adepts people who have already experienced enlightenment? And if they have experienced enlightenment, do they still need to practice?

SHIFU    Adepts may or may not have experienced enlightenment; and yes, people who have experienced enlightenment should still continue to practice under the guidance of a qualified teacher. Experiencing enlightenment does not mean that you have overcome or left behind vexations. Quite the contrary, you still may have many vexations and do not know how to move forward.

Adepts may not be enlightened, but nevertheless sincerely wish to move forward in their practice. They may still have heavy vexations, thus creating obstructions, and they may wish to deal with these vexations as well as the anxiety that stems from them.

Anxiety can come from other sources as well. Practitioners may feel anxious about not being able to move forward; for example, not being able to break through a *gong'an* (koan), or even to quiet their minds to a point where they can practice a *gong'an*. Then there are people who have solved the great matter of a particular *gong'an*, but are now anxious about what to do next. These situations are normal; they come with practice. The people who should really worry are those who do not care about progress, or who feel they have no problems. Such people are more deeply deluded, and they are much more difficult to work with.

Some people can experience deep samadhi, or sit in vexation-free stillness for hours, but when they rise from the cushion, vexations and scattered mind return. In fact, they may only be calm when they sit in meditation. There are others who have experienced enlightenment, but who have not cultivated samadhi power, and so they too suffer from vexations. Such people, whether they are old or young, can be considered adepts, but they still need to practice and work with a good teacher.

STUDENT   How do you, as a teacher, judge the experiences and levels of your students? What are your guidelines, and how do we know for sure that your observations are correct?

SHIFU   Asking such a question is already the wrong attitude.

If students have such an attitude when they look for a teacher, they will never be able to find one. Both beginners and adepts should trust teachers for whom they have an affinity. They should not hold back with an attitude of scrutiny and skepticism. For instance, some teachers might do strange things just to test a student. You must be open and sincere to learn from a teacher. On the other hand, if teachers repeatedly demonstrate wrong behavior in areas of relationships, money, or power, then you should leave them.

STUDENT   You are confusing me. First you say that students should trust teachers that they study with and not interpret questionable behavior, and then you say that students should know when a teacher is, in fact, behaving inappropriately. How are we to know? How does one recognize a false teacher?

SHIFU   The most important thing is to be able to judge whether the teacher has a correct view of Buddhadharma. If their views of the Dharma are correct, even if their behavior reveals some weaknesses, they should not be considered false teachers. On the other hand, if teachers do not have a correct view of the Dharma, they cannot be considered authentic or virtuous teachers. Of course, this presupposes that the person making the judgment has some understanding of correct Dharma. Without an understanding of the Dharma, there is no way that a practitioner can tell if a teacher is genuine or false.

Beyond this, there are some basic criteria that can be used in assessing teachers. First, consider their causes and conditions. In other words, their actions should be based on a foundation of emptiness: there should be no attachment in

what they do. Second, consider their causes and consequences, or karma. The sense of emptiness that guides the
actions of virtuous teachers (causes and conditions) should
accord with their karma (causes and consequences). That is
to say, their actions need to be guided by a sense of
responsibility. They should, at all times, be clearly aware of
the consequences of their actions. Thus, there is an intimate
relationship between responsibility and non-attachment.
These, then, are the marks of virtuous teachers: they have a
correct view of the Dharma, their actions reveal no
attachment, and they have a clear sense of responsibility.

STUDENT   In regard to misguided teachers and practitioners, I have heard the term 'wild fox Chan' and have
wondered what it means.

SHIFU   'Wild fox Chan' describes people who have not
experienced true emptiness, but nevertheless claim to have
no attachments. It means taking the false to be real—saying
one has attained something when has not, pretending to be
an enlightened when one is not, giving false teachings, and
speaking in a manner that implies one is enlightened.

The phrase 'wild fox' derives from an anecdote involving
Master Baizhang (720-814) and a mysterious monk who came
to him with a question about Dharma. Upon having his
question cleared up, the monk asked Baizhang to perform a
service for a dead fox he would find at a particular location.
It turns out that many lifetimes ago, this monk had given
false teaching about enlightenment and karma, and for his
presumption had been reborn as a wild fox ever since.
Baizhang finally corrected the monk's wrong views, freeing
him from the series of rebirths as a wild fox.

Sophisticated people with a flair for language can often feign enlightenment by talking authoritatively about emptiness. Volumes have been written about alleged exchanges between teachers and students in *gong'ans*. Some students infuse their speech with ideas from these anecdotes. Often their words are not backed up by actual experience. Unfortunately, it is usually difficult for an ordinary person, or even some teachers, to detect this. But the truth surfaces when they are engaged in conversation with someone genuinely enlightened. Without genuine experience even the most quick-witted will eventually reveal their inexperience and insincerity.

STUDENT   What is meant by guru worship, and is there such an idea in Chan?

SHIFU   In guru worship, students perceive their teachers as the embodiment of enlightenment, and they devote their practice to worshipping and respecting these teachers. It is akin to combining Buddha, Dharma, and Sangha into one person. Such a practice does not exist in the Chan tradition, but it does exist in the Tibetan tradition. In Tibetan Buddhism, the teaching, or transmission, can only be passed directly from teacher to student. In other words, without the teacher there can be no teaching.

In the Chan tradition, the role of the teacher is to assist and affirm practitioners' practice. Teachers do not transmit the teaching; rather, they determine whether or not practitioners have realized buddha-nature. Chan teachers can only guide you to realize and reveal your own wisdom, and then verify the experience. The relationship between teacher and student is more that of friends than guru and disciple. In

Chan, it is said that the relationship is three parts teacher and student and seven parts fellow practitioners.

STUDENT   To me, the behavior of Zen masters often appears the same as that of a guru.

SHIFU   This is not true in the Chan tradition. Shakyamuni Buddha himself said, "I do not lead." Shakyamuni taught people to use the Buddhadharma, but he always viewed himself as part of the sangha.

STUDENT   How does one separate the teachings of Buddhadharma from the teacher?

SHIFU   Buddhadharma consists of abstract principles that are best learned from a teacher. Furthermore, if you wish to respect Buddhadharma, then you must respect the teacher. It is through a teacher that you learn correct Buddhadharma. So, to practice truly and deeply, one must have a qualified teacher. You may say that Buddhadharma is your teacher, but Buddhadharma relies on teachers to teach it. Teachers lead and guide you, and are therefore an extremely important part of the practice. If you must separate Buddhadharma from the teacher, then view the teacher's teachings as Buddhadharma, and view the teacher's behavior as his or her own business.

STUDENT   If teachers continuously break precepts or behave incorrectly, should students remain with them?

SHIFU   That depends on the student. Is there something more to learn? Are you being hurt? If you are being hurt and still remain, then you will develop mental problems. So why would you stay? If you are not being hurt, and are still able to learn, then consider staying.

STUDENT   Is it all right to look for and learn from more than one teacher?

SHIFU   Throughout Buddhist history there have been examples of students who were not satisfied because their teachers could not help them to improve, so they left. There were also instances where teachers asked students to leave, telling them that causes and conditions were not right and that they should seek other teachers. Sometimes students felt they could not learn anymore from their teachers, but after talking to other sangha members, they gained understanding and remained with the same teacher. And there have been cases where students have left their teachers, and after going to other places and trying out other teachers, returned to their original teachers and were are able to learn from them again.

When one has many teachers at the same time, however, it will usually lead to confusion. It is acceptable if one teacher teaches precepts, another teaches sutras, and still another teaches meditation. But if one is cultivating samadhi and wisdom with a few teachers at the same time, it will likely lead to problems.

STUDENT   How do teachers continue to practice? If one becomes a teacher, but still has problems, or has not experienced enlightenment, what should he or she do?

SHIFU   I can only speak about my own experience. I became a teacher out of causes and conditions that were uniquely mine. I did not think about being a teacher. I was asked to guide some people to practice because they knew my background and knew that I was qualified to be a teacher. I was not thinking about teaching others at that time, let alone guiding others in Chan practice. But as I continued to teach others, I grew as a teacher. I was like a ship rising as the water rose. When a good student came, I would get better. Through the teaching process, I discovered areas that I needed to improve upon, and I worked at it. It is not that my students were more advanced than I was, but since each student was unique, I learned to handle each in an appropriate way. In turn, it helped my own practice. In fact, the process continues to this day. As I continue to teach my methods of guidance become clearer, more detailed, and more varied. Now, when a student has a problem, it is almost always clear right away what it is, and I know immediately what to do. The more experience I gain, the more solid my own practice becomes.

STUDENT   Can you speak more about these skills that you have developed. It is my sense that some teachers do not have the experience to lead students. Others do not have the qualifications. Are there methods to cultivate these skills?

SHIFU   Difficult to say. It is not a clearly delineated skill that one can learn as in a school. It is being able to observe the minds, behavior, and responses of others, and then being able to act accordingly. Teachers must cultivate the sensitivity to understand others as well as the ability to express and guide clearly. This does not necessarily correspond to a teacher's own enlightenment experience. There were arhats that could not teach.

As to whether teachers should continue to practice, that is not even debatable. Whether one is just a practitioner, a teacher, a master, or even enlightened, practice should continue for one's entire lifetime. There are still *gong'ans* to contemplate, there is still silent illumination, there are still prostrations to the Three Jewels, there is still sitting meditation. Every moment is an opportunity to practice. Shakyamuni Buddha continued to practice even after he became a buddha.

STUDENT  Why? There is an understanding in Chan that after enlightenment, one can put down everything, that there is nothing to do. Isn't this true?

SHIFU  If you are talking about complete and thorough enlightenment, then what you say is literally correct, but you are drawing the wrong conclusion. Essentially, after thorough enlightenment, there is nothing that the mind *has* to do. Yet, one still does things. One still interacts with the environment and with other people. One still practices. However, as I said before, experiencing enlightenment does not mean that one is free from vexations. On the contrary, one becomes more clearly aware of the vexations that are still present. One must continue to practice, to cultivate samadhi power, to experience enlightenment again and again, to develop a compassionate mind. Practice never ends.

STUDENT  What is the mind of an enlightened person?

SHIFU  That is a complex question. It depends on the depth to which someone is enlightened, and there is a big difference between *experiencing* enlightenment and *being* enlightened. Enlightenment experiences are usually momentary flashes of deep insight. They come and go, and afterward, you are left with the memory and power of the experience. Furthermore, enlightenment experiences can be shallow or deep. People with shallow enlightenment may be clear about their own vexations, but they still might not be able to control them all the time. With deeper enlightenment, one may know from where and when vexations arise, and so not let them appear. This awareness grows when one has both enlightenment experience and samadhi power. One with deep enlightenment experience and deep samadhi power would not suffer vexations because he or she would not waver even when vexations tried to manifest. That is why both enlightenment experiences and samadhi power are important. When vexations do appear, one can use samadhi power to stop them from taking hold. If one has only enlightenment experience, but no samadhi power, he or she will still suffer from vexations.

Enlightenment without the power of samadhi is not solid, and samadhi does not necessarily lead to enlightenment. On the other hand, it is likely that someone who has cultivated samadhi power will experience deeper levels of enlightenment. Conversely, someone who has experienced enlightenment will likely enter the level of samadhi that is in accordance with emptiness. In this samadhi, there is no self-center.

STUDENT   What is Dharma transmission?

SHIFU   Dharma cannot be transmitted. So-called Dharma transmission is only a confirmation. Dharma transmission and transmission to a successor are two different things.

Transmission of the Dharma is to confirm that a practitioner's mind is in accordance with the nature of emptiness. It is a seal or sanction given by the teacher to a disciple. In reality, there is no Dharma that is being transmitted. Dharma transmission from generation to generation is more a title of office.

Bodhidharma did not bring the Dharma with him when he went from India to China. Dharma is everywhere and ever-present. People receiving the Dharma have merely realized their own true mind. A teacher can only give *inka*, which is acknowledging the continuation of the lineage. It is not transmission of wisdom. While one generation may give *inka*, to the next, there is really nothing to transmit.

STUDENT   If an abbot is also a qualified Chan master, isn't it necessary that he or she pass on the position of abbotship to someone who has experienced his or her true nature? And what if there is no such student?

SHIFU   Abbots need not have experienced enlightenment. If the next generation does not have someone with enlightenment experience, the position of abbot is still appointed. After all, a temple has to be looked after. Each temple still has the transmission of that position. A Chan master then has to look for someone else to be a qualified teacher because the abbot might not have that capability.

STUDENT   Have there been cases in the Buddhist transmission of Dharma of people who did not receive *inka*, but who taught anyway because they believed that they were enlightened?

SHIFU   Such people may have done so on their own, but no such people have been acknowledged in the Chan records.

STUDENT   Are there no breaks in the Chan tradition?

SHIFU   There are no breaks in the Chan tradition. However, there have been people in Chan history who have insisted that they were qualified teachers and who have then started new lineages.

# Practicing Alone, with a Group, and with a Master

QUESTION   What are the advantages and disadvantages of practicing on one's own, with a group, and with a master?

SHIFU   Practice can occur in various settings: individual practice, group practice, short-term practice, long-term practice, daily practice, and intensive, periodic practice. Individual practice can be relaxed, periodically intensive, short-term, or long-term; the same is true for group practice. One can also look at these forms of practice from the point of view of lay people vs. homeleavers. I will try to address all of these variations.

In all cases, whether alone or with a group, whether as a householder or homeleaver, it is better to practice under a qualified master. Practice without the guidance of a master will probably not be too fruitful. For one thing, practicing with a master can save you time because a master's understanding and experience can help you firmly grasp the essentials of practice and cultivate a correct view of Buddhadharma. This enables you to more quickly free yourself from the vexations of body and mind. With a master, time otherwise spent studying sutras and worrying about following the right path can be devoted single-mindedly to practice.

There are people, however, whose karmic roots are sharp and deep; that is, they have practiced well for many lifetimes. Such people make speedy progress whether under the guidance of a master or not. They understand Buddhadharma and do not stray from the path. For example, Shakyamuni practiced with many masters before becoming completely enlightened, but as he was not satisfied with their teachings, he practiced on his own for six years. He did not attain enlightenment until he put down everything. Shakyamuni did have teachers, but his was a case of self-enlightenment. Huineng (638-713), the sixth patriarch of Chan, also became enlightened without the guidance of a master. In his case, hearing one line of the *Diamond Sutra* was enough. Fifth Patriarch Hongran (601-674) later confirmed his attainment. In essence the *Diamond Sutra* was Huineng's teacher.

Obviously, such people are rare. Unless practitioners feel they are on a par with people such as the Buddha and Huineng, I suggest that they seek the guidance of a good master. If practitioners have mental obstructions or difficulty with their practice, masters can help them to resolve their problems. Also, if practitioners have some type of meditation experience, a master can determine whether it is genuine or not. Left alone, practitioners may deceive themselves, thinking that an illusory experience is enlightenment. That would be harmful to their practice.

As a practitioner, you should have a specific method, and you should understand the goal of your practice. You should set aside a period of time each day to practice. In addition to daily sittings, you should occasionally devote longer periods of time exclusively to practice: one full day per week, one entire weekend per month, a seven-day retreat one or more times a year.

If you are a very serious and devoted practitioner who wishes to conduct a solitary retreat for a month, a year, or even several years, then certain criteria must be met. First, you should have a sound grasp of Buddhadharma and your practice. Second, your physical and psychological health must be strong enough to endure the rigors of an extended solitary retreat. Third, you should be familiar and smooth with your method; in other words, you ought to be able to cope with any mental or physical phenomena that arise, and be able to correct and refine your understanding of the Dharma as your practice develops. In most cases, heightened experiences will be illusions. The best attitude is to ignore all unusual phenomena, sensations, ideas, and feelings that arise, and to maintain a detached, non-seeking, calm attitude. Remember, I am talking about experiences that arise during practice. If you get sick or hurt yourself, you would be foolish to ignore it.

If the criteria I have mentioned are not met, the practitioner may develop serious physical and mental obstructions and will not know how to deal with them. For these reasons, beginners should not attempt a solitary retreat. In fact, I would not recommend it for most people. It is extremely demanding. Most people are better off practicing in a group—preferably five people or more—with or without a master. Again, having a master is always better, but group practice without a master is preferable to solitary practice without a master, because if one member has problems, the others can help.

STUDENT    But how do the others know that they are saying or doing the right thing? They may be harming rather than helping the person with the problem.

SHIFU    Addressing a question someone has is already helping. Of course, it is better to have at least one experienced member in the group.

STUDENT    Is the best policy to tell practitioners to ignore what they have experienced?

SHIFU    Not always. If they experience a typical physiological or psychological sensation, it is okay to tell them to ignore it; but if they have a question about the method or the Dharma, then someone with more experience should try to answer them. If you do not know the answer, then tell them so. If you think you do know the answer, then answer the question, but it would be wise to qualify the answer to reflect your level of experience. Furthermore, if a person is tired or frustrated, or is suffering from a headache or other body pains, then you must offer a method to help him or her deal with the problem. Often the best answer is to tell the person to relax or rest for a while.

Group practice is also better than solo practice because the schedule is more regular. On your own, it is easy to get lazy and miss a sitting here or there; but in a group, you will feel obligated to attend sittings and practice well. Seeing other people practicing usually sparks your own desire to practice.

As householders, you should make an effort to set up a group practice. If you live near a meditation center, then it is easier because the setting and schedule are already established. You can show up in the morning or evening, on weekdays or weekends. If you do not live near a center, then you must improvise. It is difficult to find a place where several people can sit on a daily basis, but the more often and regularly a group meets, the better it is for everyone's practice. The group should also try to set aside one day per week or one weekend per month for more rigorous practice. It would also be all right to spend longer periods of time— four to seven days—practicing energetically.

STUDENT    Is there a certain, safe time limit for retreats held without a master?

SHIFU    It is not good to practice intensely for too long without a master. Problems might arise. Participating in a several-day retreat without a master is already energetic. You should not follow exactly the stringent rules of an intensive seven-day retreat. It is better to have a more relaxed atmosphere.

There are other forms of practice that are not as intense as meditation, such as chanting or reciting sutras. It is all right to hold such retreats without a master. People at my temple in Taiwan sometimes hold seven-day recitation retreats when I am not present.

In all situations I have described, it is easier and better to sit in a group. It is difficult to hold personal retreats and keep to the schedule. Any number of distractions or vexations might interrupt your practice. To practice well on your own takes great will power.

In regard to short-term vs. long-term practice, results and progress will depend on your level of experience, your karma and causes and conditions. Practicing for a long time does not guarantee more enduring experiences, just as practicing for a short time does not preclude having an experience. So long as you practice, that is good. Focus all your energies on the present sitting. If you can maintain this attitude every time you meditate, you will make progress.

I always stress the importance of daily practice. It is important to have a regular sitting schedule, but practice does not end when you get up from the cushion. Cultivate mindfulness in all situations. Whether you are doing something you like or dislike, whether it is to your advantage or disadvantage, try not to put yourself at center stage. Put aside self-centeredness and cultivate compassion. Be helpful to others in everything you do; this will help decrease selfcenteredness. Most importantly, whenever you do something, do it with focused awareness. Do not be lazy and allow your mind to wander. This is daily practice. This is mindfulness. For most people, this type of lifestyle is impossible. In order to practice in this way, it is important to meditate every day and to periodically attend more intensive retreats.

Most householders cannot practice steadily and energetically for a long time because of responsibilities and obligations. However, if you are single and have a flexible job, you can devote yourself to long-term practice—one or more years. In most cases, such people live in monasteries or retreat centers, where the environment is conducive to practice. Many householders do so on a temporary basis. They practice intensely, leave to work a while, and afterward return to practice. Although beneficial, this is not genuine long-term practice. The best way is to live in a monastery or center and practice continuously for several years.

Until now I have been talking about lay practitioners. The correct attitude of a homeleaver is fundamentally different from that of a householder. In taking vows, monks and nuns theoretically leave behind self-centeredness and devote all their time and effort to the practice of Buddhadharma. Homeleavers do not have a family, a home, a career, or possessions. They have no worldly responsibilities and obligations. The true meaning of leaving home is to leave everything behind—intellect, emotions, ego, desire, body, and mind—in effect, abandoning everything except the vows and Buddhadharma.

Many people say that the Chan Center belongs to me—Shifu Sheng-yen. They are mistaken. I live here and work here, but it is not my place. Nor does it belong to the monks and nuns who live here. A person who has left home has nothing. If a monk or nun thinks, "This is my home," he or she should immediately remember what it means to have left home. People who have truly left home have nothing except practice: no cares, no worries, no goals. To an outsider, it may seem that they are working and acting like lay people, but to monastics, everything is practice. It would be difficult for householders to maintain this kind of attitude.

STUDENT   I have to disagree with you, Shifu. Sure, monks and nuns take vows and leave home, but that is a ritual, and it is purely an intellectual conception. Most monks and nuns are pretty much the same as lay practitioners. I see the monks who live and work here. They have responsibilities just as I do. In fact, it seems they have more responsibilities and work than I do. They have bills to pay, legal matters to deal with, visitors to greet and take care of, and a very hectic social schedule. It seems that they have replaced one home with another.

On the other hand, why can't I, as a lay practitioner, have the attitude of a monk or nun? Yes, I must go to work and earn money, but it is something I must do to survive. Whether it is work or being with my family, I try to see it as practice. I try to be mindful in all that I do. I try to live by the precepts and put Buddhist principles into practice. If lay practitioners have this attitude, why should they be any different from monastics?

SHIFU   The difference is that the responsibilities of home-leavers are just responsibilities and nothing more. Monastics should not be emotionally involved with and attached to what they do. Let me rephrase that. Monks and nuns should not be emotionally attached to anything, and they live in an environment with rules that constantly remind them of that. On the other hand, most householders are emotionally attached to their families, their work, and their possessions. However, if you can practice with the attitude of a home-leaver and detach yourself from things, then you are correct, there would be no difference. A fine example is the family of Layman Pang (740-808/11), wealthy lay practitioners of high attainment, who gave up their possessions and took up basket weaving for their livelihood.

Monastics should be able to leave behind their worldly selves. This does not happen instantly. They do not take vows, shave their heads, put on robes, and immediately master such an attitude. It is a gradual, life-long process. One cannot win or inherit such an attitude. One must cultivate it.

# Approaches to
# Daily Meditation

QUESTION    How should one approach daily meditation practice?

SHIFU    This is an important question, one that may seem obvious to some practitioners; in fact many misunderstand it. I often wonder how many people are stuck in their daily practice simply because they truly do not know how to approach it. It is important to have the correct conception of daily practice, because this is what we do most—on our own, away from centers, and without the guidance of teachers.

First, have a proper mental attitude. Second, know how to use a method correctly. Third, relax your mind before and while you use your method. This is easy to say, but many people do not know how to relax. Some try too hard to relax and become more tense. Others relax so much that they fall asleep, or drift into wandering reveries. Both extremes are wrong. That is why a proper mental attitude toward practice is important.

What is the proper attitude? Tell yourself that the time you spend every day in practice is the most enjoyable, comfortable, and pleasant of times. Since we do not spend that much time each day sitting, the time we do set aside for practice is precious. If you have this attitude, you will not feel tense or sleepy while meditating.

Do you see meditating as an obligation or a duty, or do you find it enjoyable? If you do not enjoy meditating, it will be hard to sustain a steady, long-term practice. If enjoyment does not come naturally to you, try to cultivate an attitude of enjoyment. First, before you sit, remind yourself to feel happy about what you are about to do. When I was a student, I would get up early and eat breakfast. There were six hours between breakfast and lunch. By eleven o'clock I was starving. My last class was from eleven to twelve, and when the bell rang, I was so happy knowing that it was lunchtime. My body and mind were merged in this happiness. This is the kind of attitude you should cultivate for meditation.

When you sit think of it as a time without worries. Every other time there are difficulties and responsibilities to think about. Meditation is a time to lift burdens off your body and mind. It should be a relief. One has the opportunity to let everything else go while meditating.

Make sure your posture is correct, and then forget your body. If you worry about your body, you will not be able to relax. Then tell your mind to be free. Tell yourself that you are not going to restrict your mind in any way, thinking about this or that. Let it go, but not in a daydreaming way. At that point, watch your mind; see where it goes, but do not follow it. When you follow your thoughts you are allowing them to control you. But if you do follow your thoughts, do not get angry with yourself. Once you realize that you have been following wandering thoughts, they will usually go away on their own.

When you follow wandering thoughts, you are restricting your awareness to that particular thought train. When you do not follow your wandering thoughts, your mind is free and open. Tell your mind it can go anywhere it pleases, but you will not follow it. At this time your body will be relaxed and your mind will be free because you are not restricting it in any way. This is the most enjoyable time; you have nothing to do; mind and body are at ease. If you have no thoughts, then that is good, let it be that way; but if thoughts arise, pay attention to your breath. If your breath is long and smooth, it means you are comfortable. You do not even have to continue to notice your breath. If your mind is clear, just sit. But once you start to become aware of your body, then make sure your posture is correct. I hope you can do this. Do not think you have to sit because you owe somebody something.

STUDENT   When I teach people how to meditate and tell them it is a way of clearing the mind of thoughts, some say that it is impossible not to think. They say you are always thinking, even if you are thinking of nothing. Is it possible to know something without conceptualizing it, to have no thinking or reasoning, just pure awareness?

SHIFU   Your students are right because it is difficult to imagine such a state if you have never experienced it, or if you do not meditate. When you think you are not thinking, that is also thinking. With meditation you can reach a point where there is no fluctuation, no scattering, no confusion. You reach a state of equanimity and your mind is peaceful. There are no waves. That is what being clear means. In that situation, there are still thoughts, but if you maintain clarity you will not dwell on them.

STUDENT   How do you practice when there is not enough time to sit because of a hectic schedule or other obstacles?

SHIFU   During your busy day, try to find little bits of time to sit and relax and clear your mind. It does not have to be on a cushion, and it does not have to be for thirty minutes or an hour. Take three or five minutes here and there to sit: at your desk, in a car, bus, or train. You can do this anywhere and anytime. Relax your body and mind. Breathe. Settle your mind. Let your mind and body refresh themselves.

If your schedule is too hectic to set aside even five minutes, then try to relax your mind and body while you are working, or walking, or talking. Make work your practice. Be mindful of what you do and say. I do this. There are days when I have no private time from early morning until late at night. Whenever I remember, I try to stay relaxed in body and mind. I try not to let distractions bother me. I let them come and go. It is something that all of us can do. It takes effort and time, but it is not too difficult. If I can do it, so can you.

STUDENT   Is it okay to meditate on a train while commuting to and from work? It's hard to keep a correct posture in those seats.

SHIFU    I teach how to do standing and sitting-on-chair methods. It is better not to sit with your back supported by something, but if you cannot help it, then do the best you can. It is okay to sit back on trains, planes, and buses. However, please do not meditate while you are driving. While driving, practice mindfulness; that is, be in the moment and place your mind where your actions are, in this case driving the vehicle.

STUDENT    Some people fall asleep whenever they meditate. They can be really energetic, but as soon as they sit down they become drowsy and ten minutes later they are fighting off sleep. Pain at least keeps you awake, but sleepiness sneaks up on you and drags you down. It can be discouraging. Could this be considered a karmic obstruction? Can something be done about it?

SHIFU    If you talk about karmic obstructions it becomes too wide a field, but we can help such conditions using concrete methods. You can relax your body doing exercises beforehand—head and body exercises. And when you sit, make sure your back is straight and your chin tucked in. It is fine if your back is slightly bent, but only if you are not sleepy. As soon as you feel sleep coming on, straighten your back and do some deep breathing. If deep breathing alone does not work, you can couple it with hunching your shoulders and then relaxing them. You can also stare in front of you with wide-open eyes, until they well with tears. All these techniques help to clear a drowsy mind. If you are always sleepy, sit for ten minutes and then get up and exercise. Even ten minutes of sitting is useful. After exercising, you can try to sit again.

STUDENT   Why are noontime and midnight considered not good times to sit? What if it is the only time you can sit? A well-known meditation teacher says noon and midnight are good times and one should avoid dawn and dusk. Time of day is time of day, so why are there differences? Is it individual preference, or is there a greater importance?

SHIFU   Meditating occasionally at noon and midnight should not be a problem, but it is best not to make it a regular habit. What this teacher says might be true for him. I do not know if it is just his personal preference, or if there is something more to it. Normally, though, at midnight you should be asleep or at least tired and resting, especially if you have been working all day.

Avoiding noon and midnight comes from the philosophy of Chinese medicine. It is not my personal opinion. Chinese medicine holds that the sun, the moon, the planets, magnetic fields, and the rest of the universe all influence the body. There are certain rhythms that affect all of us. If you regularly sit at noon and midnight, you may get out of balance with the diurnal rhythms of the planet, as well as your body and mind. But if it is an occasional thing, then there will not be any problems. Also, there will not be any problems if the practitioner is experienced, as in the case of the teacher you mention.

Regarding when to sit, you should not make yourself sit when you do not want to. If you force it, you will grow to hate it. If after ten minutes you realize it was definitely the wrong time to sit—not just a few scattered thoughts telling you so—then get up. Do some exercises and then try again. Do not force it. Make sure that you allocate some time to sit and tell yourself you will enjoy doing it. If you feel bad about it during this time, get up and do some exercises and then try again when you feel better. Once your time is up, you can stop. I usually tell beginners to sit for twenty-five to thirty-minute periods.

STUDENT   What you said earlier about just sitting and letting thoughts go sounds more like Caodong Chan (Soto Zen). Usually you teach methods that seem more structured. Here it sounds like what I have read in *Zen Mind, Beginner's Mind*.

SHIFU   *Zen Mind, Beginner's Mind* teaches you to just put down your mind, but that hard to do in the beginning stages of practice, when you may need a method like counting breaths to focus your mind. Some people have difficulty counting breaths, so I will have them do *shikantaza* (just sitting) practice instead. In this practice, one's total focus is on the body sitting there in meditation, and nothing else, therefore, 'just sitting.' Some people cannot use either method. They have too many scattered thoughts for *shikantaza* and they control or force their breathing. I usually advise these people to repeat the Buddha's name or recite a mantra. These two methods also allow the practitioner to stabilize the mind.

STUDENT   What kind of mantra would be good?

SHIFU   Anything can be a mantra. Some mantras have power in and of themselves, especially if many people repeat them aloud and together, over and over. The more people use them, the more power they generate. Using your own personal mantra will not gain much power, but some mantras, like the Great Compassionate Dhyana mantra, where each phrase is a bodhisattva's name, are extremely powerful. However, Chan is not concerned with personal power, so any mantra or phrase will do. As a Chan method, a mantra should be simple, and its purpose is to focus the mind.

STUDENT   Most of us have hectic lives and schedules. When we try to meditate we are extremely scattered in the beginning. You say we should tell ourselves to feel happy and relaxed about what we are going to do, but that may be difficult to do. You can tell yourself to settle down, but that does not mean you will. Would it be better to start with counting breaths until you are settled and then shift to the just-sitting method?

SHIFU   It is okay to do that. But you should still approach sitting with the attitude I explained. It is a precious and happy time. This helps your mind settle more quickly, and you are already relaxing before you begin sitting. This attitude will not become a habit overnight. You have to cultivate it. If you just had a fight you probably would not feel calm enough to sit. But if you could cultivate the attitude I have described, you will be able to say, "Let's just sit."

STUDENT   You usually tell us not to switch methods. Starting with counting the breath and then switching to *shikantaza* sounds like an inconsistency.

SHIFU   If you keep switching you will not find out which method is suitable for you. You will never penetrate a method that way. It is best to work on one method, and if your mind is clear enough, it should be easy to do so. When students reach a deeper level, I teach them other methods.

In the situation you speak of, you are counting your breath to settle your mind before entering *shikantaza*. You are using it as a stepping-stone. That is OK. What I discourage is random or frequent switching. If you start counting breaths and then switch to *shikantaza* with good results, then by all means do it, but don't keep switching back and forth. You will never develop power in either method that way.

STUDENT Sometimes you say that counting breaths is the most basic method and later on you introduce other methods. Other times you say any method can take you all the way to the 'other shore.' It seems to me that breath counting is a basic method I eventually have to give up for a better method.

SHIFU Here is an analogy, even if it is not fully appropriate. Counting breaths is basic. It is like walking. Almost everyone can walk, but people can also ride a bike, sail a ship, drive a car, fly a plane. There are many ways to get from one place to another. Walking is one of them; and although walking seems to be the slowest way, sometimes it is not the case. You know the story of the tortoise and the hare. Walking is slow but steady.

Counting the breaths is a good method. The *Agama Sutra* says it can be used to attain arhatship, in other words, full enlightenment. If you use this method for a while and then want to switch, that is okay. For instance, you can practice *shikantaza*, or work on a *gong'an or huatou*. It is like walking and then hopping a train. If you just walk, you will get there. If you switch to a vehicle, you will also get there. It is constant and frequent switching without any sustained effort in any one method that is bad.

Counting the breath is a basic method. In using this method you should be able to examine yourself better to see if you are working hard or not. It is an excellent method. If it were not, I wouldn't teach it.

STUDENT    Sitting for however long you like and getting up whenever you like bothers me. There is no discipline. Many thoughts go through the mind. If you act upon every thought that goes through the mind, you would not sit for very long. Five minutes into the sitting you might think that you are hungry. After ten minutes you might think meditation is useless. But after sitting for an extended period I may have a thought that I am having a good sitting. Really, the whole purpose of sitting is precisely to watch these thoughts come and go, to see that thoughts do rise and fall. You would never realize it if you did not sit through it. If you got up, you would never know this. Isn't it better to ride it out?

SHIFU    You do not get up when just any thought runs through your mind. I meant it only when you have an overwhelmingly uncomfortable feeling, either physically or mentally. In this case, the feeling probably is not going to go away and sitting through it would just make matters worse, so it is best to get up. When you feel hectic and tired, you can sometime sit through it. But if it gets worse and worse, it might be better to get up. The point is not to make it so burdensome to sit that you develop an aversion to it.

But if you lack determination, and come up with an excuse every other day, then it is not okay. For example, if you have work that you must get done for the next day, then that is a good reason to forego sitting. But if you put off sitting to finish a crossword puzzle, that is not a good reason.

*172*

You are only fooling yourself. You know inside when it is a good reason and when it is not, so be honest with yourself and be your own disciplinarian. It's up to you.

The approach I describe is for daily practice, not retreats. During retreat, the schedule is fixed. You sit when it is time to sit. On retreat there is a level of commitment and discipline that does not usually occur in daily practice. It is good when you can carry that energy over into your daily life. But I want people, especially beginners, to feel that daily practice is comfortable, not difficult. If people use this approach, they will not put it off or give up. They will try and keep on trying. Gradually they will be able to practice steadily. Also, during their daily routine people can become tense, confused and nervous. If they want to practice, it is difficult to settle down right away. This is a good approach for those times. After people exercise or do slow-walking meditation for a little while, they are more relaxed and it is easier to sit.

STUDENT   You said we should think of sitting as a pleasurable and wonderful time. I can intellectually say sitting is a wonderful thing. I know it, but sometimes I feel differently, and it's hard to make the feeling and the thought come together. This is true for many things, not just meditation. Sometimes I feel like two different people.

SHIFU   You have to cultivate this skill. To use an analogy, if you are learning to play tennis, initially you may feel frustrated and discouraged because you are missing the ball or hitting it poorly. But with practice you will improve. With persistence, at some point it becomes natural and enjoyable, and you look forward with enthusiasm to playing. The health benefits of tennis then become a free bonus.

You have to turn sitting practice into a habit. Give yourself a hint subconsciously. Tell yourself sitting is a pleasure, a good time. Create this attitude, this atmosphere, even though you know you will not really feel this way all the time. If you do it over and over, you will train yourself. Tell yourself this kind of enjoyment is better than other kinds of enjoyment. It is a precious, spiritual time. Train yourself. At first it will be difficult, and you might fail in the beginning, but keep trying. This, too, is practice.

# Practice in
# Daily Life

QUESTION  How do we incorporate practice into daily life? What does sitting meditation have to do with practicing compassion?

SHIFU  Daily practice consists of fixed practice and ordinary activity practice. In fixed practice, at certain designated times each day, you meditate, prostrate, recite or read sutras, or perform morning and evening services, in any combination you can manage. You should adhere to a regular schedule with these practices.

Fixed, structured practice is clear, but how do you practice when working, commuting, entertaining, socializing, and so on? It is possible to practice in all of these situations. Usually, when people think about practice, meditating or studying Buddhadharma comes to mind, but Chan stresses that you should take advantage of all moments, whether practicing in a structured manner or following a daily routine. All times, situations, and environments are opportunities to practice.

In the *Avatamsaka Sutra*, there is a famous chapter in the form of a *gatha* (verse) from which the Three Refuges were taken. This chapter speaks of all the human activities: eating, sleeping, walking, resting, talking, and so on. It says that in all activities we should have in the forefront of our minds the wellbeing of sentient beings. This is called bodhi-mind, and the teaching of bodhi-mind is the essence of the chapter.

A person on the bodhisattva path follows the Four Great Vows, of which the first is to help sentient beings. If you can consistently think of other sentient beings' welfare, compassion will naturally arise in your thoughts and actions. When people place themselves ahead of others, the greatest obstructions on the path are arrogance, greed, and anger.

Practitioners who check their pride and help others as often as they can realize that attainment is possible only with the help of sentient beings. Only through interacting with others can one cultivate compassion and wisdom. Of course, the motivation and intention behind helping others is also important. Expecting something in return, even gratitude, is self-serving and not in accordance with bodhi-mind. Indeed, as practitioners we should thank sentient beings for giving us endless opportunities to practice bodhi-mind and to cultivate merit and virtue.

Without sentient beings, a bodhisattva could not attain buddhahood. Therefore, those on the bodhisattva path should help those who need help, and be thankful to those we have already helped. In all cases, we should be grateful to sentient beings. Such an attitude will help lessen feelings of pride and arrogance.

It is easy for greed, anger, arrogance, and hatred to arise. Greed arises from wanting more. To be miserly is a product of greed—hanging on to what one has. Envy arises when we want what others have. Anger arises when something comes between us and what we want. Hatred can arise when someone is different from us, or too much like us. Arrogance grows when we think we are in some way superior to others. All these feelings are caused by self-centeredness. Thus, the way to practice is to cultivate bodhi-mind with pure intention, helping others, and not indulging in self-serving vexations.

For example, on Thanksgiving Eve, I asked Chris to come to the Chan Center and spend the night and some of Thanksgiving Day on editing and paperwork. Chris agreed, and that is good. If he was very self-centered, he might have said no. But the situation was more complex than it seemed. By Chris working at the Center during a holiday, he may have been helping me, but hurting his family. For this reason I apologized to him and his family and said that I hoped his companion, Maria, would not be upset. Chris said that she was not, and I said that it was probably because she figures I am an old man who needs all the help he can get.

MARIA    I wasn't upset. It's Chris who needs all the help he can get.

SHIFU    In that case, Chris should be grateful to us because I provided a good opportunity for him to practice, and you made it easier for him to do it.

In all our actions, we should reflect on whether our intentions are beneficial to others. Likewise, when negative feelings arise in us, we should reflect on them, to see if they are harmful to others. In this way, we will check ourselves before we act. If we put other sentient beings before our- selves, selfish feelings will not arise as often or as easily.

It is difficult for most of us to think about benefiting sentient beings all the time, and in this case, I am talking primarily about people. Imagine if I included all realms of sentient beings. For example, if one of a couple is working hard at a job all day, he or she may be in a bad mood upon returning home. On the other hand, if the other person had to do housekeeping all day, he or she may also be in a bad mood. Two people in a bad mood usually spells trouble. But, if one of the two is mindful enough to perceive that the other may also have had a bad day, he or she will be more attentive, patient, tolerant, and considerate. There will likely be fewer problems. This is an example of proper practice: thinking less about oneself and more about others. This is the beginning of compassion.

On one of my retreats, three women shared a room. One complained to me that, if there was one thing she hated, it was snoring, and both of her roommates were "snoring their heads off." I said, "Maybe you snore sometimes, too." She said, "Me? I would rather die than snore!" If she could accept the idea that she herself was capable of snoring, she would probably have more consideration for those who do snore.

To help her, I told a story: Once I spent a night in the same room with two masters. Both snored, one in a loud, roaring tone and the other in a lower, wheezy tone. It annoyed me, to say the least. I felt like poking them, but then they might have woken up and been unable to fall asleep again. I decided against that idea. Instead, I imagined that the wheezer was a frog croaking in a marsh and that the other was a tiger roaring in the jungle. On the right a frog, on the left a tiger, right a frog, left a tiger, frog, tiger, frog, tiger . . . and eventually I fell asleep. I remembered that ancient masters could enter samadhi just by listening to the sound of the wind or flowing water. I thought that if it could be done with wind and water, it could also be done with snoring. Perhaps I would not enter samadhi, but at least I would fall asleep. Being considerate of others is as much a form of practice as meditation. Do not only think of yourself; and when you are thinking of yourself, at least do the right thing.

STUDENT   How do you know what the right thing is?

SHIFU   Base your decisions and judgments on the teachings of Buddhadharma. If you are not sure whether something is right or wrong, or good or bad, then try to determine if it accords with Buddhist teachings and precepts. If it does, then do it. If it does not, refrain from doing it. Use Buddhist teachings as a guideline. If you are still unsure, ask your Dharma teacher for advice. Also, use society's laws, ethics, morals, and customs as guidelines. If your intentions are in accord with society's standard, then you are probably not off track; and, if you have common sense, you can also use that.

Be aware of your changing mental and physical conditions. See how they affect your thoughts, words, and actions. Usually, if we are unhealthy or physically hurt, we will be in a bad mood. The whole world looks ugly when you are in a bad frame of mind. During these times everything and everyone seems to be lacking. It is easy for anger and hatred to arise. Despite this, from moment to moment, and with everyone, try to give rise to feelings of gratitude.

Greedy people are usually unaware of their own greed. The same is true for people filled with anger, arrogance, or pride. But, sooner or later, practitioners will recognize that they have been greedy, angry, or arrogant. At that time, they should practice repentance. If you can do this every time, you will recognize these and non-virtuous feelings more often and they will naturally arise less and less.

As a practitioner, you repent because you realize that these mental states result from your strong attachment to self. Of course, you must use your self-centeredness to repent, but afterward, your self-centeredness should lessen, at least temporarily. If the situation allows, it is best to repent in front of a Buddha statue. While bowing or prostrating, reflect on the things you thought, said, or did that were wrong. When you become aware of your wrongdoings, acknowledge your errors and vow not to repeat those behaviors. Likewise, whenever something good happens or someone is kind to you, make a conscious effort to feel grateful.

In the temple in Taiwan, I tell many of my students to use two sentences in their daily lives. Whenever they meet or receive help from anyone they should say, "Amitabha Buddha, thank you." They are not giving thanks to Amitabha Buddha, but to the person who helped them. However, because their method is to recite the name of Amitabha Buddha, giving thanks reminds them of their practice and so helps them to cultivate mindfulness and bodhi-mind in their daily lives.

The second sentence, spoken when aware of a wrong action, is "I'm sorry." To say "thank you" is gratitude and to say "I'm sorry" is repentance. If people can truly hold these two attitudes in their minds and act on them, then they will have fewer vexations. If you can do this with genuine concern for sentient beings, then compassion will arise.

To summarize, be mindful of the welfare of sentient beings. Remind yourself not to be self-centered. Repent wrong actions and feel gratitude toward others. What I have described is, in fact, daily practice. If you consistently strive to hold these ideas and incorporate them into your daily life, you are doing daily practice. At the same time, it is important to continue to meditate so as to be more aware of your mental state. If you are scattered and unaware, you will not see your negative feelings arising. With meditation as an underlying discipline, you will be more mindful of your actions, intentions, feelings, moods, and thoughts.

STUDENT   To be mindful of our behavior, should we set up an objective observer in our minds that monitors our intentions, thoughts, words, and actions?

SHIFU   No. That would make you tense and tired. With meditation you will gradually cultivate an inner stillness, so that in any situation you will not get too excited or emotional. If your mind is relatively peaceful, you will naturally be more aware of your thoughts and you will know what to say and do. You will not lose control. When controlled by your emotions and impulses, you are in fact out of control, saying and doing things before you think about the consequences. This is how trouble starts. This is how vexations arise for you and for others. Therefore, try to stay peaceful and exercise restraint in your words and actions. This comes gradually, from regularly meditating, from being mindful during your daily practice, and from using Buddha-dharma to guide your behavior.

On the other hand, if you are always watching yourself like a hawk or a critic, you will drive yourself crazy or make yourself miserable. If there is an observer constantly watching, you will not be able to function smoothly. If piano players always watched themselves play, they would not be able to play with spontaneity.

STUDENT    Every day I ride the subway and I see a procession of beggars, homeless people and sick people, and they often ask for money. What attitude should I have in such situations?

SHIFU    This is a difficult question to answer because every situation is different. It depends on who you are, what you can do, how much you can give. If you are poor and have no money, then you cannot do much. Perhaps you can help an individual person here and there: give food to a homeless family or clothing to someone dressed in rags. If you have money, power, or influence, then you can do more. Perhaps you can help to create a better society and environment. But you must remember, no matter what kind of help you give, there will be those who do not care, who will not listen, and who will not change. You do what you can. You do your best.

If we merely use money to help these people, the help will be minimal. Our financial resources are limited. Besides, money will not help them in a fundamental way. We have to figure out how we can better the environment and help them improve their karma, which has led them to where they are now. We have to help them understand the principle of cause and consequence, so that they will better understand their situation. In this way we can help them in a fundamental way. Buddhism takes the long view and concerns itself with fundamental issues. We as practitioners cannot dwell only on short-term solutions. We have to dig beneath the superficial. To do this we have to think about how we can spread the Dharma.

STUDENT   It doesn't sound realistic. Most of these people are already too far gone to listen to ways in which they can change their lives. It's too late. Even if they believed in future lifetimes, I'm sure they are thinking about today and tomorrow, not about years down the road. And they don't want to know about their root problems. They want food, clothing, shelter, drugs, medicine. These people need immediate help. Are you saying we should become street-corner evangelists and preach Buddhadharma to passers-by?

SHIFU   No, you should not evangelize. That is not the Buddhist way. It will only bring more problems—for you, for others, for Buddhism in general. The best way is to practice Buddhadharma. If you live it, then you do not have to preach. It will flow from you naturally. If you are of a mind to give, the giving will come naturally. Those who have affinity with you will benefit. This is helping of the highest order. You do not have to evangelize. If you live the Buddhadharma, people will come to you.

STUDENT   What about the other side of the coin? Suppose you work in a dog-eat-dog business. How do you deal with competition with other businesses? It is your job to outdo the competition. Isn't this causing your competitors to suffer? But if you helped your competitors it would mean losing your own job or business. How should one act in these circumstances?

SHIFU    Honest competition is not necessarily evil. It depends on your attitude. In what way are you competitive? The correct attitude is to strive forward and, at the same time, wish your competition to strive forward as well. It is like a swim meet. I do my swimming and you do yours. We do not try to knock the other person dead and then go ahead. We encourage true competitive spirit. This is healthy. It encourages one to perform at higher levels.

An environment where everyone mutually stimulates one another is healthy. In any area of competition, some will get ahead, and some will fall behind. Inevitably, some will fall so far behind they will not be able to continue. That area of competition, then, is not for them. They will have to switch to another field. That is neither your fault nor your concern. People who fail in one area will survive, and they may go on to succeed in another area.

If you are in a dog-eat-dog or unethical business, you should consider getting another job. Right livelihood is part of the Eightfold Noble Path. Your livelihood should accord with your sense of Buddhadharma.

STUDENT    Constantly trying to think of the benefit and welfare of sentient beings seems to be a great burden. Wouldn't this attitude itself become a vexation?

SHIFU    It will not be a burden or vexation to one who understands the teachings of Buddhadharma, especially the principle of causes and conditions. As you try to help others, remember that sentient beings have their own causes and conditions, their own merit and virtue, their own karma. You cannot change that. You cannot take on other people's karma.

For example, two months ago about eighty of us went to India. An older woman in the group was knocked down by a water buffalo and she broke her leg. In spite of her handicap, she insisted on continuing with the group. She said, "I want to go, even if it kills me!"

I said, "If you really want to die, you are better off in Taiwan. If you come with us, the whole group will suffer. As a Buddhist, you should understand karma. Your being knocked down by this buffalo could mean that you owed the buffalo something from a previous life, perhaps your own life; but because you were on a pilgrimage, you only suffered a broken leg. That is your karma. If you insist on going on, you will be a burden to the whole group and you will only be creating more bad karma for yourself." Hearing this, she decided to return to Taiwan.

The key word is 'try.' Of course you should not do anything that would harm others, but you should try to help in any way you can. Whether or not you truly help them is another story, and it really is not your concern.

STUDENT    Trying to be compassionate all the time can become a mental burden, especially if it must be pounded into the brain moment after moment. Wouldn't it cut into all of our other thoughts, words, and actions? Can we always be thinking about other people? Even when we are sitting on the toilet? It can be oppressive. Is there another way one can think about it?

SHIFU    You are forgetting what I said earlier. Do not do anything that will make you feel tense, tired, or miserable. If you whip yourself all the time, you will be of no use to others or to yourself. Be as mindful as you can. With meditation as a supporting discipline and Buddhadharma as your guideline, compassion will grow naturally. Do the best you can, but do not push too hard.

STUDENT   Is it possible to go about your daily activities and perceive the world in a non-discriminating manner, like a camera or mirror, without being enlightened?

SHIFU   There is the mind of intuition and there is the mind of non-discrimination. Unenlightened people can, to varying extents, rely on their intuition—knowing, saying, and doing things in a direct way, without relying much on the thought process. With a truly non-discriminating mind, there are no vexations, but with the mind of intuition, vexations can still arise. A mind of intuition can be cultivated and strengthened with meditation. It is not enlightenment, but it is a good state of mind.

# Is the View of
# Practice More Important
# than Practice?

QUESTION    I have heard a Chan aphorism that goes
something like this: "Practice is important, but the view of
practice is even more important." This seems to contradict
everything I have ever heard about Chan. Chan says to drop
the ego and subjective views. Any view I can possibly have
must be subjective and therefore a distortion of the truth. It
becomes yet another obstruction.

Also, isn't an experience an experience, regardless of what
the person practices or believes in? If the ego goes away, the
ego goes away. What does it matter if the person is atheist,
Buddhist, Christian, Hindu, Jewish, Muslim, or anything else?
If you say that only Buddhists can have experiences where
the ego drops, isn't this elitist?

SHIFU    The saying is a paraphrase of a line that reads: "What one knows or sees is more important than where one is stepping." The phrase, "What one knows or sees," should not be replaced with the word 'view,' because view is something that can come from one's learning. The phrase refers to those things that come directly from one's experience. In the *Lotus Sutra* there is a saying, "To open what the Buddha knows and sees; to reveal what the Buddha knows and sees; to realize what the Buddha knows and sees; to enter what the Buddha knows and sees." What the Buddha knows and sees is emptiness, no form, no attachment, and no phenomena.

The line should be interpreted thusly: "What is known and seen is more important than what one is doing." And "what is known and seen" refers specifically to what the Buddha knows and sees. How should a practitioner relate to this? First is the case of one who has experienced enlightenment and has entered into what the Buddha knows and sees. How does one really know that what one sees is actually what the Buddha sees? One must gauge the experience against the teachings of the Buddha—the sutras. Practicing diligently, studying the sutras, and keeping the precepts fall under the heading of "What one does." In this case, what one does is not as important as what one sees or knows. If the experience is not real enlightenment, then one cannot know and see what the Buddha knows and sees.

If one has a good, qualified teacher, it is not absolutely necessary to read the sutras for proper guidance. Such a teacher should be able to determine if the experience is real or false, shallow or deep. If it is not enlightenment, then the teacher can point directly to the problem or sticking point—the obstruction or the attachment.

The aphorism is not advising people to abandon practice; rather, it is saying that practice is important, but that which the Buddha knows and sees is even more important. Without the guidance of the Buddha's experience, people would not be practicing Buddhadharma correctly. They would be practicing outer-path teachings. So, before enlightenment, practitioners need the guidance of what the Buddha knows and sees. After enlightenment, they still need to check their experiences against the teachings of the Buddha and see if their experiences are truly what the Buddha knows and sees.

If you have intellectually grasped what the Buddha knows and sees without actually being enlightened, you will at least not be likely to venture down the wrong path. You can even guide others in practice, but you will not be able to confirm someone's possible enlightenment. At least you can help people in the correct way of practice. On the other hand, if a teacher is not enlightened and does not conceptually understand what the Buddha knows and sees, he or she is probably practicing and leading others down outer paths. People often practice with some attachment or expectation in mind—an idea that there is something to gain. This can lead to problems.

From this perspective, I say that without the guidance of what the Buddha knows and sees, practitioners of other religions cannot experience the Buddha's enlightenment, no matter how deep their experience. Such people will still have an idea of, or an attachment to, an eternal and omnipresent totality. Whether this is called God or something else does not matter; it is not what the Buddha knows and sees.

Even to experience totality is extremely difficult and a sign of progress. Many practitioners, including Buddhists, have shallow experiences of this nature. They feel a lightness or peace; they might believe that they are free from self-centeredness, but they still have attachments. This is why one needs the guidance of a good teacher.

Many practitioners misinterpret this kind of experience, which indeed, corresponds to elementary levels of attainment. For example, there are four fruition levels in the Hinayana tradition, the first of which is *srotapanna,* the 'stream winner' who has entered the 'stream' of enlightenment, but still has attachments; and the fourth of which is arhatship, liberation from samsara. But even prior to these there are four preliminary levels: level of warmth, top level, level of wisdom, level of first in the world. Only after these four levels can someone enter the fruition levels of the Hinayana. Many practitioners, Chan included, think they are already enlightened, when in fact they have only experienced the first level of warmth.

STUDENT   Is it possible to practice outside Buddhism and experience no-self?

SHIFU   No. No matter what non-Buddhist path you choose, you will have some attainment or expectation in your mind.

STUDENT   Is it possible that such a person can practice without any idea of gain?

SHIFU   Yes. Such a person would be called a prayeka-buddha—someone who becomes enlightened without the Buddha's teachings. But in the sutras it is said that it is only possible to be a pratyekabuddha in a world where there is no Buddhadharma.

STUDENT   You mention shallow and deep enlightenment. When you mention experiences, are you referring exclusively to experiences of no-self?

SHIFU   Not necessarily. If I am talking about Chan enlightenment, then I am talking about experiences of no-self. However, I often use the word enlightenment to refer to experiences from many spiritual and non-spiritual traditions. People from many different traditions often have the experience of a great totality. These can be considered enlightenment experiences, but they are not experiences of no-self.

A shallow Chan experience will last for a short time and a deep experience will last longer. Also, with a deeper experience a person sees emptiness more clearly. His or her sense of emptiness is solid, whereas the shallow experience is not as clear or solid. The deepest enlightenment is when you are not just seeing emptiness, but are, in fact, in the midst of emptiness. The stages of enlightenment experience may be compared to a person's gradually increasing experience of wine. The first stage is a person who has never seen or tasted wine. In the next stage the person has seen it and knows what it looks like, but has not yet tasted it. Next, the person tastes it and now knows the flavor. Later, if still interested, the person may want another taste, or a whole glass. Last is the stage where the person jumps into the barrel of wine. At this point there is no separation from the wine. To speak of thirst is no longer relevant.

STUDENT   Is it possible for someone who does not know Buddhadharma to experience no-self? Is it possible that they do have the experience, but because their background is different they interpret it differently? Perhaps they see it as God or totality.

SHIFU    It is impossible for such people to have the true experience of no-self. One who experiences no-self enters into the realm of what the Buddha knows and sees. Such a person would not interpret or explain it as God or totality.

STUDENT    I read an anecdote about a woman who was not practicing at all, just going through an intense period in her life. What naturally arose in her mind was the question, "Who am I?" She had an experience from it and it changed her view of herself and the world. Some time later she read some books on Zen Buddhism and saw the connection between her experience and Zen. She talked to a roshi and he confirmed her experience.

SHIFU    If it happened as you say and a legitimate roshi confirmed her experience, it would mean she is something like a pratyekabuddha because she had no preconception of emptiness. On the other hand, if the roshi encouraged her to practice further and then guided her, and then she experienced more, that is perfectly understandable.

I knew an American who had an experience twenty-five years ago. He went to a master and his experience was confirmed. Ten years later he felt some of his problems were not resolved so he went to another master and his past experience was again confirmed. Another fifteen years went by and still he was not satisfied. He was a teacher at a center, so he left and came to me. I told him there were certain problems with his understanding. I told him that he probably had a legitimate experience and that was good, but he was clinging to a memory. If someone thinks the memory of a long-gone experience is the experience itself, then that is a problem. I told this man to practice hard and say, "No good," to whatever experience he might have. If he practiced in this manner and later needed guidance, I would gladly help out.

The woman that you speak of was open-minded and flexible and had no attachment to her experience. Therefore, she probably could practice in a smooth manner after her initial experience. But this man had expectations, so he had problems.

STUDENT    In the Chan sect there are numerous examples of people who had genuine experiences of no-self and yet still encountered many problems afterward. Does this mean that the initial experience was not genuine?

SHIFU    No, these experiences could very well have been genuine. A good teacher would be able to ascertain the authenticity of the experiences and help these people to have more and deeper Chan experiences. But there are no guarantees. A person's practice might slip. Perhaps a teacher and student do not connect. There can be any number of reasons. A person who experiences no-self can regress. A perfect example is the story of the American teacher. He had an experience that was confirmed by a teacher, but he still had problems later on. He came to me to see if the right causes and conditions, or karmic affinity, existed between us, but I felt not, so I gave him a method and advised him to return to his old teacher.

STUDENT    You said in order to have a no-self experience, one needs to have an understanding of Chan and also have a qualified teacher. In the case of the woman, what if she had been a Buddhist nun or monk in a previous life, or had a deep experience in a previous life, and in this life the causes and conditions finally came together in an enlightenment experience?

SHIFU   Even if you have practiced in previous lives, in this life you still need a teacher and teachings; but if you practiced well in previous lives, things will likely progress more quickly. Before he became the sixth patriarch of Chan, Huineng was a young monk working in the kitchen. Because he had good karmic roots, he was suddenly enlightened when he heard a line from the *Diamond Sutra*. Still, he regarded Fifth Patriarch Hongran as his teacher, and went to him for guidance. But Huineng did not hear an ordinary line from an ordinary book; it was pure Buddhadharma that he heard.

One could argue that a person who has never heard of Buddhadharma lives in a world without it, so he or she could in fact be a pratyekabuddha. If so how would this person's attainment be gauged? We use Buddhist criteria to gauge the level of Buddhist attainment. If such a person claims to be enlightened by Buddhist standards, then likely he or she is not. Since the time of the Buddha, there have been many people—scholars, leaders, and philosophers, who had experiences and who claimed that they were enlightened in the Buddhist sense. They were probably wrong. Their experiences must be judged against the principles of Buddhadharma. The fact is that certain aspects of Buddhism are different from all other religions. Therefore, people who do not have a clear understanding of Buddhadharma will not have Buddhist enlightenment experiences.

STUDENT    You said that a person who has the correct understanding of Buddhadharma, even without enlightenment, could guide others in their practice. How does one know if one has a correct understanding without the experience to go with it?

SHIFU    If you have a good teacher and are a sincere practitioner, then you ought to be familiar with many principles of Buddhadharma. Much of Buddhism is not too difficult to understand and communicate. Also, you can develop a sound, intellectual understanding of the Dharma through appropriate literature. Armed with such knowledge, you can teach others on a rudimentary level. However, you should not deal with big issues. Obviously, and most importantly, you have no capability of confirming or disavowing someone else's supposed enlightenment experience. I must also stress that if you are intent on teaching others about Buddhism or leading others in meditation, you should first get permission from your teacher. This holds whether you are a lay practitioner or a monastic.

Problems arise when people use their own religious experiences to explain or interpret the sutras. That is reversing the correct procedure, and it is dangerous. One should not use one's own experience to interpret sutras; one should use sutras to interpret one's experiences. If people use their own experiences to interpret the sutras, then there will be problems. That is why it is best to study with a good and qualified teacher.

# Can Intelligence be a
# Hindrance to Practice?

QUESTION   One often reads that Chan and Zen masters disdain displays of intelligence. Master Dahui (1089-1163) made fun of scholars, and modern master Suzuki Roshi said that an expert's mind has few possibilities, whereas a beginner's mind is limitless. On the other hand, many Westerners who take up Chan practice are initially lured by the intellectual richness of Buddhist philosophy. Is there a contradiction here?

SHIFU   Since the earliest days of Buddhism, I doubt that there has ever been a genuine Chan practitioner who was dull and stupid. Also, I doubt that there has ever been a single person who entered the path of Chan practice on blind faith. Most people practice Chan as a result of a rational decision. Furthermore, Chan does not emphasize pure meditative practice at the expense of intellectual learning. If you meditate, but have no idea why you do it, at best your practice will be a hollow, foundationless shell.

Chan emphasizes personal experience from meditation, but it is also important to have a correct understanding of Chan practice and principles. Without understanding the Dharma, a person would derive only limited benefit from the practice. It could even be harmful. For this reason alone, Chan does not oppose intelligence. However, the question is why Chan masters often seem to put down intelligence and learning.

Chan masters acknowledge intelligence and learning, but taught that they must be transcended. Intellectual knowledge is not ultimate truth. The enlightened state that Chan speaks of is beyond thinking, words, and symbols: it cannot be described and it cannot be understood through deductive reasoning. Ultimately, thought and language are man-made constructs based on symbols. By definition, a symbol is not the thing it symbolizes. Symbols, then, cannot explain or grasp enlightenment and one cannot reach enlightenment solely through the use of symbols. It is hard enough using symbols to explain the world around us, let alone as a means to attain enlightenment. Besides, each person views the world differently, with his or her own set of experiences and understanding. Chan masters must caution their students that enlightenment cannot be reached, described, or imagined in a purely intellectual way, whether by language, thought, or symbol. Ordinary words are insufficient. Quoting Shakyamuni is insufficient. Relying on the words and sayings of the patriarchs is insufficient. Such descriptions are not the reality of enlightenment itself.

Chan masters teach their students to leave behind all concepts so they may *directly experience* enlightenment for themselves. Most people can intellectually accept this explanation, further demonstrating that Chan is a rational approach.

I can whet your intellectual appetite with Chan philosophy, but when you practice seriously, you cannot rely on knowledge and intelligence. It is impossible to practice Chan correctly and at the same time hold on to previous ideas. You cannot reflect on this or that saying, nor can you dwell on your experiences, wondering if you have tasted enlightenment. The only way to experience enlightenment is to leave everything behind. In fact, leaving everything behind is itself enlightenment. If there is anything to which you still cling, then you cannot become enlightened. Intelligence, thoughts, words, and language are all attachments that are difficult to transcend, even for a moment. If they cannot be left behind, they become obstructions to practice.

Ironically, enlightened beings use reasoning, intelligence, and language to help others practice. To communicate the benefits of Chan, they use tools based on knowledge and experience. Before practice, you need learning, knowledge, and experience. The more intelligent you are, the better. After enlightenment, you again need knowledge and experience. During actual practice, however, learning is of little use.

Most of the Chan patriarchs were learned and intelligent. Before enlightenment they had only worldly intelligence. After enlightenment they possessed true wisdom. Intelligence before enlightenment is intelligence with attachment. Wisdom is intelligence without attachment.

STUDENT I have heard that some Hindu traditions regard meditation as a secondary, supportive practice, whereas intellectual study and debate of sacred texts are regarded as the superior practice.

SHIFU    There are Buddhist traditions like this as well. When Xuancang (600-664) went to India in the seventh century to retrieve sutras and sastras, he discovered two major Buddhist traditions, Yogacara and Madhyamika. Masters and disciples of these traditions constantly engaged in Dharma debates. In fact, they spent all their time in detailed intellectual analyses of Buddhist philosophy, using the ancient Buddhist logical system as the tool of their investigations. The more they engaged in their studies and debates, the more lucid their minds became, until they clearly and fully understood all Buddhist concepts and principles. Quite naturally, through such rigorous training their vexations lessened as well.

In a sense, however, this type of practice is elitist. Engaging in debates and study is easier if you live where you can do it all the time. A monastery is conducive to such practice. There is plenty of time, many fellow practitioners with similar aspirations, and few disturbances and temptations. Lay practitioners cannot do this; they have other responsibilities. Only scholars and academics would have the facilities, desire, and time for such practice. It is not suitable for the ordinary person.

I know a master in Taiwan who never meditates. Once I asked him, "Do you have any method of practice?" He replied, "What do you mean by practice? I spend all of my time reading Buddhadharma, writing about Buddhadharma, thinking about Buddhadharma. My whole life is spent in the midst of Buddhadharma. What other practice do I need?" For him the answer is none. He has a clear understanding of

Buddhadharma, so he feels no need for meditative practice. His is a path quite different from that of Chan.

If people pursue the intellectual path and forego meditation, they also forego the spiritual experience of the practice, which directly affects body and mind. Intellectual stimulation only engages the mental faculties. People would lose the physiological and direct mental benefit from meditating. Even the Hindu traditions do not completely neglect meditation, and incorporate it as a supportive, auxiliary practice.

Furthermore, just because you are intelligent does not mean you are proficient or trained in the skills of logic and deductive reasoning. A non-scholar probably would not be suited for a practice that involves intense analysis. On the other hand, anyone can practice the methods of Chan. Chan practice is rational, but it does not require scholarly skills. If it did, there would not be many Chan and Zen practitioners. Even someone who has never read a book can practice Chan.

STUDENT   You say the modern master you spoke about has a perfectly clear understanding of Buddhadharma. Is this the same as being enlightened?

SHIFU   That depends on his mental state. If he has no obstructions or attachments in his mind, then he is enlightened. If he still has attachments, then at best he only intellectually understands enlightenment. This is not true enlightenment. However, there are limitless approaches to Dharma. If you relentlessly continue with a method based on logical investigation until you have dropped all attachments, including the deductive habit itself, then you will experience enlightenment, just as you would through Chan methods.

One can reach a certain level of intellectual enlightenment through reasoning and dialectic, but if there are still any attachments, it is not Chan enlightenment.

Two Tibetan lamas once had a debate. In the end, the younger lama had the last word and the elder just smiled. Seeing this, the younger lama laughed. Who won? You will never know, because you were not there. And even if you were there, if you saw it with a mind of attachment you still would not know who won the debate. Perhaps the young lama did win, but perhaps the elder's silence was the true answer. You must be enlightened yourself to know who won.

STUDENT    Charles Luk described a person deep in practice as being dull, even stupid. It seemed his regular intellectual ability had been impaired by the practice. From Charles Luk's words it seemed that it is a common occurrence among serious practitioners. Is this true? Is this dull intellectual ability what it is like to be enlightened?

SHIFU    There is a famous Buddhist saying: First mountains are mountains and rivers are rivers. Then mountains are no longer mountains and rivers are no longer rivers. In the end, mountains are again mountains and rivers are again rivers. This describes three stages of practice.

In the first stage, before or just beginning practice, practitioners have intelligence, but discriminate with a mind of attachment. They know mountains are mountains, and rivers are rivers. The second stage refers to people who are practicing diligently and deeply. They are not always able to make clear distinctions between this and that, and indeed they may appear dull or stupid to an outside observer. The third stage describes enlightenment, and once again practitioners clearly discriminate between this and that. The difference between the first and third stage is that in the first stage people have a sense of self. In the third stage there are no more attachments to self. Charles Luk was describing the second stage of practice.

Enlightenment is not a hindrance to intelligence. Indeed, it usually sharpens one's intellectual ability. However, reliance on the intellect as the sole tool or guide to practice can easily become an obstruction.

# Chinese Chan
# and Japanese Zen

🍃

QUESTION    What are the similarities and differences between Chinese Chan and Japanese Zen?

SHIFU    Chan was transmitted from China to Japan during the Northern Song Dynasty (960-1127). When Chan was assimilated and altered by Japanese culture, this resulted in Zen. Remember that Chan itself had evolved over the centuries. There were noticeable changes in Chan Buddhism from the Tang Dynasty (618-907) to the Song Dynasty (960-1278), from the Song to the Ming Dynasty (1368-1644), and from the Ming to the present. Chan in the Northern Song Dynasty was probably very similar to Japanese Zen of that same period, but over the centuries they have evolved along different paths.

Most people in the West who know about Buddhism are more familiar with Zen than with Chan. There are two main schools of Zen, the Rinzai which evolved from the Linji School of China, and the Soto which came from the Caodong School of China.

There is a marked difference in the flavor of Japanese Zen before and after World War II. Before the war, Zen displayed a more martial spirit. After the war, this characteristic was not as evident, but compared to masters from other countries, Japanese Zen masters, or roshis, exhibited forceful personalities. It would not be difficult to point out a roshi in a gathering of monks. It is common for a Japanese man in a position of power to have a commanding personality, like that of a samurai. It is not necessarily the trait of a roshi; it is the trait of a Japanese man in a position of power. In recent times, however, Japanese men have not exhibited the samurai personality as in the past. Today, roshis of both genders have emerged in the West. No doubt, these masters will have personae reflecting their own cultures.

On the other hand, except for their dress and appearance, Chinese Chan masters would not stand out in a crowd. In general, Chinese masters do not have fierce or forceful personalities. If a Chinese master is fierce, then it is that particular master's personality. Chan masters will take charge while they are guiding others in practice, but they will not carry this kind of behavior over into daily life. During retreats Chan masters might scold some people, but it would be rare to witness this behavior at other times. Outside of the Chan Hall, they live ordinary lives and are indistinguishable from everyone else.

In the Chan tradition, there are, in general, two types of Chan masters. One tends to scold, and sometimes beat practitioners while guiding them. These masters are usually of the Linji tradition. The other type of master uses gentle words and mannerisms in teaching. Generally, these masters are of the Caodong tradition. Again, however, we emphasize that masters exhibit such behavior only when guiding others in practice.

In Chan and Zen monasteries, practice is very much part of daily life. Work and service are important aspects of practice. Of course, there are times devoted completely to meditation. At those times there may be a few hundred monks and nuns practicing together formally. In Chan retreats, there are usually no regularly scheduled personal interviews with the master. When a practitioner feels something important has happened he or she may request a personal interview. At other times, a master teaches to the entire gathering at the same time. People may stay in a Chan monastery for years without a single occasion to meet and speak personally with the master. During Zen retreats, on the other hand, masters usually interview their disciples daily.

Through the centuries, Chinese Chan monasteries have not placed as much emphasis on appearances and specific forms of practice. For example, Chinese monasteries do not issue sets of uniforms and robes to sangha members. Monks and nuns wear their own clothes. Of course they have ceremonial robes for special occasions, but for the most part, there are no strict rules governing clothing. Emphasis is placed on following precepts and adhering to the daily schedule.

It is only natural that there be differences between Japanese Zen monasteries and Chinese Chan monasteries. The same is true for Chan centers and Zen centers in the United States. If people see our Chan Center as being different from a typical American Zen center, it should come as no surprise. Our Chan Center in America is even different from a traditional Chinese monastery. A typical zendo in this country is different from a traditional zendo in Japan. This is normal, since such centers would naturally have some of the flavors of the local culture.

Actually, traditional zendos in Japan are quite similar to traditional Chan Halls in China. A typical Chan Hall, where meditation practice takes place, is usually only one of several buildings in a Chinese monastery. Here at the Chan Center, we only have two buildings, and one is a dormitory for nuns and lay women residents. Therefore, we have to fit everything else into one building.

In a traditional Chan monastery, there may be several buildings and thousands of residents. A large group may live in the building holding the Main Hall. Only a hundred or so may stay at the Chan Hall, which is usually austere in its appearance, and may not have a single Buddha statue. On the other hand, some Chan practitioners may never go to the Main Hall to attend its activities.

I am a product of twentieth-century China, so when I came to the United States I brought some flavor of modern China with me. In the same way, American Zen centers founded by Japanese teachers carry the spirit of modern Japan. I have not adhered completely to the style of Chinese Chan. Certain elements of the Chan Center have been borrowed from Japanese teachings. For example, the cushions (zafus) we sit on are from the Japanese tradition.

Traditionally, practitioners of the Chinese Linji and Caodong, and the Japanese Rinzai sects, sit facing each other. Here we sit facing the wall, after the Japanese Soto tradition. I also have practitioners do variations of hatha yoga exercises in between sittings. This is not found in any Chinese or Japanese tradition. It is just that I feel stretching exercises are healthy for the body and necessary for modern practitioners.

My attempt to give each retreatant several personal interviews is adopted from Zen. I will interview each practitioner a couple of times during retreat, but not every day. I often leave it up to the practitioner. If he or she wishes to speak with me, I am usually available.

Chinese Chan monasteries are predominantly closed to lay practitioners. In a traditional Chan monastery monks or nuns live and practice together for many years. One would not often find householders attending weeklong retreats and then returning to their regular lives and daily schedules. Our Chan Center in New York is open to and frequented mostly by householders.

Things in the United States will never be the same as they are in China, so I have had to restructure things and modify the way I teach. Chan and Zen will have to change and adapt if they are to survive in modern cultures, whether Eastern or Western.

STUDENT   On retreats at the Chan Center, we do prostration practice. Is this also an element of the Zen sect?

SHIFU   Prostration is a generic Buddhist practice. Zen uses prostration, but not to the extent of other Buddhist traditions. In a Japanese monastery, prostration practice is not emphasized, but monks and nuns will prostrate three times before and after services. However, it is up to the individual how he or she wishes to practice during private time. There are four kinds of samadhi practice: sitting, walking, chanting, and prostrating, so prostration is a legitimate form of practice.

STUDENT   Do Zen practitioners do slow-walking meditation?

SHIFU   Yes, but not fast-walking meditation. In Chan monasteries, practitioners fast walk but do not slow walk. At the New York Chan Center we do both forms of walking.

There are other differences. Japanese Zen does not use the method of reciting Amitabha Buddha's name, whereas the Chinese tradition does. This method was taught by Fourth Patriarch Daoxin (580-651). Today, most people recite Amitabha Buddha's name, but any buddha's name will do. After the Song Dynasty, many people used this method as part of their Chan training. In Japan, reciting the Buddha's name is practiced mainly by the Pure Land sect.

In Zen, people begin to practice by counting the breath, or meditating on a *wato* (Chinese: *huatou*). In general, the Rinzai sect uses the koan (Chinese: *gong'an*) and *wato* methods. A roshi will give a student a series of koans or *watos* to work on, one after another. The main method used by the Soto sect is *shikantaza* (Chinese: *zhiguandazuo*), which means 'just sitting.' Shikantaza is often described as the method of no-method.

When teaching beginners, I usually ask them to count or follow the breath. If newcomers have been using *huatous* for a long time and are doing well, I will advise them to continue. If people are accustomed to reciting Amitabha Buddha's name, I will advise them to continue, but not to recite with the desire to be reborn in the Pure Land.

As a Chan method, reciting the Buddha's name, or a mantra for that matter, is no different from counting the breath. Its purpose is to help calm the mind. When a reciter of the Buddha's name reaches a point where the mind is calm and concentrated, he or she can then start to ask, "Who is reciting the Buddha's name?" In essence, the method turns into a *huatou*. Some have said that if you turn reciting the Buddha's name into a *huatou*, it is simultaneously a Chan method and a Pure Land method. I disagree. In reality, it is Chan practice.

Followers of Linji Chan usually begin by collecting their minds, the most common methods being counting breaths, reciting Buddha's name, or using a *huatou*. In the beginning, however, a *huatou* is recited like a mantra or Amitabha Buddha's name. Eventually, practitioners progress to contemplating a *huatou* in order to arouse the doubt sensation. Whereas the normal practice for Rinzai Zen students is to work on one *huatou* after another, Linji Chan students may work on the same *huatou* for their entire lives.

In my opinion, it is easier to collect the mind using methods other than a *huatou*, so I rarely instruct beginning practitioners to start with one. Giving rise to a sense of doubt is the purpose of a *huatou*. If it does not happen, then the method has not served its purpose.

Practitioners of the Caodong sect usually begin by counting breaths or reciting the Buddha's name. They will not, however, turn the method into a *huatou*. Instead, when their minds are calm, practitioners will practice silent illumination, which is similar to *shikantaza*.

STUDENT    When Pure Land practitioners recite the Buddha's name and attain a level of one-mindedness, is it the same as a Chan experience of one-mindedness?

SHIFU    It is not the same because the Pure Land practitioner is seeking to be reborn in the Pure Land. A seeking attitude presupposes that there is attachment. If there are any attachments involved, it cannot be a Chan experience. When a Chan practitioner recites the Buddha's name, there should not be any element of desire. A true Chan or Zen practitioner would not ask a buddha for help.

STUDENT   Why then do some Chan practitioners call on Guanyin (Avalokitesvara Bodhisattva) for help?

SHIFU   Chan is part of Buddhism and is therefore not completely devoid of religiosity. Practitioners who are in situations where they feel hopeless or helpless may call on Guanyin for help or strength. It is human nature to sometimes feel weak or at a loss. The question is, would Chan masters ask Guanyin for help? Chan masters, even if they have no attachments and are not seeking anything for their own sake, may at times find they cannot do something for the sake of sentient beings. In these situations Chan masters may invoke the name of Guanyin. However, in my study of Chinese Buddhist history, I have never come across any reference of a Tang Dynasty Chan master reciting names of buddhas and bodhisattvas. It is possible that the attainment of contemporary masters is not as deep as that of past patriarchs. A genuinely enlightened master would not need to call on Guanyin for help.

STUDENT   If Soto Zen derives from Caodong Chan, then how come Soto is considered a gradual school of practice whereas Caodong is considered a sudden approach?

SHIFU   Where did you hear that? There is no such distinction. You should not confuse 'soft' with 'gradual.' The Soto and Caodong sects are gentler in their approach to practice than are the Rinzai and Linji sects. But they are all sudden methods of practice. There are two ways to look at this. First, I always stress that practice is both the process and the goal. If the goal is to practice, then it is automatically a sudden method. Second, whether you practice forcefully or gently—whether you break through illusion with a *huatou* or you gently calm the mind until self disappears— enlightenment always comes suddenly. Chan enlightenment never appears little by little.

If you insist on calling the Caodong sect a gradual approach, then you must also call the Linji sect a gradual approach. Caodong practitioners practice silent illumination steadily for years. Linji practitioners investigate *huatou*. They may do so for years. What is the difference?

STUDENT    Japanese Zen monks can marry. What is the difference between a Zen priest and a Zen monk and why is there no such distinction in Chan? Are there any other obvious differences?

SHIFU    In Japan the tradition of celibate monks receded with the coming of the Meiji Restoration, when Zen monks were encouraged to marry. Such practitioners are referred to as priests. The difference is that priests can marry and live with their families in a temple. They might follow the monk lifestyle, but if they marry, they are not monks. A married monk is a contradiction in terms. On the other hand, Japanese Zen nuns cannot marry. Presently, they are struggling for this right.

STUDENT    But I thought one of the first precepts for becoming a Buddhist monk was to take a vow of celibacy.

SHIFU   Zen priests take most of the traditional Buddhist vows, but celibacy is not one of them.

STUDENT   When you become a monk or nun in China, you are a Buddhist and not specifically a Chan Buddhist or Pure Land Buddhist. Monks and nuns can try different practices during their lifetimes. Is this also true in Japan?

SHIFU   In China, once you become a monk or nun, you can practice any Buddhist tradition. You are not even limited to Chinese Buddhism. You can practice Theravada Buddhism, Tibetan Buddhism, or any other tradition. This is not the case in Japan. When you join the sangha in Japan, you choose whether you want to be part of the Zen sect or Pure Land sect. This may be a good idea. In China, it is so easy for monks and nuns to dabble with different practices that many of them never advance in any one tradition. It is like what I say about changing meditation methods all the time. You never get anywhere. It's like window-shopping.

The few years that I lived in Japan were spent intensively studying and practicing. I did not make it a point to analyze the similarities and differences between Zen and Chan. Likewise, my contact with American Zen centers and with people who follow the Zen tradition in the United States has been limited, so everything I have said must be considered in this light.

Furthermore, we have limited our discussion to China, Japan and the United States, but there is also a strong Son (Chan) tradition in Korea, and masters from Korea have come to the United States as well. My guess is that in each of these places, the tradition of Chan Buddhism carries qualities unique to those areas and environments. A basic principle of

Buddhism is that all things change. Why should the different Chan traditions be immune to this fundamental principle?

I prefer that we explain to people what we do and why we do it. It is pointless to say, "Chan does this and Zen does that." Inevitably, it leads to unfair comparisons, disagreements, quarrels, and competition. If such discussions spark controversy and animosity among people who want to believe that one style is better than another, then they are not good practitioners. Such behavior is foolish. Practitioners should be concerned with their own practice and with helping others.

Looking beyond whatever differences exist, Chan and Zen are both within the Mahayana tradition, whose followers meditate and practice for the sake of helping sentient beings. This is more important than any differences.

American Buddhism owes a debt of gratitude to Japanese Zen masters and authors, who were among the first to come to the West with teachings of Buddhadharma. Their initial work and success made it possible and easier for other Buddhist traditions to become established.

# Chan and the Absurd

QUESTION   The records of Chan are full of examples of bizarre dialogues and incidents between masters and disciples. Frequently these seem to have a quality of absurd wit or humor. What is the origin of this quality that appears to be unique to Chan, not only among religions but also within Buddhism itself?

SHIFU   In training disciples, Chan masters employ methods that are appropriate for everyday practice, as well as methods that are used only during special situations. They do not regularly employ *gong'ans* that Westerners read about when they first encounter Chan literature and study the historical records. These *gong'ans*, which sometimes appear comical, are meant mostly for special occasions. If it were in fact true that Chan masters trained disciples only in ways described in these records, strangers visiting a Chan monastery might think that they were in an insane asylum. In reality, life in a

Chan monastery is a solemn affair. You would most likely never see a Chan master burning a Buddha statue to make a point, or to emphasize a particular principle of Buddhism. As it turns out, however, these unusual incidents are precisely the ones that have been recorded.

Life in a Chan monastery is ordinary. The daily life of the master is the same as that of the other monks and nuns. All live according to a strict and full schedule that allows few opportunities for the master to engage in dialogue with other sangha members, especially newcomers. There are times for group gatherings, but even these are for specific purposes. The senior disciples would usually sit in front, closer to the master. If the master asked questions, only those who had some attainment in practice would dare to answer. Sometimes a dialogue might develop that would seem humorous to an outsider.

Sometimes newcomers would arrive at a monastery and sit at the back of these gatherings. If they were experienced and confident, they might later come forward to answer questions, or to raise some of their own. At those times, even beginners might come forward, seeking direct guidance from the master.

The dialogues in these circumstances were not always conclusive. They were not always resolved with a clear true or false response. If a monk made apt responses and needed further guidance, the master might grant him an interview. An exception would be when the master felt the monk's responses were the product of mere book learning, in which case the monk would be chased out of the room.

A private interview with a master has far more significance than discussions in the Chan Hall. At an interview, the master may pitch questions at a high or low level. If the monk's mind is bright and clear, his response will be spontaneous no matter what the master says. This indicates that the monk's mind is in correspondence with the master's.

The master may say that fish swim on mountains and birds fly in the sea. No matter what words are used, the master is interested in one thing: determining the disciple's level of understanding. Through dialogue, the master may find opportunities for guiding the disciple, but not by explanation. The master will use what is called 'opportune sharp action'—something that cannot be explained by words or described by appearances. Still, the master uses language, and sometimes gestures, to guide a disciple. If the disciple does not grasp the master's meaning, he is told to leave the room immediately.

Or, the master may say, "All dharmas are reduced to one. To what is this one reduced?" The disciple may say, "I want to take a leak." There does not seem to be any connection between the question and response. But a master may recognize the disciple's level of experience from the exchange. Perhaps the master may feel that the response is not genuine. The dialogue might continue with, "Who is it that wants to take a leak?" To this the monk may say nothing, and, instead, empty his bladder. Surely this seems insane from a conventional perspective.

If the monk appears to be feigning, the master may strike him with the incense board. The disciple may seize the board from the master, who might say, "Before you strike, tell me why you want to beat me." Or the master might say, "All right, I won't hit you now, but you have thirty blows coming your way." To which the disciple might say, "You are the one who deserves a beating."

All such interactions would be unintelligible to a third party, but an alert master will immediately understand what is transpiring. A lesser master, on the other hand, may dish out punishment or make pointless remarks, and thus risk exposure to a clear-minded disciple. But this is not common. If it did happen, the master should, by all means, take instruction from the disciple. There is an anecdote from the Chan records that illustrates this possibility.

Baizhang (720-814), a famous Chan master, had a disciple who originally studied with another master, but later became enlightened under Baizhang. Later, when the monk was visiting his former monastery, he saw his first master reading sutras. At that moment, a bee trapped in the room was dashing itself against a paper window. The visiting monk said, "There is a wide road out there, yet all you can do is fly into old paper." Seeing the monk looking at the bee, the old master assumed the remark was directed at the bee. Later, the master was bathing and asked the monk to scrub his back. The monk said, "What a pity, in such a beautiful Buddhist temple not to have a buddha." Surprised, the old master wanted to know the meaning of such a strange remark. The monk said, "Master, at Baizhang's place I found a place of entry. Now I have returned to repay my debt to you."

The master ordered a feast to be prepared and invited his former disciple to speak at the Chan Hall. Again, the monk said, "What a pity, in such a beautiful Buddhist temple, not to have a buddha." When the old master heard this, he had an enlightenment experience. Was the monk saying the old master was not enlightened to begin with? Nobody knows except the two people involved. But we can say that when masters recognize that they can learn from disciples, they should do so, without necessarily reversing positions. This is another one of those stories that has a humorous or witty aspect.

Because Chan is a direct method, it is impossible to use language or description to show the degree of clarity of one's mind. To say or do nothing are also out of the question, so a seasoned master will directly and spontaneously use any means available. The words and actions are tools in the hands of the master, and their meanings cannot be ascertained from their conventional usage.

Phrases like, "It's raining in the east but the west gets wet," or "Mr. Li drinks, but Mr. Lo gets drunk," are easy to understand. Words, language, and concepts are all man-made artifacts. If we do not stick to the conventional meanings of words, there is no reason why a 'bird' could not be a fish, or a 'fish' a bird. Besides, from the point of view of unified mind, there is no coming and going of phenomena, and no distinction between this and that.

A Chan master determines a disciple's level of understanding by asking questions and gauging the responses. A simple question, "Have you eaten yet?" could be answered in a number of ways. The disciple could simply say, "Yes," or, "I've never been hungry." These are completely different responses, and might indicate different levels of experience. If the master then says, "Have you washed the dishes?" and the disciple says, "I just did," it is irrelevant whether or not the disciple actually washed the dishes. It is the response to the question that matters. The dialogue has nothing to do with 'true' or 'false.'

While washing rice one day, Dongshan (807-869) was approached by his master, who asked, "Are you using water to wash rice, or rice to wash water? When done, do you throw away water or rice?" The answer came, "I throw out both." The master said, "Then what will the monks eat?" The monk replied, "I don't care," and he walked away. Does it sound like Dongshan had gone crazy? Actually, the response reveals Dongshan's detachment from everything around him. It reveals a certain level of attainment, though not an especially deep level. This sort of dialogue cannot be imitated, because it arises out of the unique circumstances of the moment. An alert master can sense when an 'opportune sharp action' can cut like a knife into the disciple's mind and reveal what is inside.

Things like this seldom happen in a Chan master's lifetime. Being the method of instantaneous enlightenment, Chan is realized in moments when masters cannot rely on logic and discrimination to help a disciple. They must then rely on the most direct means available, and use whatever words are on the tips of their tongues. To people unfamiliar with Chan these stories may appear to be humorous, but the humor is superficial, or coincidental. Chan is actually sober and practical. The real Chan practice is the practice of daily life. The story of Dongshan occurred during the mundane daily activity of washing rice. If, in daily life, you conduct yourself without attachment, that is already Chan practice. Practitioners do not dwell on ideas of gods and buddhas existing apart from daily life. In this sense, Chan is more a humanistic philosophy than it is a formal religion. But in its human aspect, it is detached from the happenstance of transient moods and feelings. It is a pure life.

Once, a patriarch said to his disciples, "For thirty years I have been saying things to deceive you." One of the disciples responded, "You should have retired long ago." The next day, the patriarch dug a hole large enough for a body. He called the monk who made the remark and said, "If it is true that I should have retired, then bury me. Otherwise, I will bury you." The monk ran away. Is the problem with the master or the monk? This sounds like a crazy Chan story, but there is meaning in it. I will let you contemplate it.

# Chan Sickness

♥

QUESTION   I have heard of people falling into a state of mind called Chan sickness after practicing hard for a long time. What is Chan sickness?

SHIFU    First of all, Chan sickness is rare. People who meditate an hour or two a day simply do not practice intensely enough for problems to arise. Even if you have psychological problems or are anxious for attainment, there will not be any serious problems. Only when you practice hard and continuously for a long time are problems likely to arise, but most of the time they will not. If people know they are prone to have weird mental visions that they do not understand, it is probably best that they not practice too intensely.

Chan sickness can result from four kinds of causes: the first is physiological, the second is psychological, the third is karmic obstruction, and the fourth is outside sources, such as spirits. Depending on the cause, Chan sickness may manifest in different ways. If the source is physiological, the problem should also be observable when the person is not meditating. In fact, it is likely that the problem existed before the person started to meditate. Meditation sometimes brings such problems to the fore.

Chan sickness of the body can arise from many causes. One is an incorrect attitude toward the practice. For example, if you are hoping through meditation to develop supernormal powers, you are in for trouble. Some people hope through meditation to stay young forever or to develop super-sexual powers. Such attitudes if taken to the extreme can lead to health and possibly mental problems as well.

Other reasons for physiological problems are incorrect posture and unnatural breathing. If you sit with a curved back, you may experience back and neck pain. If you force or try to control your breathing, you may stress your diaphragm. Improper nutrition, such as when food intake is not regulated, may also lead to problems. Some people try to sit for a long time without eating or drinking. If you reach a point in meditation where you have no sense of time, as in samadhi, lack of nutrition may not matter, but if time still exists in your mind, you should not skip meals.

Lack of sleep can also cause Chan sickness. Some people think that meditation is a replacement for sleep, so they forego sleep altogether or cut back on their sleep time. This can lead to serious problems, especially with the nervous system. If one sits for too long without adequate movement or exercise, the body's energy channels can become blocked.

Many people hear that meditation will improve their health, alleviate or cure ailments, and release blocked energy channels. This is possible, but it takes time. People who are in poor health before they start meditating have to be careful. If people are looking for quick results, and spend too much time meditating before they are able to handle it, their condition could worsen.

The second source of Chan sickness, psychological problems, can occur if one is over-anxious about achieving results. Someone may desperately want to achieve enlightenment or acquire supernormal powers. Sickness of this nature comes from vexations, stemming from obsessive greed, hatred, pride, or doubt. Everyone encounters these feelings and desires, but in most of us it does not get out of hand. Such obsessions can lead to Chan sickness unless there is proper guidance.

If you are overly anxious about getting results from your practice, it will be easier to experience bad psychological states or become physically ill. If such problems do arise, say this to yourself: "Whatever comes I do not need and do not want. Whatever appears I will neither like nor fear." It is difficult advice to follow, but it is the attitude you should cultivate.

The third source of Chan sickness is karmic obstructions. Everything may be fine until people start practicing with intensity. Then they suffer headaches, a tightening in the chest, fearful hallucinations, or other symptoms. Such Chan sickness comes from previous bad karma. Medical or psychological care will not help. It is best to stop meditating intensely. It is not necessary for such people to give up meditating altogether, but they should approach it more casually. They should also recite repentance verses before and after meditation. If a person can do repentance practice with sincerity, then the sickness may gradually disappear. Repentance, however, is not enough; they must also make vows. Repentance is for past bad actions. Making vows is for the future. One should vow not to practice solely for one's own benefit, but for the benefit of all sentient beings.

STUDENT    Some so-called teachers claim that they can take your bad karma away from you so that you can live a less burdened life. I thought that one's karma was one's karma and could not be given or taken away.

SHIFU    It is possible to take someone's karma away by transferring merit to them, but only for a short time. It is like owing someone money when you are in a tight squeeze. Someone can pay for you, temporarily getting you off the hook, but you still owe the money. In the end, you are responsible for your own karma. Only when your practice is extremely deep and your mind and world-view changes can your bad karma go away. You may still suffer, but you will no longer see it as suffering.

SHIFU    The fourth source of Chan sickness, demonic obstructions or *maras*, is extremely rare. Demonic obstructions can refer either to external forces or to internal mental conditions. When I talk about demonic obstructions and demonic states, I am usually referring to something that people conjure up in their own minds. It stems from wrong thinking, following the wrong path, having the wrong view or attitude. For most people, interference by external spirits simply does not happen. However, in those rare circumstances when there is external interference from spirits, it goes hand in hand with wrong thinking. Practitioners who follow the correct path, have a correct view of the Dharma, and who are not over-anxious or greedy, will not be disturbed by such forces.

People who are disturbed by outside influences usually have bodies and personalities that are accessible to spirits. They serve as mediums or channels for outside entities. They are vulnerable even if they do not meditate, but when they meditate, they may be even more vulnerable. Spirits may attach themselves to people and direct their thinking and actions as if they were puppets. Discontinuing practice would likely have no affect upon the spirit's influence.

Interference from outside entities can take place with or without the awareness of the practitioner. Being aware of an outside influence is better than not being aware. People may think that there is a spirit, deity, bodhisattva, or buddha using their bodies to spread the Dharma. They know they are not the ones who are acting. The second situation, being unaware, is more serious. Such people may think they are enlightened. If they are told that their experiences and behavior do not stand up against the teachings of the Buddha, they will not believe you. Such people have tremendous confidence in themselves and can usually influence many people. These people are said to have fallen into demonic states.

Most serious is when a person feels he or she has reached buddhahood. Insanity is not even as bad. At least then it is clear that there is a problem and the person can be helped. People who think they are buddhas or bodhisattvas do not believe they need help and can lead many others down erroneous pathways.

If the problem were due to external spirits, it would be quite useless to seek help from physicians or psychotherapists. Other methods are necessary. One method is to drive away the spirit with another external force, such as a mantra or a spell. This is not reliable, however. The second method is for the disturbed person to do repentance practice. If the person is not capable of doing it, others can repent instead, but it will not be as effective. The effectiveness of repentance practice depends on the severity of the case.

As we said before, Chan sickness is very rare, and in most cases, they are of more mundane origin, such as physical, psychological, and karmic influences. If the problem is physiological, then seeking help from a doctor can be useful. If the problem is mental illness, guidance from an appropriate therapist or teacher is needed. The practitioner, however, must have faith that the therapy will be of benefit.

If the problem is psychological, so long as misconceptions are corrected, there will be no problems resulting from meditation. Self-doubt, anxiousness, or anger in moderate amounts, are not severe psychological problems. If the problem is physiological, it is possible that the person will not heal completely. It should be understood that I am talking about severe and special cases. Most people never encounter such problems. Pain in the legs, or trouble with energy channels, are not severe physiological problems.

Whether someone recovering from Chan sickness can continue intensive practice depends on the person and the situation. If all symptoms disappear, then it is all right to continue. If the symptoms persist to any degree, it is best to forego intensive meditation until symptoms disappear altogether.

STUDENT   Is it possible that a person could be deemed insane by society, but in fact only be in a Chan state of realization?

SHIFU   Yes, it is possible. Such people are neither insane nor suffering from Chan sickness. Rather, they temporarily view the world so differently their words and actions may seem odd. Others may think them insane, but in fact they are fine. This stage will pass and they will return to what is considered normal behavior.

STUDENT   Can a practitioner who does not have the proper guidance suffer from Chan sickness if he or she has a no-self experience?

SHIFU   It is possible. If the teacher is not around and the person has an experience of emptiness, but not necessarily enlightenment, he or she could develop mental problems or become deeply confused. That is why practice traditions such as Chan, Zen, and Tibetan Buddhism stress the need for a qualified teacher. That is why there is a tradition of transmission from teacher to student. There is a process that one needs to go through when one walks a spiritual path. Be wary of someone who claims to be enlightened and offers to teach you, yet has not received transmission or has not been recognized by a qualified master.

STUDENT   You have said that whenever we experience anything strange, we should just ignore it. You have also said that we should regard anything or anyone that helps us as the gift of a bodhisattva.

SHIFU   When practitioners encounter interference from external things—people, situations, other beings—and it does not obstruct their practice, but in fact makes them practice even harder, then external obstructions are beneficial. As such they should be thought of as gifts from bodhisattvas.

# Chan and Psychotherapy

QUESTION   How is Chan similar to and different from psychotherapy? Is the relationship between student and master similar to that of patient and therapist?

SHIFU   There are similarities and differences. The goal of Chan is to eliminate ignorance and vexation, to see into one's intrinsic nature, and to realize bodhi-mind. The goal of psychotherapy is to eliminate or alleviate a person's internal conflicts, confusion, contradictions, sense of helplessness, etc. Thus, Chan and psychotherapy are similar in that they address issues of the mind and that their goals are to help people become clearer and more stable. The difference is in the degree of clarity.

Psychology does not speak of intrinsic nature and spiritual awakening; it tries to help a person become more stable and to understand and deal with his or her problems.

If the therapy is successful, the person can be somewhat wiser and happier. Not having studied Western psychology and psychoanalysis in depth, I do not have a good understanding of what therapists do. It is better to talk to psychologists about therapy. I am, however, qualified to talk about Chan. With that in mind, I will try to answer the questions you pose.

STUDENT    In Chan, how does one deal with personal problems? Does one just treat the symptom or does one not bother with it at all? The advice I usually get is to ignore whatever arises in my mind while I meditate. Causes and conditions and causes and consequences are many and complex, so that it is difficult to find the direct source of a problem. Could you say that the Chan attitude is, if you cannot find a cause, do not bother with it?

SHIFU    Chan does not address specific psychological problems and their causes. Chan masters will rarely analyze a personal situation. Rather, Chan masters lead people to pose their own questions. When people are vexed, stuck, or restless, they should find the questions and answers themselves. It is for students to realize that, after all, problems exist because an individual is attached to a partic-ular idea of self. People create problems for themselves. Therefore, they must come to realize and resolve problems themselves.

There are two categories of practice. One is the practice of no method and the other is practice with a method. The practice of no method can be summed up by the words of the patriarch, Huineng: "Thinking of neither good nor evil, where is your mind right now?" This no-method approach ultimately leads to the silent illumination of the Caodong

(Soto) School. In this practice you neither respond to nor suppress thoughts that arise. The meditator simply maintains awareness of the thoughts, and lets them pass. Eventually, thoughts lessen until wisdom manifests.

Practice with a method may be based on counting or watching the breath, or the methods of *gong'an* and *huatou*. In practice with methods, the student also ignores vexing thoughts, but, by concentrating on a method, the mind becomes one-pointed. Eventually, the method itself disappears and wisdom manifests. The goals are the same: the meditator realizes that the problems that cause vexations, restlessness, and instability are rooted in, and created by, the illusory self. For Chan, analysis and explanation are unnecessary.

In some forms of psychotherapy, the therapist dialogues with the patient to find out what has been happening in the patient's mind; both aspire to come to some understanding of the problem. Therapists may try to determine patients' problems by associating symptoms with the systems or theories in which they are schooled or familiar. This is not always reliable because everyone has a different life history and experiences. Therapists may believe their analysis and approach are objective, but they may be wrong.

When they undergo therapy, people may come away with a feeling of ease or consolation; the problems may not be solved but there is temporary relief. This is not to say that therapy is ultimately useless in resolving problems, but for many patients therapy can become a crutch to get through the day or week. Furthermore, to rely fully on science is limiting. There exist things not measurable or observable. For example, if therapists were to cope with problems deriving from karmic force or demonic obstructions, their theories may not be able to handle the problems.

The Chan master does not try to solve personality problems, but guides the student with the teachings of Buddhadharma, the methods of practice, and as an exemplar. Everybody should be able to use Chan methods, but there are those who are not interested, or who do not have the confidence, or who are not willing to make the effort. Until these people change, they simply cannot and will not be able to resolve their problems through the methods and teachings of Chan. We also need to recognize that there are people with psychological problems that Chan cannot help.

I guide students in their practice. I really do not have to put on the hat of a therapist, but there are people who have been on several retreats and have been unable to solve certain persistent problems. Therefore, during retreat interviews, I may ask questions and play the role of therapist even though I have no formal training. I base my teaching and guidance on my own understanding of the human mind and Buddhadharma. For this reason some retreatants may feel that they have gotten benefits similar to those obtainable from therapy.

What I do, however, is not typically Chan. The typical role of the Chan master is to throw the problem back at the practitioner, with the advice to just continue practicing. Here is an analogy: there is a leech that attaches to the body and sucks your blood. If you find your body covered with these parasites, one way to help yourself is to pick them off one by one. That would take a long time and require much effort, not to mention a significant loss of blood. A much simpler solution is to treat the body with salt so that all of the parasites fall off at once. Chan methods are like the salt treatment for parasites; it treats the whole person, and does not address each individual problem.

To deal with problems in each instance is to try to remove the parasites one by one. It is messy and sometimes dangerous. While you are picking one off, the rest have time to penetrate further. Or you may have only stunned them; or worse, you may cut one into three pieces only to find that it has regenerated into three new parasites. Psychological problems can be like this. When you think you have finished dealing with a problem, it reappears in another form, or in many forms. There is also the added danger of parasites infecting the therapist. It is better and easier to throw salt on the body. This is getting to the root problem, which is the attachment to a sense of self.

For this reason many therapists have expressed interest in Chan and Buddhism. Numerous analysts and therapists have come here to practice and have developed more insight. They tell me that Chan reinforces and supplements their methods. A therapist who incorporates Buddhist teaching is like a tiger with wings.

STUDENT   I have been in therapy for ten years. There is a concept in psychoanalysis called denial. For example, somebody in an office yells at everyone and then thinks no one likes him. He does not realize that he is causing people to dislike him. He is totally unaware of his problem. That is denial. Is this like ignoring your problems in Chan?

SHIFU   It is not the same. With Chan you are aware of what you are doing, thinking, and saying. It is just that you detach yourself from your problem. Most problems are due to attaching to a view of self, or to a recurring thought or behavioral pattern. If you acknowledge the thought and do not respond to it, eventually it will cease to come up and bother you. For most problems that arise during meditation, ignoring them is the best method. If you have another method for dealing successfully with problems, then use that method.

If during retreat you encounter problems and do not know how to deal with them, it is probably best to ignore them. Or, you could ask me for guidance. I may also tell you to ignore the problem, or I may give you a method to deal with it.

STUDENT   Should this way of dealing with problems while meditating carry over into daily life as well?

SHIFU   If you meditate on a regular basis, yes. I am not saying that people should go through life ignoring and denying their problems and difficulties, but most problems are not very serious. By dwelling on them, we blow them out of proportion. These minor problems are best ignored. Problems that have been around for a long time and show up in many forms need to be addressed. Such problems need special attention. If you need help, I will listen and perhaps offer guidance, or you could go to a therapist.

STUDENT   Psychotherapy usually deals with neuroses, not psychoses, so things like demonic obstructions usually do not come up, although I am sure there is a lot of stuff from people's past karma that comes up and influences problems.

Psychotherapy deals with motivation. If you are supposed to write to a friend and you procrastinate for no apparent reason, then there might be something blocking your motivation, and it could be classified as a neurosis. Psychoses prevent one from dealing with reality even on a simple level.

Good therapists do not tell you your problems. They try to get you to realize what your problems are. They also deal quite often with early childhood. A child who had difficulties dealing with parents may find similar but magnified problems arising in adulthood.

Finally, psychotherapy is in the realm of small self or ego. It has been helpful for me. It helps me get through everyday problems. But I could not exist only with therapy. It's like running around in a dark room bumping into objects. Therapy may give me some bearings, but I am still in a dark room with the objects.

SHIFU    Thank you for enlightening me on the role of psychotherapy. I like that therapists allow patients to figure out their own problems. I am happy to be corrected. I also like your last remark. One can get a lot of benefit from therapy, but if one depends exclusively on it, it is still like running around in a dark room.

Therapy has its uses, but it is not enough. Models of therapy are often developed by a single person. That person's life, experiences, and karma influence what he or she thinks and feels. Therefore, a psychological model can also be a study of the mind of its inventor, and not necessarily an accurate picture of people in general. Also, therapies are often based on the scientific method, so they have to do with things that can be observed, measured, proven. If it cannot be proven, it is not science. Therefore, it is difficult for analysts to accept things like demonic obstructions and karmic force. On the other hand, symptoms like hearing voices are not necessarily caused by demonic obstructions.

It is useful for us to know something about psychotherapy. Some who cannot benefit from practicing Chan would be wise to seek help from therapists. I have sometimes advised people to seek out therapy before attempting intense practice. There is no harm in meditating an hour or two a day no matter what your problem is, but going on intensive retreats is another story. Chan and psychotherapy can work hand in hand.

STUDENT   I am still not clear on one issue. How is the Chan way of ignoring a problem different from denying or repressing problems?

SHIFU   One does not ignore problems in the ordinary sense. You do not repress your thoughts and desires. You do not force them out of your mind. You allow thoughts to enter your mind and leave your mind. Watch them, but do not follow them. This is difficult to do, and only people who practice diligently on a regular basis can develop the clarity and will power to do it.

You cannot make thoughts and desires go away. They will come, in one form or another—disguised, in dreams, intermittently, in floods. Meditators must use their experience and knowledge of Buddhadharma to identify and come to terms with their problems. Also, it is best to perform some type of repentance practice, such as prostrations, to help reduce self-centeredness. These are all useful techniques, but there are no guarantees that they will work all the time.

Meditation makes you clearer as to when thoughts and feelings arise as well as to the motivations behind them. You begin to see the roots and seeds of vexations within you, and with such clarity comes the ability to deal with them better. You can refrain from acting on these thoughts and feelings. If you do not water weeds, they will not grow. If you do, then your garden will be overrun. Some people do not mind this. Many weeds produce beautiful flowers. In such cases, however, at least you will know who is responsible for the consequences.

Awareness brings control and power to deal with your vexations; you may give in to them anyway, perhaps because you have no choice. There is the saying that ignorance is bliss. Those who are completely controlled by their thoughts and desires have no idea why they do what they do. They say, "This is who I am," and suffer the consequences time and again. Some blame others. Some resign themselves to a life of suffering.

Hopefully, practitioners are different. Hopefully, meditation, repentance, and the Dharma can bring one greater self-awareness, self-control, and humility. Buddhists, however, are not perfect and the spiritual path is not always smooth, straight, or clearly marked. That is why it is called practice. For all of us there will be times when the flood comes. The best advice I can give for such times is to stick with your practice, learn how to swim, keep your head above water, and get to higher ground. You must learn how to survive your own floods.

# Why Read Sutras?

QUESTION   Do you recommend reading sutras as part of Chan practice?

SHIFU   One can read sutras in two ways. One way is to read the sutras as you would any other book. In this sense, reasoning and intellect are involved, and the reader's intention is to understand what is being said. The second way is to recite or chant the sutra. In this approach, you are not trying to understand the content of the sutra; you are using the power of the sutra's words to cultivate samadhi.

If you read a sutra for intellectual understanding, naturally you will encounter parts you do not understand. If the problem is terminology or a philosophical idea, you can check reference sources. If, after checking references you still do not understand, you should pass over it and continue to read. There will be parts in every sutra that will be beyond your comprehension. The purpose in chanting sutras is not to intellectually understand its contents, but if certain concepts come across, that is fine. You do not have to shut your mind to them.

If your purpose in reading sutras is to gain an intellectual understanding of the Dharma, it would probably be better to read sastras, or treatises. Written by enlightened patriarchs, sastras present Buddhist concepts in a more rigorous, systematic, and logical manner than do sutras. No matter how long, sutras usually express only one or two ideas. The *Mahaprajna Sutra* consists of six hundred fascicles, or chapters, but the entire sutra speaks of only one concept: emptiness. The same is true for most other sutras. As one might expect, the repetition of the same idea can become tiring, but the repetition serves a specific purpose: to allow Dharma concepts to sink deeper and deeper into the reader's mind. The sutra presents the idea from numerous angles and uses many illustrations and analogies; but, in essence, it is always the same concept. Because of the focus on just one or two ideas, sutras are perfect for chanting. If, however, you wish to read a sutra for intellectual reasons, you will still benefit immensely from the experience.

There are too many sutras to mention in this discussion. For Chan practitioners, I recommend the *Heart Sutra*. It is short and concise, but it is sufficient. I also recommend the *Diamond Sutra*. For reading purposes, the *Heart Sutra* is better, because it presents more concepts than the *Diamond Sutra*. On the other hand, it is better to chant the *Diamond Sutra*, precisely because it contains fewer concepts and more repetition.

I also recommend the *Sutra of Complete Enlightenment* and the *Surangama Sutra*. Although these are better to recite, they are also excellent sources of Dharma principles, and in fact, are close in format to sastras. They present many concepts without too much repetition. These two sutras emphasize practice, talk about levels of meditation and discuss the experiences associated with practice. They also analyze the nature of ordinary sentient beings and the world. If you do not have a master to check your progress, you should refer to the *Surangama Sutra* to ascertain what you are experiencing, and to determine if you are proceeding in the right direction.

The *Vimalakirti Sutra* is also good, because it discusses two important ideas. It states that the Pure Land is innate in one's mind, and it explains non-duality, which means positing neither this nor that, neither something nor its opposite. When the *Heart Sutra* says, "Neither pure nor impure," it means that purity and impurity are not separate; to the enlightened mind, they are the same. In the same way, the Pure Land and the world of ordinary sentient beings are the same.

STUDENT   Would you recommend reading or reciting the *Avatamsaka Sutra*?

SHIFU   The *Avatamsaka Sutra* is good to read or recite. It takes a 'mind only' perspective of Buddhism. It also talks about the last and most profound stages of bodhisattvas, from the first through tenth *bhumi* levels. It does not talk much about the human realm, or how ordinary sentient beings can practice to attain enlightenment. For these reasons, it is considered a difficult sutra. But it is still worth reading.

STUDENT   As I understand it, Shakyamuni Buddha spoke the sutras, except for the *Platform Sutra*, which consists of the teachings of Huineng. Sastras, on the other hand, are commentaries on sutras written by patriarchs. Is this correct?

SHIFU   Sastras are written by patriarchs and scholars, and are of two varieties. In one type, a patriarch takes a few sutras that contain similar concepts and synthesizes a more encompassing system. The second type of sastra is a commentary on one particular sutra. In principle, Shakyamuni spoke all the sutras, but this need not be the case. For example, the *Vimalakirti Sutra* and *Avatamsaka Sutra* may have been spoken by incarnations of other buddhas or bodhisattvas. They are considered sutras because they do not deviate from the Dharma.

STUDENT   What is your opinion of modern writings, such as *Zen Mind, Beginner's Mind?*

SHIFU   Writings like this are good. If, years from now, these writings are still considered important and worthwhile, then they will be considered patriarchs' writings.

STUDENT   Is it okay to chant the sutras silently?

SHIFU   If you chant silently, you must still mentally make the sound. If you do not you will lose concentration, and perhaps fall into a trance.

STUDENT   Should we chant the sutra in its original language, either Sanskrit or Chinese? Or is it all right to chant in English?

SHIFU    If you do not care to know the meaning of a sutra at all, then it would be better to chant mantras instead of sutras. Although mantras may have meaning in their original language, it is not necessary to know the meaning. Reading sutras is different. Even though you do not intentionally try to analyze the concepts, the meaning naturally and spontaneously sinks into the mind. As you recite sutras, simultaneously your mind calms down and your understanding of Buddhadharma is corrected and refined. Therefore, it is best to chant sutras in the language you understand best.

A patriarch of the Tiantai School was reciting the *Lotus Sutra*, and while he read the chapter on the Medicine Buddha, he suddenly saw that very Dharma assembly, with Shakyamuni Buddha presiding. It was as if the Dharma assembly was still in session. He even saw his own master sitting in attendance. After that, his wisdom increased tremendously, and in fact, he became known as the "Minor Shakyamuni of the East."

In more modern times, Master Daishi (1890-1947) was reciting the *Mahaprajna Sutra* during a solitary retreat. Suddenly, he lost all sense of time. Sometime later, he returned to his normal state. After that experience, his wisdom welled up like water from a spring. These are examples of enlightenment, and in both of these examples, the masters were not analyzing the sutras. They were reciting them over and over, that is all.

In the late Ming Dynasty, Master Ou i (1561-1626) had many experiences from reading sutras, but none came from meditation. Once, he was writing a commentary on a sutra when suddenly, wisdom welled up within him. He wrote things that he had not originally intended, and it all came out spontaneously.

Reading as well as writing can lead to enlightenment, but of course, it depends on what you are reading and writing. Reading sutras without having thoughts in your mind, without analyzing their meaning, can lead to enlightenment. Do you think reading a bestseller can lead to similar experiences? This is highly doubtful. At those times, you are not in the right state of mind. Also, when you read sutras, each word and phrase is like a key that opens a door, enabling you to sink deeper into practice.

Mantras are different. Reciting mantras helps to calm and focus the mind. A certain amount of power can be generated from reciting a mantra as well as from reciting a sutra; but can reciting mantras alone and exclusively lead to enlightenment? Chan does not support this belief.

STUDENT    Where does the power of the mantra come from? Do the actual words have power, or does power manifest from repeating the mantra over and over again?

SHIFU    Both. The mantra is a symbol. It represents a buddha's or bodhisattva's power, and therefore the mantra itself has power. In this sense, the power comes from the sound of the mantra. Also, people who single-mindedly recite the mantra can generate power from within, even if they have no intention of doing so.

STUDENT    Must the mantras be recited in Sanskrit?

SHIFU    The mantras should be recited in their original language. However, there are Chinese Daoist mantras as well as Sanskrit mantras.

STUDENT   Do mantras come from Shakyamuni Buddha?

SHIFU   Shakyamuni did not teach mantras. They were taught by the incarnations of enlightened beings.

# Chan and the
## National Culture

QUESTION   Why does it seem that there were so many more masters and advanced practitioners in ancient China than there are in our present time? Was it different, perhaps easier, practicing centuries ago? Is the Eastern culture more suitable for practicing Buddhism?

SHIFU   Of course, culture and history have had a strong influence on Chan. China was ripe for a change when Chan emerged during the Tang Dynasty. Confucianism and Daoism, China's native philosophic traditions, had reached their saturation points. It was difficult for gifted practitioners and scholars in these traditions to make further breakthroughs. In contrast to the familiar traditional doctrines of Confucianism and Daoism, Chan offered a fresh, direct perspective. Those who switched to Chan were already well prepared intellectually and in practice, so they adopted the teachings and methods of practice in a solid, determined manner and were therefore able to make quick and steady progress.

Even so, though conditions were ideal, only a few people in the many large monasteries achieved profound insight through Chan. By the time of the Song Dynasty, there were far fewer practitioners, and therefore far fewer accomplished masters. This occurred in part because Confucianism had lured many people back to its tradition by adopting some of Chan's characteristics. However, there were a few great masters during the Song Dynasty, among them Rujing (1163-1228), the teacher of Dogen (1200-1253), who was instrumental in founding and spreading the Soto sect in Japan.

The cultural milieu also influenced the success of Chan. During the Tang and Song Dynasties, practitioners were able to isolate themselves from society and practice in the mountains. They were not bothered by the government, and did not rely on offerings and on followers for their livelihoods; their lifestyles were stable and simple. Furthermore, they had a sincere attitude and a strong, focused commitment to practice. Many people who moved to the mountains to cultivate wisdom did so for life. Their determination was enduring.

Now let's talk about Chan and Zen in the West. There are a few similarities that America has with China. For one, many Westerners have turned to Chan and Zen because of dissatisfaction with their prior religions and philosophies, just as Confucians and Daoists did during the Tang Dynasty. The teachings of Chan and Zen are appealing to intelligent, receptive people. For those people who are searching for a different spiritual path, an understanding of these teachings is positive and beneficial.

On the other hand, Westerners who have accepted the teachings of Chan and Zen without too much difficulty have not fared as well with the practice. For Americans, serious practice is difficult in terms of attitude, environment, and willingness. In regard to willingness and attitude toward practice, Westerners differ from the Chinese of the Tang Dynasty. The concept of practicing the Dao or The Way was already deeply ingrained in the Chinese culture, so the transition to the practice of Chan was smooth. Americans are not as fortunate. For the most part, Western culture has not been exposed to the idea of intense personal practice as a means of discovering and solving the problems of human existence. In Western religions, people tend to rely on the authority of God, or the love of God, to solve their problems, although this may be changing.

Americans who practice Chan often do not have a clear understanding of what personal practice entails. For instance, the idea of sudden enlightenment is appealing, but many Westerners do not fully appreciate that years, perhaps a lifetime of practice may be necessary for such an experience to occur. Because the concept of personal practice is not ingrained in Western culture, people in the West appear less willing to commit themselves to the long term practice of Chan.

How much time is needed to devote to practice? It depends on what you want to accomplish. Progress can best be made if a person devotes several years exclusively to Chan practice. It would be best to do this while still young because a great deal of energy is required.

Practicing a couple of hours a day would be beneficial in

daily life, but deep enlightenment would be highly improbable, if not impossible. Setting aside a few months of the year for practice is better than practicing a couple of hours a day. However, being a householder presents a problem. If a person has an enlightenment experience, but must return to family and normal daily life, it would be almost impossible to retain the power and insight derived from that enlightened state.

Most of the practitioners during the Tang Dynasty were homeleavers. Are practitioners in America willing to become monks and nuns? In Japan today, most practitioners are householders. However, in Japan, entire families can live in monasteries, or the practitioner can live in a monastery while the rest of the family lives in a regular community. I am not sure that a similar environment can be created in the West.

In America, I feel that Chan will be practiced and taught mostly by householders, because few people seem willing to become monks or nuns. Householders will be the ones who will have enlightenment experiences, become Chan masters, and lead others. If this occurs, what will be the level of practice and attainment? It would be wrong to say that householders cannot have high levels of enlightenment, but if they live with their families while practicing, how much time and effort can they devote to practice?

The cultural environment also poses a problem for most Americans. To make profound progress, Chan practitioners should lead a stable lifestyle, one not too hectic and cluttered. A simple existence is necessary. There was once a very learned practitioner named Xiangyan Zhixian (d. 898) who was posed a question by his master. Even with all his knowledge and practice, Xiangyan could not answer the question, so he abandoned Buddhism and moved to the mountains, where he lived alone. He existed, nothing more. One day as he was sweeping his hut, a pebble he had swept struck a bamboo stalk, and upon hearing the noise he became enlightened. Although he had abandoned the formal teach-ings of Chan, the question his master had asked stayed in his mind. His enlightenment was possible because he had a simple mentality and lived a simple life in a simple environment.

A similar situation would be difficult to come by in our present time. It is hard to isolate oneself. Yet, there are places where one can live and practice undisturbed. Actually, in terms of physical environment, America is a good place for practice. There is abundant land and material, and the government is stable and accepting of people with diverse interests. What is necessary is the right attitude toward practice. If you were given the opportunity to live and practice without interruptions, would you have the mentality to follow it through, or would you abandon your com-mitment after a few months?

Another problem for Americans is inconsistency. People here constantly look for new teachers and teachings, and if they do not find success after a short time in one system, they move on to another. In hopping from one master to another, it would be difficult to make progress, no matter how hard one practiced. Fundamental to making progress in Chan is practicing under the guidance of a master. Dahui Zonggao (1089-1163) was considered deeply enlightened, yet he was advised to seek out Master Yuanwu Keqin (1063-1135). Dahui was fortunate to meet such a great man, for within a year, he had two more profound experiences. Master Yuanwu was a necessary factor in Dahui's development.

At present, it is quite difficult to have great masters appear in the West. This does not mean that there is no hope for the future. Buddhism is still in its infancy in the West. People must first adopt the correct mentality. They must properly understand the practice of Chan and the importance of cultivating wisdom. When this happens, great masters will appear.

During the Tang Dynasty, China was ready for the emergence of Huineng, who became the sixth patriarch of the Chan lineage. But had it not been for the work of Hongren, the fifth patriarch, the situation would have been much different. The ground was fertile, ready for a seed such as Huineng. When the ground is fertile enough in the West, great masters will appear here also.

STUDENT    Are you saying good masters have not yet appeared in the West because Westerners' karma is not ripe enough?

SHIFU   Yes, but I am not restricting my view to the West. There is no such thing as one culture being inherently better for Chan. Chan is universal. If a person or an entire culture has the right karma to meet a good master, it will happen. China as a culture during the Tang Dynasty was collectively ready for good Chan teachers. If Chinese culture had continued to remain well suited for Chan, then there would still be good masters in abundance right now. But there aren't. Perhaps the West is the next fertile ground. Maybe we are planting the proper seeds for this to happen in the near future. The West seems to be embracing the ideas and practices of the East while the East seems to be doing the opposite. Perhaps the next flourishing of Chan will be in the West. I look forward to it.

# Living with Entertainment

◆

QUESTION  One of the precepts for monks and nuns is to abstain from certain kinds of entertainment, such as going to movies or concerts, listening to music, or reading novels. Should lay practitioners avoid entertainment too? Would it be against Buddhist precepts to spread the Dharma through entertainment? I feel that I see Dharma in many non-Buddhist arts—music, film, literature. Is this beneficial or am I just rationalizing my desires?

SHIFU  Monks and nuns take many precepts, one of which is to abstain from entertainment. Certain forms of entertainment become occasions for people to vent their emotions or moods. Obviously, actors vent feelings and emotions when they work, as does the audience if it connects with their performance. That is a primary function of entertainment.

Homeleavers should avoid involvement either as performers or audience. It may seem overly strict, but the more one experiences such activities, the more attachments associated with them will persist. A person may experience short-lived catharsis after a performance, but there will be a strong desire to repeat the process. In this sense, these activities can be addictive.

Monks and nuns should aspire to leaving all desires behind. If they participate in entertainment, it is difficult or impossible to cut off desires. Monks and nuns should use their practice and guidance from the Dharma to lessen and eventually eliminate desires. The precept serves as a guideline and reminder for homeleavers.

If monks and nuns are not serious about leaving desires behind, there is no reason or need to leave home. However, it is difficult today to avoid all forms of entertainment. One would have to go into seclusion. The walls of the Chan Center cannot keep out the sounds of music on the street, and although monastics do not participate in different forms of entertainment, they are not opposed to other people engaging in such activities.

If getting involved in entertainment is unavoidable, a monk or nun should use expedient methods. The solution is simple with visual entertainment—do not look. The solution is not as simple with sound. It depends on one's practice. Advanced practitioners can be within range of the sounds and yet not hear them. Homeleavers in situations like this must do the best they can.

There were two young monks in Taiwan who originally came to my temple to try out the sangha lifestyle. During the first year there were times when they became restless. They felt that doing prostrations and meditation would not help.

Finally the two of them decided to see a movie, knowing it was a major infraction of the monastic precepts. I found out about it, and when they returned I asked, "What's going to come of this?" They said, "We knew it we were breaking a precept, but we decided to go anyway." Since then they have become good monks, not overwhelmed by restlessness, and no longer with a desire to go to the movies.

Lay practitioners are not required to abstain from entertainment. Watching movies and engaging in other activities like this can help to relieve restlessness or other moods. Even if they decide to take the eight precepts of the layperson, which are the Five Precepts plus three abstentions, they only have to avoid entertainment six days out of the month. This gives lay practitioners a taste of what the left-home lifestyle is like. However, lay Buddhists can engage in singing, dancing, going to the movies or watching videos with no fear of breaking precepts.

However, monastics sometimes bend the rules. In Taiwan, I observed a monk chanting loudly. I asked, "Are you practicing?" He answered, "No, actually, I feel uncomfortable and restless. I want to sing, but I cannot, so I'm letting out my frustrations this way." I replied, "That's not the right way to chant. When you chant you should do it respectfully, and you shouldn't sing so loud." This monk was not breaking any precepts, but he was not behaving the way a monk should. He said, "These days one can hear chanting being broadcast on the radio. Is that normal?" I said, "They're doing that to spread the Dharma to as many people as possible. Whom are you chanting to?" "I'm trying to get rid of the uneasy restlessness within myself. I guess you could also say I'm singing to the ghosts."

From a Buddhist point of view, I am not opposed to

people singing, dancing, or performing. In fact, at our Center's Buddha birthday celebration, people perform, and I watch as well. I do not crave entertainment, but it is a celebration and I want other people to feel good.

It is all right for monastics to engage in some forms of entertainment if it is part of their job. For example, two movies were produced in Taiwan, one on the life of the Buddha and one about Bodhisattva Avalokitesvara. After the movies were completed the producers invited me to the previews to see if they were in accordance with the spirit of the Dharma. Naturally, I went. On the other hand, if a monk or nun went to the cinema one evening to see it, it would not be acceptable, because that would be for personal gratification.

I think it is fine to use singing, dancing, and acting, as well as other art forms, to spread the Dharma. I encourage people to use modern language to tell stories from the Buddhist point of view. These stories need not come from the sutras. In India, a famous Buddhist master named Asvaghosa composed poetry and songs based on the life of the Buddha for others to sing. During the Song and Yuan (1271-1368) Dynasties, Buddhist masters composed similar songs so others could sing and spread the Dharma.

There are numerous cases where literature has been used to spread the Dharma. There is a chapter in the *Avatamsaka Sutra, Entering the Dharma Realm*, which tells of a bodhisattva who learned cultivation from fifty-three different masters, but it reads like a long, entertaining novel. There are stories in the *Lotus Sutra*, which are elegantly written, and many of the sutras convey the Dharma in a very literary manner.

The modern Chinese novel has its roots in the historic novels written in the Ming and Qing (1644-1911) Dynasties, but they in turn adopted literary styles found in the sutras.

Buddhist sutras often use a format where a long paragraph of teaching is followed by a verse. In many Chinese historical novels, the order is reversed, chapters beginning with a verse and followed by a story.

STUDENT    Is it possible to derive results and benefits from music, plays, art, and literature that are similar to what can be derived from practice?

SHIFU    I think it is possible with music. For example, during retreat we chant in the morning and evening. Chanting, after all, is music. I am talking about types of music that excite people. Music conducive to practice should help people settle down. It can help the mind move from a confused and scattered state to a calmer, more concentrated state.

I have heard that a Korean woman has choreographed a Chan dance, and supposedly a person watching it can become settled, clear, and calm. If that goal can be attained, then people should be encouraged to watch the dance being performed.

Similarly, if the intent of a written work is to convey a Buddhist idea, that is useful. I doubt if people could become enlightened just by reading a novel, but if they can cultivate a better understanding of Chan teachings and attitudes through reading, that is good.

One can view these examples from the standpoint of art or from the standpoint of practice. From the artistic point of view, people would be listening, watching, dancing, singing, or reading for their enjoyment. From the practice point of view, people would engage in these activities as a means to help move beyond the confusion and restlessness of the ordinary mind.

STUDENT   There have been times when I have focused so fixedly while reading difficult poetry that afterwards my mind feels clear and light. The feeling is similar to what I experience after a good meditation session.

SHIFU   When your mind is concentrated you will experience a sensation like that. But that is as far you will get when reading poetry or novels. They cannot take you beyond a certain level of concentration. After a while the mind will veer out of focus or you will be moved in some way by the material you are reading.

STUDENT   Isn't contemplation part of practice? Sometimes during retreat you have us contemplate thoughts we call up. Why can't we contemplate a story, poem, or painting?

SHIFU   The contemplation I ask you to do should not involve logical thinking; rather, you should place your mind on one point and look directly into things. It is hard to explain, but it is different from using logic or following a chain of thoughts to a conclusion.

Through music, dance, and literature, it is possible to experience things similar to that which comes from practice. One can understand practice as helping a practitioner move from a scattered mind to a concentrated mind, from a concentrated mind to a unified mind, from a unified mind to no-mind. Through art forms it is possible to reach concentrated mind. But it would be quite difficult to experience unified mind through such activities, not to mention no-mind.

STUDENT   It seems that most traditions that have been

around for a long time resist change, and yet I feel that if the Buddha were alive today, he would probably make use of modern technology—videos, radio, television. It would be especially useful for people who are not at all aware spiritually. One could reach so many.

SHIFU   My organizations do in fact distribute Dharma talks on CD's, tape, and videos. However, these are not for entertainment, but for teaching purposes.

STUDENT   What about left-home people who do not have access to the teachings of masters? Many temples do not have teachers.

SHIFU   Entertainment videos are out of the question, but educational videos are fine, especially if shown in a temple or training center. A theater may draw a mixed crowd, which could lead to distractions.

STUDENT   There are already many meditation tapes, some with music, and some with speech. I feel they can only teach up to a certain level, perhaps to the point of a concentrated mind. But it is shallow. Wouldn't Chan meditation tapes defeat the purpose of teaching Chan? Chan emphasizes practicing with a master. People might think that a video can replace a teacher or a retreat. Videos like this could mislead people, especially if endorsed by a Buddhist group.

SHIFU   It is possible to make meditation tapes of varying levels, but the higher stages of practice cannot be conveyed in this way. At a certain point you must study with a master. However, I would endorse learning tapes for beginners.

STUDENT   What about calligraphy and painting?

SHIFU   These are also included in the arts, and the same thing applies. Through such art forms one can reach a certain level of concentration, but to experience Chan enlightenment would be extremely difficult. Precepts for monks and nuns do not forbid painting, calligraphy, poetry, or even photography. In general, however, left-home people should not spend too much time on such things. Monastics who spend a lot of time with their art probably will not devote enough time and energy to practice.

There were many monks who are well known for calligraphy, painting, and poetry, but with few exceptions they have no significance in Chinese Buddhist history because they were not outstanding practitioners.

STUDENT   What about Hanshan (Cold Mountain)?

SHIFU   Hanshan happened to write poetry, but he did not think of himself as a poet.

STUDENT   Earlier you said that entertainment helps people vent their emotions. For example, listening to an orchestra perform a symphony might move someone to cry. What is the difference between this and the occasional emotional outbursts one might encounter during retreat?

SHIFU   There are similarities, but it is not the same thing. When people cry or laugh on retreat, they often do not know why they do so. It is more an adjustment within the body rather than a venting of emotions. People who cry at a symphony know why they are crying.

It is also possible for people on a retreat to think of things that cause them to vent their emotions in a particular way, but afterwards they usually feel relieved and peaceful. People at a symphony who cry may also feel relieved and peaceful afterwards, but it is probably not the case most of the time. Besides, feeling peaceful on retreat is conducive to better practice. People who feel peaceful after crying at a symphony are probably not going to make use of their calm condition. Have you ever cried at a symphony?

STUDENT    No, but on retreat I did, and I did not feel peaceful afterward because I did not get it all out.

SHIFU    You are right. You did not allow all of it to come out. If you did, you would have felt better and more at ease. If you do not let it out, then you will feel uncomfortable, almost as if you were suffocating.

# Poetry and Wangwei

QUESTION    Wangwei, one of China's most famous poets, lived during the Tang Dynasty. He was a government official, a devout Buddhist practitioner, and a strong supporter of the Dharma and Sangha. Can you tell from his poetry if he was a highly attained practitioner? Can we learn anything important from his poetry that is related to the Dharma?

SHIFU    First, I must admit that I have never spent time studying Wangwei's poetry, but I have read a few of his poems. Actually, throughout much of Chinese literature and poetry, there have been works that have the flavor of Chan. Wangwei is famous, so people are likely to remember him better than other poets. He is well known for his calligraphy and poetry, and because of his interest in Buddhism, he has been called 'the Buddha of the Poets.' We should not assert that he was the best of poets, or that he was enlightened, but simply that he was a poet who happened to be a Buddhist.

Much of Wangwei's poetry talks about nature and the poems express an air of tranquility, freedom, spontaneity; but there are other poets who did the same, some of whom preceded Wangwei and who were influenced by other things, like Daoism. We should not immediately surmise that Chinese poems about nature are influenced by Buddhism. Poems that are truly influenced by Buddhism must have the characteristic of selflessness, of no attachment, of something that is at once empty and at the same time dynamic.

We come across many Buddhist themes in Wangwei's poetry. We also know that the lifestyle and demeanor of monks and nuns impressed him. His poems sometimes contrast the lifestyle of monastics with that of householders, and his poems convey deep respect for the sangha. We can conclude that he was an admirer of Buddhism, but we cannot say with certainty that he was a highly attained practitioner. I have not read anything by him that would indicate this, but he definitely knew about methods of practice.

Whether or not one can determine Wangwei's attainment from his poetry would be difficult to say. It would also be highly subjective. Likewise, whether or not one can gain deep Buddhist insight through his poetry would also be difficult to say.

STUDENT  In one of his poems, *Kalapati Lay Ill in Bed*, Wangwei makes use of Buddhist terminology. Is it genuine or is it artistic showmanship?

SHIFU  This poem contains many references to the *Vimalakirti Sutra*, and it also describes certain attitudes that have a Chan flavor. Then again, I have read poetry written by intellectuals who have never practiced Buddhism at all, yet

268

who are capable of conveying high levels of Chan. This poem does not prove anything one way or the other. For instance, two lines of this poem read:

> *Not one single dharma is real*
> *Not one single dharma is defiled*

These lines are taken directly from the sutras. Can we say that the lines come directly from Wangwei's practice?

STUDENT Here is a poem that seems to convey some sort of attainment. Would you comment on this?

*Visiting the Temple of Gathered Fragrance*

*I do not know the Temple of Gathered Fragrance,*
*For several miles entering cloudy peaks*
*Ancient trees, paths without people;*
*Deep in the mountains, where is the bell?*
*Noise from the spring swallows up lofty rocks,*
*The color of the sun chills green pines ...*
*Toward dusk, by the curve of an empty pond,*
*Peaceful meditation controls poison dragons.*

SHIFU Poets, through their artistic vision, look at the world and attempt to convey what it inspires within them. Readers, through poets' words, can then enter the world described by them. If poets succeed in this, that is good. That is the function of art. It is vexation too, but there are different levels of vexation.

Buddhism sometimes speaks of three levels of emotion. The first or lowest level consists of the coarse, abrupt, and often violent moods that arise arbitrarily in people's minds. It is an immediate response to different stimuli and so it is abrupt and uneven. The second level includes the more stable and refined emotions, and usually refers to the more positive emotions, such as enduring love. However, this level is still subject to fluctuation. At the third, and highest, level are highly refined emotions with very little attachment. It is a kind of aspiration toward something good, beautiful, noble. Sometimes it is called an artist's enlightenment or an artist's vision. To attain such a level is indeed very good.

Poetry and painting are similar in that, if they are good, the reader or observer can enter the world and feel the emotion sought to be conveyed by the artist. Wangwei is this caliber of poet. It can be very useful for people who have an affinity for art. It can also help those people who cannot practice sitting meditation in that it can ease their vexations while they are engrossed in the work.

STUDENT   Here is perhaps the most famous of Wangwei's poems:

*Deer Park*

*Empty mountain, no man is seen . . .*
*Only heard are echoes of men's talk.*
*Reflected light enters the deep wood*
*and shines again on blue green moss.*

By the end of the poem any human presence is gone. All that remains is light. Would Shifu comment on this poem?

SHIFU   It is poetry, so you can interpret it any way you want to. For example, many Chan masters recognize everything as being perfect or the highest. If you interpret this poem from that vantage, you can say that it describes a Chan state. But even if it does so, it is not a high level of Chan. It speaks of empty mountains in the sense that there are no people. Then it mentions the sound of human voices. Finally it leads to light shining on moss. Who is seeing all of this? There is still an observer. As long as a self remains, it cannot be a high level of Chan.

STUDENT   There seems to be a mutual sharing or correspondence between Daoism and Buddhism. In fact, there is a story of Laozi going to India and becoming the Buddha. Chan is different from earlier Theravada Buddhism. Much of this difference seems to be the influence of Daoism. Daoism is nature oriented; it speaks of the tranquility and ever-changing yet eternal quality of nature. The *Avatamsaka Sutra* speaks about the interpenetration of the universal and the particular. Likewise, one of the goals of Chan practice is to unify the mind and become one with nature. Is my last statement correct, and was Daoism an influence on Buddhism?

SHIFU   There will always be influences from other cultures and traditions. Laozi and Confucius were contemporaries of Shakyamuni Buddha, so Daoism and Confucianism were both well established when Buddhism entered China. People naturally interpreted Buddhism in the light of what they knew. Chan, especially the southern school, was influenced by the naturalistic tendencies of Daoism. For example, the idea that all beings, sentient and non-sentient, can attain buddhahood is not found in the original Indian sutras. There is a legend of Master Daosheng (355-434) giving a talk to no one while everything nodded its approval, including the rocks. These are Daoist influences. Such ideas show up in the writings of monks after the sixth patriarch.

Wangwei was probably influenced by Daoism. At the same time, monks were producing Chan poetry and painting that convey a state that seems to have no substance and yet is still dynamic. The artistic works convey the idea that any dharma includes all of totality. Such paintings would tend to be impressionistic or abstract. These works differ from the nature-influenced art. They are influenced directly by the Chan teachings.

As to unifying mind with nature, there is a point in one's meditation when body, mind, and environment become undifferentiated. There is no internal or external, and no differentiation between the previous and subsequent thoughts. It is possible for art and poetry to convey this feeling, and it is also possible for an artist and poet to experience this without practicing, but it is extremely difficult to achieve.

STUDENT    Buddha-nature is everywhere and everything. Can artists, by way of their intense involvement with their art, attain some level of Chan without even knowing about Buddhism?

SHIFU    It is possible for an artist to attain a state that may be called an artist's enlightenment, a kind of unified mind, where the artist merges with the art, but the experience is still grounded in existence, not emptiness. We can consider an artist's enlightenment a shallow level of Chan attainment, but it is not the same as seeing one's intrinsic nature.

STUDENT   What about the third bodhisattva vow, which says there are limitless approaches to Dharma? You once said anything, even intellectualism, can be a path to enlightenment if you have no vexations or obstructions in your mind.

SHIFU   If you have no vexations or obstructions in your mind, then you are already enlightened. You have already seen your intrinsic nature. Just because it seems you have no emotional disturbances does not mean you have no vexation.

STUDENT   What if art becomes a method? Can you become so involved in the work that you experience the state of no-self?

SHIFU   Almost impossible. If you become completely absorbed in your art, then art becomes the totality of your world and your life. You may think you have no self, but you are still attached to art.

STUDENT   So then what is the meaning of the third bodhisattva vow?

SHIFU   The third vow says there are limitless approaches to Dharma. The idea is that a bodhisattva will learn limitless Dharma approaches for the sake of helping sentient beings. It is not for the sake of the practitioner. For example, if someone is only interested in dancing, a bodhisattva might learn dancing in order to help the person understand Buddhadharma.

# Balancing Responsibilities and Practice

QUESTION   Practice requires a lot of time and effort, and most people who practice are lay people. It seems there would be more time and fewer obstacles if our lives had a minimal number of responsibilities. Could Shifu address this issue of freedom and responsibility, using marriage and children as examples?

SHIFU   For a Chan practitioner, accepting responsibilities is a part of practice whether you are a homeleaver or householder. Family life is a part of practice. If you are a married, whether your spouse is Buddhist or not, you must accept the additional responsibilities of being a wife or husband.

If your partner does not understand why you spend so much time and effort practicing, you should see him or her as a bodhisattva helping you cultivate patience and tolerance.

This attitude, however, is quite difficult to maintain. If you are not a bodhisattva, you will probably not be able to recognize and accept someone else as one. Most people under such circumstances will try to evade their responsibilities and problems, or they will avoid them before they arise.

Earlier, one of you mentioned that it was difficult to practice while your marriage was failing. Of course, I do not know the reasons for the break-up, but in most cases the failure of a marriage is the result and responsibility of both individuals. If wanting fewer responsibilities and more freedom is causing your marriage to fail, you may need to change your attitude.

You may think that the only type of practice is sitting meditation, but that is incorrect. While meditation helps you to become less vulnerable to the swings of moods and emotions, every other aspect of your life—work, relationship with your partner, family life—is also an opportunity for practice. It is wise to accept those responsibilities as practice.

Even for a monk or nun, practice would not be limited to meditation. I do not meditate all day. My day is filled with responsibilities. In fact, leaving home to become a monk or nun means that you formally let go of your own indulgences and devote your time and effort to helping others. All this is part of practice. A sangha member may not have family responsibilities, but they have taken on even greater responsibilities—all sentient beings.

STUDENT    What about the responsibility of having and caring for children? As a serious practitioner, would it be better not to have children?  If you followed this direction, would it then be shirking the responsibility of being a householder?

SHIFU    First, from a Buddhist point of view, if you give birth to a child, you are creating the occasion for another sentient being to begin yet another cycle of birth and death. On the other hand, if you do not give birth to this child, the sentient being will still be born through other causes and conditions because it has the karma to be born again.

The question of intention arises. If you avoid having children because of a sincere desire to practice intensively, that is acceptable. This implies that you are actually spending most of your time practicing, and has nothing to do with grasping or avoiding. However, if you say, "I don't like kids. They'll interfere with my practice," that attitude implies aversion toward children, and is self-centered and wrong.

There is also a realistic question. If you do not have any children, does it really mean that your practice will be better? And if you do have children, does it mean that your practice will be distracted? If you do not have children, you may spend your time doing other things anyway. On the other hand, if you do have children, you will have to cut out many other interests to care for your family, and you may end up with more time to practice.

One of the members of the Center says she has cut down on her practice because of her children, but is it because of the children? In her case, it has to do with the way she arranges her time and priorities. She spends much of her time working, earning extra money so that the children will be able to someday go to college. In the meantime, she has to hire baby-sitters to take care of the children while she works. Work, not children, has interfered with her practice.

STUDENT    But if parents do not work so that they can

practice, and then discover that their children cannot go to college, is this right?

SHIFU   When you have children, how much do you have to do in order to fulfill your responsibilities to them? It depends on you and the situation; your capabilities and your resources may be limited. If you are poor, you may not be able to send your children to an expensive college, or any college. In the case above, the mother wants certain things for her children and she is working for them. She cannot practice as much. That is the reality of the situation. It is her choice, her karma.

On the other hand, there is another member of the Center who has a child and is doing quite well with the practice. She sits every day, she contributes a great deal to the Center and she attends nearly every retreat. She is still able to set aside the time. That is her choice and her situation. It has been my observation, at least in Taiwan, that house-holders should have children, because if they do not, especially after a few years of marriage, it will be quite difficult for them to have a happy relationship.

STUDENT   Why?

SHIFU   If there are conflicts between the couple, the children act as a buffer. With such a common bond, such a shared interest, a couple cannot make a big deal of trivialities and they will not split up because of minor differences. Of course, it is easy to get divorced in the U.S., but as practitioners, such an extreme situation should rarely arise.

In China in the old days, there were well-known household practitioners who did well in their practice while simultaneously raising large families. It never was the case that their children stopped them from practicing. I see that trend in China and this present trend in the U.S. as transient periods. Now, people here are involved in many activities and they are keeping their families small, but in the future things will change, and perhaps they will change to something similar to that of old China.

Of course, realistically, children take up a great deal of your time, and with few exceptions in this Center, people who have children find it difficult to come to many of the functions here. My opinion is this: if you are just beginning to practice, not having children is a preferred situation.

STUDENT    So, you are saying that that for beginning practitioners, it would be best not to have children?

SHIFU    I would not say it that way, because if that were the case, then people might consider themselves beginning practitioners for their entire lives, and they will never have children. Realize that, for many people, the main function of having children is to strengthen the tie of the marriage and family. If there are relatively few difficulties in a marriage, if a couple is progressing in a happy, productive relationship, then not to have children is fine. Nevertheless, having children can strengthen the bonds in a marriage, sometimes even saving a marriage.

STUDENT    If we think of having children as a way of strengthening or saving a marriage, then what is our responsibility to the child?

SHIFU    Do not think of having children as a means of

solving the problems of a marriage. It is that when you have children, your enhanced responsibilities will naturally help to strengthen the tie of the marriage. In this case, the children are helping out. On the other hand, if a couple accepts the responsibility of having a child, they are also helping the child.

A couple who quarreled a lot had a child. I asked them how things were going. The husband said, "Things have changed. Previously we argued all the time. Now the kid keeps our hands filled with his own difficulties, so we have no time or energy left over for our own arguments." So, if you want to calm your marital relationship, having a child may be a wise choice. He or she will take the majority of your focus and energy.

STUDENT   In Carlos Castaneda's books, don Juan advised his followers to avoid having children if they wanted to follow the path of a spiritual warrior. He said that when a child is born, it takes away a lot of the life energy from the parents, making them weaker. He also said that if you want to maintain personal power, then do not have children. What is your opinion?

SHIFU   Chan does not believe or recognize such ideas. Sure a child takes away energy from the parents, but in a natural way. The child is growing and demands attention and care. Devoting such time and energy drains you. As I said earlier, if you are a beginning practitioner, it might be difficult to practice and have children. It would take an enormous amount of power, energy, time and effort to collect your mind and concentrate. But, even being married without children might cause problems. You might create your own interference and obstacles. In this case, it would be better to live the life of a monk or nun, or at least that of a single person. From a Chan point of view, I must stress again that practice is not just sitting meditation. All aspects of life should be part of practice.

STUDENT  When I was single, my practice was erratic at best. Now I am married and I practice every day. In my case, marriage helped my practice.

SHIFU  It is not that getting married helped you in the practice, but, rather, it is your change of attitude. As a single person, you might have had many interests and probably did not know how to spend your time wisely or efficiently. Now that you are married, you are mentally prepared to settle down, and as a consequence you can channel your energy better.

STUDENT  Meditation is not the only aspect of practice, but if one wants to attain deeper levels of practice, then meditation is important. In this sense, can marriage and children have an adverse affect on one's practice, and would it prevent one from becoming a master?

SHIFU  When the Buddha taught the Dharma, he knew it was impossible for all people to become monks and nuns. Leaving home helps to leave behind one's desires. This is possible for only a small minority of practitioners. For this reason, the Buddha had separate teachings and precepts for lay people and sangha members. There are many differences between lay practice and left-home practice. Lay people are more connected to family, career, possessions, and personal affairs. Monks and nuns have taken vows to abandon these things. Ideally, they should have no belongings, including their own bodies.

The strongest attachments of ordinary people are to other people. A young girl is most attached to her parents. Later, her boyfriend or husband becomes the most important person. When she has children, they become most important. In time, her children will leave to start their own families. Even so, she will continue to have deep feelings for them and their children. An ordinary person's life is full of attachments stemming from relationships. It is difficult to have all these attachments and still devote oneself wholeheartedly to practice. Sex may not even be part of it, but if it is, it too becomes an extremely sticky attachment. Sexual activity makes it difficult to cultivate samadhi.

Love and marriage can become a source of vexations, but they are not necessarily obstructions to being a good practitioner. On the other hand, while it is possible, love and marriage make it difficult for someone to become a good Chan master. The person may be a good teacher, but it may be difficult to cultivate a deep, pure wisdom. There are exceptions. In the Tibetan Nyingmapa tradition, there have been exceptional masters who were married. However, these masters relied as much on the blessings of their *yidam*, or spiritual guide, as on their personal practice for power.

Having a supportive spouse or partner who will practice with you is an excellent arrangement. That would be a life based on mutual care, respect, and love, without over-reliance on sex to define the relationship. Such a life is a good foundation for achieving liberation.

# Raising Buddhist Children in a non-Buddhist Society

QUESTION    We are going to have a child soon. As Westerners who have incorporated Buddhism into our lives, we wonder how we should raise our child. Many people turn to Buddhism because they are dissatisfied, for whatever reason, with their previous faith. We fall into this category, and we are wary of preaching our beliefs to others, including our children. How would you recommend that an American Buddhist couple raise a child in an environment that is largely ignorant of Buddhism?

SHIFU    First, we must accept and affirm that religion can help the baby. With this in mind, parents should begin transmitting the Dharma even before the child is born. The unborn child is aware of the external world and is capable of receiving blessings and merit.

The mother can begin conditioning the child during pregnancy by avoiding temperamental behavior or emotions of grief and anger, and by maintaining an even, happy state of mind, with a readiness to help others. In this way, there is a better chance that the baby will be born with a good disposition.

If a couple were Catholic, they would have a child baptized after it was born. The child would receive blessings, a name, and godparents. In Buddhism there is no such ritual. However, the parents should still have the child blessed. A monk or nun or master can do this. Also, the parents should accumulate meritorious deeds for the sake of the baby. They can read sutras, or repeat the names of buddhas and bodhisattvas, doing so with an open, generous, compassionate mind, with the clear and sincere intention of transferring the merit to the baby.

Actions are not restricted to reciting sutras and the Buddha's name. You can do volunteer work, social work, or donate money, and then transfer the merit to the baby. You can help in spreading the Dharma, thus helping all sentient beings, including your child. The transfer of merit comes from your mental energy through the functioning wisdom of the buddhas and bodhisattvas. If you are people with good practice and strong mental power, then you can focus your mental energy directly, with the sincere intention of helping the child.

As the child grows, you can begin to talk about the Dharma, the Buddha, and the great bodhisattvas. You should explain these ideas at one point or another, so that the child will have some understanding of Buddhism, and be better able to make a choice later. You will have to tell the child that although most people in America follow the Judeo-Christian religions and ethics, there are other religions, and that you chose to follow Buddhism. Understand that you are not forcing the child to accept Buddhism; you are not compelling the child to take refuge in the Three Jewels. You are informing the child about the alternatives, and about what you chose to follow. That is all.

At the age of seven, if the child wishes to receive the Three Refuges, then he or she can do so. This is the tradition, but seven is a young age, and the child may not be clear as to what the Dharma is. There is no problem if the child changes his or her mind later on. You should never make children feel as though they have committed sins because they have chosen not to accept the Dharma, or because they have chosen another religion. Accepting another religion is still good.

As parents, you can tell stories of other religions to your children. Along with Buddhist and Chan stories, there is no harm in relating tales from the Bible and other sources. It is also a good idea to bring your children to other churches—to the church of your original faith perhaps—to expose them to different beliefs, customs, and ideas. As it stands, you will probably be going to a Buddhist temple or monastery most of the time, so your children will be familiar with Buddhism. You do not want your children to grow up hostile to other religions. This would be unfortunate, especially if it is a result of lack of exposure toward other beliefs.

It is also important to not tell your children what to do with respect to religion, but, rather, explain to them what you are doing, and why you are doing it. Explain to them why you meditate, but do not force them to sit. As Buddhists, we would like all sentient beings to have contact with and accept Buddhadharma. Of course, you want your children to enjoy the benefits of the Dharma, but you should not coerce them.

I understand that many people who have converted to Buddhism from other religions have done so through their own will. Nobody forced them. They may think that all people should encounter and accept the Dharma in the same way. Parents may feel, "Well, we discovered the Buddha-dharma through our own karma and causes and conditions. We should allow our children the same freedom, and if they discover the Dharma, that's great. But we won't interfere at all." This is not the right attitude.

Very few people make their own decisions or choose their own path. Most people are affected by and follow what others tell them. It is important that you explain to your children, as they are growing, what Buddhism is, why you follow the Dharma, what differences and similarities exist between Buddhism and other religions. Remember that the first bodhisattva vow is to deliver innumerable sentient beings, and your children are sentient beings. How can you best do this? In addition to providing the basic care—food, shelter, love, a good education, helping them become useful members of society—be concerned with their states of mind. Can you show them how to have peace of mind? Can you help them understand and accept the Three Jewels? Can you introduce them to and help them with methods of practice? If you can do these things, you have done all you possibly can do.

We live in a hectic, heterogeneous, constantly changing society that is confusing even for adults. Instead of telling children what to do or not to do, explain what you are doing in a given situation, and why you are doing it. Explain why others do what they do. Do not make judgments for children;

try to help them understand. If you can do this, then based on your example, your children of their own accord will probably turn to Buddhadharma.

It is good to do these things before children reach fourteen or fifteen years of age. If you start early, it will be easy for your children to develop faith in Buddhism. But if you wait beyond this age, it will be difficult for children to develop the same kind of faith. Besides, around this time, children will begin to rebel against you, so it is better to get most of your teaching out of the way by then.

Adults who turn to Buddhadharma are unusual. Why they turn to Buddhism varies, but usually, they found something lacking in their previous faith, and encountering the Dharma, felt an attraction toward it. It is the result of previous good karma, but also a rational, conscious decision. Most adults, however, do not change. If you have not succeeded in interesting your children in the Dharma by the time they become adults, chances are you are never going to succeed. At that point, they are on their own. Emphasis on teaching the Dharma to your children should begin well before they reach fourteen.

Your aim is not to make your child accept Buddhadharma, but to instill a sense of responsibility for all people and all sentient beings, to instill moral principles and the courage to face life. With proper morality, children will not do or say things to harm themselves or others. With proper courage, children will put their best foot forward, and accept whatever happens; they will also accept the idea of causes and consequences in past, present, and future lives. Concentrate on these things. The kind of people your children will turn out to be, what religion or path the will follow, is ultimately up to them, not you.

STUDENT   This is a hypothetical situation: a teen-age boy says to his parents, "I've decided to become a monk. I want to leave home and devote myself to the practice." How should the parents handle this situation?

SHIFU   I left home when I was twelve. Many Dharma masters of the present and past left home when they were very young. It is not completely unreasonable that a teen-age child might have this desire. If this were to happen, the parents should ask the child what his reasons are. If he gives a strange reason, that is not good enough. If his reasons are sound, that is fine. Also, if he has no reason at all, if he just has a strong urge to go, then that is also acceptable. In fact, that was the case with me.

Actually, in our present society, there are certain rules about attending school. The best course of action would be to have the child finish their high school education. Meanwhile, the child can visit a temple or center and begin to study under a master. If after finishing school he or she is still interested, the child should attend a school for Buddhist studies. In this way, the child will gradually learn about Buddhism and the practice, and will be in a better position to know if being a monk or nun is something they want.

STUDENT   How deep is the parents' responsibility or obligation to teach their children about Buddhism?

SHIFU   The depth of the obligation should be the same as for your own self. Children start by knowing nothing. You have to feed children information and knowledge. It is like food. Some children are picky eaters, taking a little food here, rejecting food there. Others will eat whatever you put in front of them. The same is true with teaching. Feel your children out. Give as much as they are willing to take, but do not force-feed them.

STUDENT   I was raised as a Catholic, and part of my upbringing included saying the rosary several times a day, reciting prayers, reading stories about God and Jesus. As a Buddhist parent, would I want my child to learn the Buddhist equivalent, like chanting, prostrating, and so on? Also, should I make my children meditate?

SHIFU   The fewer the formalities you have, the better. In the Orient, many parents try to get the whole family doing that sort of thing—waking up early, lighting incense and prostrating, repeating the process before meals, before leaving the house or going to bed. It can get out of hand. The ritual side of Buddhism can be as involved as in any other religion.

Formalities are not that important. Emphasize maintaining a Buddhist spirit in daily life, and instilling a sense of compassion. Constantly educate them in this matter. For example, when they see a small animal, they should not be cruel to it. They should try to help all living things. Tell them that this is compassion.

Teach them not to be wasteful, that what we have comes from our previous karma. When we are wasteful, we squander accumulated merit. As parents, you should not be wasteful, and you should pass on this trait to them. Teaching children to meditate is not a bad idea, but realize that it is difficult for children to sit still. If they show an interest, show them how to sit and have them try it for five minutes. If they wish to continue, that is fine. If they want to get up and play, or do something else, that is fine too.

# Chan Practice
# and the Elderly

🍃

QUESTION   Chan meditation methods can be strenuous. In dealing with elderly people who are new to the practice, would you alter your techniques to better suit the practitioner? Also, how do you address the issue of elderly people who are newcomers to Buddhadharma?

SHIFU   The Buddha was still a young man when he left home and later became enlightened. Most of the Buddha's original disciples were young as well. However, there were a few elderly lay and monastic disciples. Mahakashyapa, one of the Buddha's greatest disciples and Buddhism's first patriarch, was an old man when he became a monk; and a great lay practitioner named Sudhatta was very old when he came in contact with the Buddha's teachings.

Just before the Buddha's death, the disciple named Subhadra, already past eighty, wished to visit the Buddha and hear his words. He knew that time was short, both for himself and for the Buddha, who was about to enter nirvana. Some of the Buddha's disciples tried to turn him away, saying, "You are already so old, what good would the teachings be for you? The Buddha's time is too precious to waste on one such as you."

The Buddha heard this and told his disciples to admit Subhadra, saying, "It is precisely because he is so old that he should hear these words." Subhadra entered the group and listened, and after hearing only a few phrases he attained arhatship. He was the last man to be ordained a monk in the Buddha's lifetime.

In the Chan sect, Master Zhaozhou (778-897), who is famous for the *gong'an*, "Does a dog have buddha-nature?" was eighteen years old when he had his first enlightenment experience. After that he studied under many masters to deepen his attainment, but he did not become a master himself until well into his eighties, when he began to accept disciples.

Buddhism makes no distinctions based on age. Karma can ripen at any time, and if one acquires the urge to practice, no matter what the age, that person should start practicing immediately and diligently. When one is old, it is even more urgent, because there is that much less time to practice. There are some physical differences. Usually, younger people will have greater endurance, strength, and energy. Older people have already expended a great deal of life energy and will be weaker in terms of the physical demands of practice.

Younger people, however, have their disadvantages.

They are usually attracted by many things in the environment, and are usually much more ambitious, wanting to accomplish things. Hence, there energy is often more scattered. Generally speaking, older people usually are not as ambitious or caught up in the world. They are more stable and may find it easier to approach the practice with a more focused single-mindedness.

STUDENT   What about people who have been practicing Buddhism and are now older? Should there be a difference in their approach to practice?

SHIFU   As practitioners get older, their practice should become more stable. There were likely many diversions when the practitioners were younger, making their practice inconsistent. There would have been times when practitioners had to put the practice aside to attend to other things. Assuming a solid foundation, practice should become more stable, with fewer interruptions, and older people will most likely not stray from the practice.

Of course, these are generalizations. As some get older, situations change in ways that make practice more difficult. A person may become ill or weak. On the other hand, some people get more energetic and high-spirited with age. The environment may change and disrupt their practice. If a retired person has practiced Buddhism as a side-interest all along, he or she may continue to consider it secondary, while filling his or her spare time with a new primary interest. Or, he or she may make practice the number-one priority.

Some people may have the wrong view of the Dharma right from the start. They think that practicing necessitates having some kind of experience. These people are not well grounded in Buddhadharma. As they get older, they might think, "This is for young people. I haven't had an experience yet, so it's ridiculous at my age to continue looking for one." Remember that practice is not limited to this lifetime. It continues, life after life, until one attains buddhahood. Even after buddhahood, one is always working hard, to benefit one's own practice and to benefit other sentient beings. The Buddha continued after his enlightenment for another forty years, working hard, helping sentient beings.

STUDENT   Isn't it also true that the proper attitude toward practice is not to be goal-oriented, but to view practice as a process? It is meditation itself that is worthwhile. In other words, the goal of meditation is meditation.

SHIFU   That is correct. We see this in the great practitioners of the past, none of whom had the attitude of practicing with the desire to experience something. They just practiced. One never knows when karmic obstructions will fall away. One person can practice for decades and not experience the dropping of karmic obstructions. Others, like Subhadra, only need to hear a few words for obstructions to disappear. You cannot predict such things, so you should just practice.

STUDENT   What attitude, then, should an older person have toward Buddhism and the practice?

SHIFU   There are no prescribed methods and answers. Some people maintain or increase their vigor as they get older. Others get weaker. There are people who have always been weak. We should not distinguish people by their age, but rather by their individual situation.

A 78-year-old man who attended a retreat thought he was in good health. I told him to take it easy, but he insisted on doing everything with the same intensity as the others. After he confessed that the retreat was taking its toll, I told him to "give rise to a sense of shame"—to contemplate one's frailty as a human being and to be aware of one's illusory self. The man followed my directions and his situation changed. No longer did he try to compete with the younger practitioners. He sat for hours at a time, in a settled manner with no pain or stress. Becoming clearly aware of his delusions, he cried, and after that his body was no longer an obstacle. Afterwards, he came to me, fatigued, saying that he felt he had accomplished what he had set out to do and that the retreat was over for him. I agreed and he went home.

On the other hand, a younger woman in poor health wanted to attend a retreat. I turned her down the first time, but the second time she convinced me that her health had improved, so I allowed her to come. In short time it became apparent that she was in terrible condition. I told her that she could do whatever she wanted: walk around, meditate, get up when she wanted, and rest when she wanted. She was disappointed, but she followed my instructions. After a while, a sense of shame arose spontaneously within her. On the fourth day, the sense of shame was so strong that she sat for half a day. In the afternoon when she came to me, her appearance had changed radically. Previously, she had had a pale, sickly, dispirited, worried look. Now, her face was bright, open and full of life. She said, "I feel like I've passed a test."

I answered, "You're right, you have. The retreat is over for you. You can go home now."

I relate these two stories to show that there is no clear distinction between young and old practitioners. It depends on the individual and on causes and conditions.

What about everyday life? Again, there is no difference. It is a mental problem, not a physical problem. You should practice in accordance with your health and vitality, not in accordance with your age. As long as you are not lazy and not diverted by other interests, practice should improve with age. Even if people engage in other activities, they should never lose sight of the practice. They should not partake in things so much that they forget about practice and the Dharma. If their minds are stable in this respect, their practice should improve.

Generally speaking, why do we put more emphasis on training younger people in the Dharma and on practicing with great effort and intensity? It is because the minds of the young are more easily scattered and diverted. Energetic practice keeps them busy and helps them to better channel and focus their energy.

In the end, physical frailty is just one more obstruction. The two greatest Japanese Zen masters, Dogen and Hakuin (1689-1769), were both men of poor health. Dogen died in his fifties after a prolonged lung disease. Hakuin was unfit physically, but, like Dogen, he became a great practitioner. It is clear, then, that people can practice, regardless of their age, health, or physical condition.

# Buddhism and
# Material Success

❧

QUESTION    Are material success and benefits a detriment to practice, or can they be of help?

SHIFU    Whether one has material wealth is not the issue. What is important is the attitude one has towards it, and how one handles it. The Bible says that it is easier for a camel to pass through the eye of a needle than for a rich man to enter the gates of Heaven. In Buddhist sutras there are no such sayings. On the contrary, there are numerous examples of wealthy and powerful people who were excellent practitioners. In Shakyamuni's time, wealthy people played an important role in supporting the Buddha. Some wealthy people, men and women alike, were both Dharma protectors and good practitioners. In fact, a few attained the third of the Four Fruition Levels of the arhat path, which means that their current life cycle in the realm of desire, which is the world as we know it, would be their last. They did not yet attain the fourth fruition because they did not take the monastic vows, but they did have the proper attitude toward material wealth.

From a Buddhist point of view, the proper understanding of material success is that everything in the world belongs to you, and nothing belongs to you. Some things belong to you in a conventional sense, but it is only a consequence of your karma. You are simply in charge of these possessions for the time being, and you have an obligation to handle them well. On a grand scale, one can say that the entire Earth is a possession of all sentient beings. But it is not ours to keep and abuse. It is ours to care for, to honor, and to pass on to future generations.

With the proper attitude, wealthy people are in a good position to help the Dharma. They can make beneficial use of their possessions. Shakyamuni Buddha stayed in the homes of several wealthy people, including kings; and he was a member of royalty himself.

If you are rich and accept the that wealth belongs to all sentient beings, perhaps you will think, "I'll give all my money away to whomever is around and needs it." That is not the correct thing to do, since this may be wasteful. Good judgment should be part of such decisions. Wise people will know how best to use their wealth; others will not. People with wisdom and wealth handle their possessions in a planned manner and follow prescribed principles. It takes a wise person to properly handle wealth.

Wise and wealthy people will not frivolously give away their wealth. It is all right for wealthy people to stay wealthy. Buddhism does not advocate poverty or communism. On the other hand, Buddhists should not say, "Everything that is mine absolutely belongs to me. I will use any means to protect my possessions." Buddhism encourages people to make offerings and help others. Strict capitalism, where people try to accumulate as much wealth as possible, is not in accordance with the Dharma. It is also quite destructive.

There are other attitudes toward wealth that can be detrimental, such as thinking of material wealth as a guarantee of personal security, or as a symbol of success, achievement, and status. People with these attitudes will try to accumulate as much wealth as possible. If they have a thousand dollars, they will want ten thousand. When they have tens of thousands, they will want millions. They will want to accumulate for themselves as well as their descendants. They hope their children and grandchildren will keep their wealth and, in fact, help it to grow. They constantly think of ways to enhance their material wealth, and worry about losing what they already have. With so much on their minds, they have little time for anything else, least of all spiritual practice.

Furthermore, such people have a deep impression that money is hard to come by, so they are reluctant to part with it, to help others. The idea of accumulating more and more of anything is contrary to practice. The opposite attitude, being careless and reckless with one's possessions, is also contrary to practice, and irresponsible. The sutras encourage people to make good use of what they have, and to be able to do without. You should not depend too much on your wealth or derive all your pleasure from such wealth. You should learn to be content in any and all situations.

There is a story concerning the famous Chan practitioner, Layman Pang, who was supposedly, very wealthy.

After enlightenment, he took all his wealth—gold, silver, jewels—loaded it in a boat and dumped it in a river. His family ended up with not even a house to live in. They survived by weaving and selling baskets. People asked, "Why didn't you give your money to the needy?" Layman Pang replied, "I didn't want to harm anyone. If you give people wealth, they will likely create a lot of bad karma. If, instead, you tell them to practice, they will gain true wealth." The story is probably fabricated, but it makes a good point: it is best to have few desires, to live simply and be content.

If you are materially wealthy, you are potentially adding to your burden of responsibilities. It takes time and energy to accumulate and manage possessions. There will be less time for practice. However, if you see yourself as being the guardian of your wealth, wealth that really belongs to all sentient beings, then you can practice well. You will see wealth as something to be used without attachment, without a sense of gain or loss.

You need not be afraid of having or accumulating wealth, nor should you overly indulge in the pleasures brought about by wealth. Use what you have with restraint, help those in need, and support the Three Jewels—Buddha, Dharma and Sangha.

# *Is Enlightenment Lasting?*

QUESTION   Some people who have seen their intrinsic self-nature—who have experienced *kensho*—say that they continue to have vexations. Does *kensho* have any lasting effect, or does the benefit eventually recede, leaving practitioners where they started?

SHIFU   Seeing into one's nature is seeing into the nature of emptiness, seeing that there is nothing to be attached to. It is realizing that the four forms described in the *Diamond Sutra*—forms of self, forms of others, forms of life, forms of sentient beings—are all empty. It is realizing that the four views—that of eternity, bliss, self, and purity, are erroneous and inverted. These four views are common attachments for ordinary sentient beings, whether they are practitioners or not. People want to believe in immortality, in an unchanging self that will continue through eternity, either in some form of heaven, or in another life. They believe that such a state will be eternally blissful, but they are defining bliss from their own experience, which is one of attachment. They believe that this state, where an unchanging self enjoys the bliss of eternal life, will be one of purity—no more suffering or defilement. However, when people speak of purity or impurity, it is usually from the perspective of physical enjoyment in the realm of desire.

Most people, including serious practitioners, cling to these four inverted views. People with such attachments have not truly seen into their intrinsic nature. It is a fundamental Mahayana principle that nothing is permanent or absolute. There is no eternal self, and there is no absolute bliss or purity. This is stated very clearly in the *Heart Sutra* and in the *Diamond Sutra*. There are no distinctions between eternity and impermanence, self and others, happiness and suffering, purity and impurity. If, in your practice, there is still attachment to any of these inverted views, then you have not truly experienced *kensho*, at least not deep *kensho*.

Some people may think, then, that there is no such thing as seeing into one's nature, or that it is impossible to experience *kensho*. It is definitely possible to experience *kensho*, but it depends on the practitioner, and it depends on the master who is providing guidance. If a master keeps a tight watch over the gate of Chan, time and again turning practitioners away, telling them that they have not yet entered, then at a certain point they will have no more expectations; there will no longer be an urge to seek enlightenment. They will just practice diligently. In such a situation, practitioners will be more likely to experience genuine *kensho*. But after the experience, what? When you experience *kensho*, you have not seen anything or attained anything. You realize that what you have seen in the past and what you are seeing now are identical, except that now there is no self involved.

With a few questions, a good master can determine if a student's report of experiencing self-nature is genuine. A lesser master, however, can be deceived. In most cases, such experiences are not genuine. Rather, they are psychological and physiological responses that arise during the practice. Again, I must stress that it takes a very good master to determine the validity of an experience.

As to vexations, they do not disappear after you experience *kensho*. They will continue to manifest as they always have. The difference is, after genuine *kensho*, you will be more aware of your vexations. You will know when vexations are about to arise. When you are in the midst of vexation, you will know your situation very clearly. It is as if there is a separate person keeping constant watch, always alert.

People who have not seen their true nature will often find themselves buried in vexation, and they will complain about their predicament. People who have seen their true nature, however, will not have this problem. They will be aware of vexations rising, and none of their vexations will be very great. In this sense, from the point of view of vexations, a person who has experienced *kensho* is much better off than one who has not.

STUDENT   Isn't it possible to see vexations rising and to know that you are in the midst of vexation without having seen your original nature?

SHIFU   It is not the same. People who have not seen their intrinsic nature are not clearly aware of their vexations. They might be able to recognize obvious vexations, but they would not be aware of the milder, subtler vexations. People who have experienced *kensho* recognize anything that involves self-attachment. It is an immediate, direct awareness. People who have not experienced *kensho* might recognize large vexations, but it is through a rational process, not through direct awareness.

Sometimes people believe that they have seen their true nature. They may even guide others in practice, believing that they are now teachers or masters, but in their own lives, they continue to indulge desire, or break the precepts. Others might question them saying, "Master, if you know these are bad habits, why do you continue?" They might answer, "Yes, I have these habits, but being enlightened, I am not attached to them." Do they know something we do not? People who have truly seen their intrinsic nature may have many desires, but before the desires overtake them, they will recognize what is happening and check themselves.

Some people feel that they have as many vexations after *kensho* as they did before. They feel that the results are not worth the effort. These people do not have the correct understanding of *kensho*. Seeing into one's true nature does not necessarily eliminate vexations. It only makes you aware of what your vexations are. To offer an analogy, a person searches for a mountain, but it is hidden in clouds and darkness. Suddenly, the sky brightens and clears, and the summit is visible. The person is happy because he or she has seen the mountain, but it is still far away. There is still much work to be done. Seeing the mountain is like seeing into one's intrinsic nature. Some people succeed in seeing the mountain without much practice, but to reach the peak requires great effort.

Some people practice long and hard and never see the mountain, not knowing that they are very close, even in the foothills. Then with a gentle nudge or the slightest guidance, they suddenly realize that they are already there. This is the equivalent of deep enlightenment. It is rare, but it demonstrates that there are many levels of enlightenment.

Seeing the mountain, even if it is still far away, is good. People with such insight will practice with more conviction and greater faith. They will understand what vexations are, and they will understand what selflessness is. Their understanding will not come from their intellect, but through direct awareness.

There is no rule as to how long you must practice before seeing your true nature, and there is no rule as to how long the effects will last. If you have been practicing a long time, then the effects may last a while, in the sense that vexations will not arise and the feeling of selflessness will persist. But it is possible that the experience will be brief—like a flash, and its effects short-lived. Rather than the clouds parting and the sky clearing, it would be like a bolt of lightning revealing the mountain for an instant, and then disappearing, leaving the traveler in darkness again. But at least, one has seen the mountain.

Depending on one's karma and strength of practice, enlightenment experiences may be shallow or deep. What is the relationship between seeing into one's intrinsic nature (*kensho*) and enlightenment? The first enlightenment experience is called 'seeing self-nature,' but subsequent enlightenment experiences are not described in this way. Each successive enlightenment experience gets deeper. For this reason, the Caodong (Soto) sect describes five different levels of attainment.

Also, from the Ming Dynasty onward, the Linji (Rinzai) sect speaks of three barriers of attainment. The first barrier is equivalent to seeing into one's intrinsic nature for the first time. The second barrier is the multiple barrier, at which you experience enlightenment over and over, gradually eliminating vexations and revealing wisdom. The experience of no-self remains longer each time.

The third barrier is the prison barrier, the equivalent of thorough enlightenment. Here, you break out of the prison of samsara, transcending the cycle of birth and death. It is as if everything has disappeared—the universe and the self. It is said that at this point even the king of the underworld, who is in charge of life and death, cannot find you. If feelings of self and attachment return, then it is not thorough enlightenment. There is still a self, and the king of the underworld will be able to find you.

Do not place much emphasis on seeing your self-nature—place your emphasis on just practicing. Do not waste time fantasizing about the 'ultimate experience.' On the other hand, it is not easy to see into one's true nature, so do not be lazy or apathetic in your practice.

Be wary of the master who confirms a lot of so-called enlightenment experiences. Sometimes a master gives false confirmation. This is not only true today; it has been happening frequently since the Ming Dynasty. Since that time, there has been an apt phrase to describe false confirmation—'the seal made from winter melon.' When a master confirms an enlightenment experience, it is like giving a Dharma seal, called *inka* in Zen. A seal should be made of diamond or jade, something enduring. A seal made from the winter melon, however, is flimsy and transient.

Inappropriate confirmations reflect the lack of skill and insight of Chan masters. Perhaps the masters have not truly seen their own original nature. Or perhaps they are mediocre practitioners who still have many vexations. Attachments influence some masters negatively, leading them to confirm experiences that are not genuine enlightenment. Maybe they are ambitious, desiring more disciples to increase their power in the Buddhist community, and their chances of having Dharma descendants. Such masters are using the seal of a winter melon, or worse, the seal of soft tofu. Really, how many disciples a master has does not matter; a few very dedicated practitioners are enough. If a master has no Dharma descendants, all it means is that his or her lineage will end. It is of no great consequence. Bodhidharma, the first patriarch of Chan, had only four Dharma heirs, three men and one woman.

In earlier times, masters who gave false confirmations were sharply criticized. They were called weak generals. Strong generals protect the 'gate' well; they do not allow people to sneak past them. They cannot be bribed, and they are not easily fooled. Only those who are strong can pass. Weak generals, on the other hand, are not steadfast and vigilant.

False confirmations are unfortunate, especially for practitioners, who would find it difficult to progress further if they thought they had already seen their true nature. And, should they discover that their experiences were not genuine, they may lose faith in Buddhadharma.

STUDENT    Can people who have seen their true nature feel worse afterward because they are more aware of their vexations? Before the experience they were ignorant of their vexations, so there was nothing to be upset about.

SHIFU    That is not the case. If you are aware of your vexations, it follows that you will be less attached to them. To be aware of vexations means that you understand your condition as an ordinary sentient being. Because you understand that it is natural for sentient beings to have vexations, you will not be upset by your own.

STUDENT    Do people who have seen their intrinsic nature have more control over themselves and their vexations?

SHIFU    We can only say that people who have seen their intrinsic nature have greater faith in themselves and their practice. They know that having vexations is normal for sentient beings, but they have faith that, through practice, vexations will lessen and disappear.

STUDENT    Do false masters knowingly deceive others, or do they really think they are good masters?

SHIFU    Both cases are possible. There are those who truly believe they are good masters, even though they are not, and there are those who are aware of their mediocrity, yet they continue deceiving others because they desire fame or wealth.

STUDENT    By what standard and whose judgment is a master considered good or bad?

SHIFU    Sometimes it manifests in the form of a double standard, where masters teach one way but practice and live another. It is not serious if masters sometimes demonstrate some bad habits, as long as they are aware of their actions. After all, they are still ordinary sentient beings. If a master were to say "This is the way of a Chan master," or "I'm a bodhisattva, so I can act this way in order to help others," that is a different story. It is also not good if a master gives preferential treatment to certain practitioners; a master should treat everyone equally, although not identically.

Remember, though, it works both ways. If practitioners travel from center to center looking for weaknesses in masters just so they can say, "This one's no good, that one's no good," then they also are behaving wrongly. Preoccupying oneself with a master's virtues and weaknesses is not a good attitude. It is also a waste of time and energy.

# *Glossary*

❧

**Agamas**   The collections of early Buddhist teachings. The *Agamas* are distinguished as: *Dirghagama* (long discourses), *Madhyamagama* (medium discourses), *Samyuktagama* (miscellaneous discourses), and *Ekottaragama* (numerical discourses).

**Alaya**   See **Eight Consciousnesses**.

**Amitabha Sutra**   The principle scripture on which the Pure Land practice is based. Reciting Amitabha Buddha's name is the most accessible and simplest form of Buddhist practice. According to the Pure Land teaching, through Amitabha Buddha's vow, any person who sincerely invokes his name and expresses the wish will be reborn in the Pure Land of Amitabha, also known as the Western Paradise. The Pure Land is a place of bliss, but should not be confused with nirvana, which is a higher state.

**Anuttara-samyak-sambodhi**   Unexcelled perfect enlightenment of the buddhas.

**Arhat**   "Worthy one." In Buddhism, the arhat is thought of as having completed the course of Buddhist practice and attained liberation, or nirvana. As such, the arhat is no longer subject to rebirth and death. Arhat is also one of the ten epithets of the Buddha. See **Ten Epithets of the Buddha.**

**Asamskrita**   Lit. "unconditioned." The term refers to a state of mind that is not caused or influenced by phenomena, therefore, free from any kind of karmic future, or "outflow."

As such, it is the opposite of samskrita. See **Samskrita** .

**Asura** One of the types of beings in the six realms of existence. Asuras, sometimes translated as "titans," are beings who have the merit to travel to the heavenly realms but are afflicted with jealousy of the heavenly devas, or gods.

**Avalokitesvara** Perhaps the most important bodhisattva in Asian Buddhism. The embodiment of compassion who hears and responds to the cries of all living beings, Avalokitesvara is depicted as either male or female. In China, Avalokitesvara (Guanyin) is usually depicted in the female form. In Zen the bodhisattva is known as Kanzeon or Kannon, in Tibetan Buddhism as Chenresig or Chenrezi.

*Avatamsaka Sutra* see *Huayan Jing*

*Avici* The last of the eight hells in which suffering continues without interruption. Once the retribution exhausts, the individual is reborn somewhere else.

❧

**Bhikshu/Bhikshuni** Fully ordained Buddhist monk and nun, respectively.

*Bhumi* The *bhumis* (ground, regions, or stages) are the ten stages of the bodhisattva's path to full buddhahood.

**Bodhi** Lit. "awakened." The principal wisdom that severs all vexations and defilements and realizes nirvana, or the wisdom that realizes the truth of every conditioned phenomenon.

**Bodhi-mind**   The mind of wisdom, a central idea in Mahayana Buddhism. The meaning of the word varies by context: 1) The arousal of altruistic mind which aspires to buddhahood for the sake of sentient beings, 2) the actual realization of enlightenment as an awakening to the true nature of reality, 3) selfless action, a meaning extremely important, yet often overlooked.

**Bodhisattva**   Lit. "enlightened being." The role model in the Mahayana tradition. The bodhisattva is a being who vows to remain in the world of samsara, postponing his/her own full liberation until all other living beings are delivered.

**Buddha**   Lit. "awakened one." Generically, a buddha is a completely enlightened sentient being. The specific historical Buddha is the religious teacher, the Indian Sakyamuni Gautama, who founded Buddhism as we know it.

**Buddhadharma**   See **Dharma**

**Buddha-nature**   The nature or potentiality for buddhahood, synonym for the "nature of emptiness."

❧

**Caodong (Wade-Giles: Ts'ao-tung, Zen: Soto)**   One of the two major "sudden enlightnment" schools of Chan to survive to the present, stressing silent-illumination practice (*shikantaza*) over *gong'an* practice, but not exclusively. The other surviving major school of Chan is the Linji (Wade-

Giles: Lin-chi, Zen: Rinzai). See **Linji.**

**Chan (Zen)**   Chan is one of the main schools of Chinese Buddhism to develop during the T'ang Dynasty (618-907). The designation derives from the Sanskrit *dhyana*, transliterated as *chan-na* in Chinese, and as *zen* in Japanese. Chan can mean meditation, but it can also mean enlightenment. See **Dhyana**.

**Deva**   Lit. "shining one." A sentient being who dwells in one of the six realms of rebirth, the godly, which is free from suffering but still subject to rebirth. The five other realms are the human, the jealous gods, the animal, the hungry ghosts, and hell.

**Dharma**   By convention, 'Dharma' (upper case) refers to the teachings of the Buddha (Buddhadharma), while 'dharma' (lower case) can refer to a thing, an object, an event, any physical or mental phenomenon. In Sanskrit, with no upper or lower case, the specific meaning is determined by context.

*Dharmadhatu*   The dharma realm, the infinite realms or worlds of reality; it can also be regarded as the ground or nature of all things.

**Dharma Ending Age**   A period of time when the teaching of the Buddha is weak, and although there may be practitioners, no one is able to gain realization.

**Dhyana**   Sanskrit for certain states of meditative

absorption cultivated as a technique for attaining enlightenment. In some sutras, dhyana refers to a practice after enlightenment, in which one solely cultivates the non-dualistic,
quiescent, and still nature of mind. 'Chan' and 'Zen' are the
Chinese and Japanese transliterations of dhyana, respectively.

**Diamond Sutra**  Sk: *Vajracchedika-sutra*. A sutra belonging
to the *Prajnaparamita* (*Perfection of Wisdom*) system of
literature, which expounds the ultimate truth of emptiness.
With the *Heart Sutra*, it is one of the most important
scriptures in the Mahayana tradition.

❧

**Eight consciousnesses**  A central idea in the Yogacara
(Mind-Only) School of Buddhism, which understands
consciousness as having eight modes of operation. These
eight modes are further divided into three categories:

*1)*  *Vijnana*, referring to the first five sense consciousnesses
(the "knowing" that arises from contact between the
sense faculties and their corresponding sense objects),
plus the sixth sense consciousness, the faculty of mental
discrimination (*manovijnana*)

*2)*  *Manas*, referring to the seventh consciousness, that of
the sense of self

*3)*  *Citta*, referring to the eighth consciousness, the *alaya* or
store-house consciousness.

The first six consciousnesses are named after the sense
faculties that serve as their support: 1) eye consciousness,
2) ear consciousness, 3) nose consciousness, 4) tongue

consciousness, 5) body consciousness, and 6) mind consciousness. The sixth consciousness, our ordinary mind, is characterized by discrimination and has all dharmas as its object. It utilizes the previous five consciousnesses in order to identify, interpret, and define the world. The seventh consciousness is the source of the belief in a separate self; it takes the eighth consciousness as its support and its object of attachment. It can also be said to be the center of these eight consciousnesses. The eighth consciousness operates as the underlying continuum of the mind's workings and functions, on which delusion is ultimately based. It is a "repository" or "storehouse" that contains all experiences as karmically-charged "seeds," which ripen under the proper causes and conditions as acts of body, speech and mind. These acts in turn create new seeds. Therefore, the eighth consciousness is unceasingly conditioned by the previous seven consciousnesses. When one is thoroughly enlightened, these consciousnesses become the function of wisdom.

**Eighteen realms**  The eighteen realms collectively refer to the domains of the six sense faculties (sight, sound, smell, taste, body, and mind), which in contact with their corresponding six sense objects, results in the six sense consciousnesses.

**Eightfold Noble Path**  The Eightfold Noble Path was expounded by the Buddha at his first sermon, in which he gave the teachings of the Four Noble Truths to his five disciple-friends. As an extension of the fourth noble truth (the way out of suffering), the Eightfold Noble Path consists of right view, right determination, right speech, right conduct, right livelihood, right effort, right mindfulness, and right concentration (meditation).

❦

**Five Skandhas**   The Five Skandhas (heaps or aggregrates) are the factors that operate together to make up a sentient being: form, sensation, perception, volition, and consciousness. The first skandha, form, is the material factor; the remaining four are mental in nature. Buddhism holds that, since the Five Skandhas lack permanence, and have no enduring reality, the sentient being they comprise is also lacking in self-nature.

**Four fruitions of the arhat path**   The four progressive stages or fruition levels of a practitioner on the way to arhatship are: 1) the stream winner who has entered the stream of enlightenment; 2) the once-returner who will experience one more cycle of rebirth, 3) the non-returner who will be reborn as a deva, or deity, in the heavenly realm; and 4) the arhat, an enlightened being liberated from samsara (the cycle of birth and death).

**Four Great Vows**   The Four Great Vows of the bodhisattva are: I vow to save all sentient beings. I vow to cut of all vexations. I vow to master all approaches to the Dharma. I vow to achieve supreme buddhahood.

**Four Noble Truths**   The four basic principles preached by Buddha in his first sermon: 1) existence is marked by suffering, 2) the cause of suffering is ignorance, 3) there is a way out of suffering, and 4) the way out of suffering is the Eightfold Noble Path. See **Eightfold Noble Path**.

❦

***Gong'an* (Zen: koan)**   Lit. "public case." A Chan method of meditation in which the practitioner energetically and single-mindedly pursues the answer to an enigmatic question usually posed by the master. The question can be answered only by abandoning logic and reasoning and through directly generating and breaking through the "doubt sensation" under natural causes and conditions. Famous *gong'an* encounters were recorded and used by masters to test their disciples' understanding, or they served as a catalyst for enlightenment. The term, *gong'an* is often used interchangeably with the term *huatou*.

❦

***Heart Sutra***   One of the most important sutras of Mahayana Buddhism, which expounds the meaning of emptiness, or the absence of self-nature in sentient beings.

**Hinayana**   The Hinayana is the path of individual enlightenment or liberation, as distinct from the Mahayana path, in which one postpones enlightenment and practices for the good of all sentient beings. The early Mahayana practitioners used the term 'Hinayana' to distinguish themselves from the earlier schools of Buddhism. It is not a term used by practitioners of early Buddhism, including the Theravadin, to their own practice. See **Mahayana**.

***Huatou*** Lit. "source of words" (before they are uttered), a method used in the Chan School to arouse the "doubt sensation." The practitioner meditates on such baffling questions as: "What is nothingness?" "Where am I?" or "Who is reciting the Buddha's name?" In this practice, one does not rely on experience, logic, or reasoning. Often, these phrases are taken from *gong'an*; at other times, they are spontaneously generated by the practitioner. The term *huatou* is often used interchangeably with the Japanese koan.

***Huayan*** One of the most influential schools of Chinese Buddhism of the T'ang dynasty (618-907). Based on the *Avatamsaka Sutra (Huayan Jing)*, the fundamental teaching of this school is the equality of all things, and the unobstructed interpenetration of, and interrelation between, absolute reality and all phenomena.

***Huayan jing*** Chinese name for the *Avatamsaka (Flower Adornment) Sutra*, a massive Mahayana Buddhist sutra translated from Sanskrit into Chinese in the fifth, seventh, and late eighth centuries. The sutra was popular among Chinese Buddhists, who believed that it was a revelation from the Buddha's enlightenment while he was in samadhi under the bodhi tree. The sutra has always been held in high regard among Chan sects, and became the basis of the Huayan School of Chan. See **Huayan.**

❧

**Karma** Lit. "action." Basically, the law of cause and effect to which all sentient beings are subject. Karma is broadly construed in Buddhism to include physical, verbal, and mental actions. It is also the cumulative causal situation affecting one's destiny as a result of past acts, thoughts, and emotions.

**Kensho**  Zen term for the first enlightenment experience, in which one perceives one's own true self-nature as "empty," devoid of fixed reality.

**Koan**  See *Gong'an.*

🌢

**Linji (Wade-Giles: Lin-chi, Zen: Rinzai)**  One of the two major schools of Chan to survive to the present, stressing *gong'an* practice, over silent illumination (*shikantaza*), but not exclusively. It is however, in the tradition of sudden enlightenment Chan. The other surviving major school of Chan is the Caodong. See **Caodong.**

**Lotus Sutra**  In Sanskrit, *Saddharmapundarika-sutra (Sutra of the Lotus of the True Dharma)*. One of the most influential scriptures in the Mahayana, translated six times into Chinese between 255-601 A.D., the *Lotus Sutra* describes the bodhisattva ideal and holds that the perfect vehicle to ultimate liberation is the Mahayana.

🌢

**Madhyamika**  Lit. "the middle way." A Mahayana school founded by Nagarjuna and his followers. The core teaching of Madhyamika stresses dependent origination and emptiness based on the *Prajanaparamita* system of thought.

**Mahayana**  Lit. "great vehicle," whose followers vow to follow the bodhisattva path for the sake of delivering all sentient beings from suffering. See **Hinayana**.

✦

*Nidanas*  See **Twelve Links of Conditioned Arising.**

**Nirvana**  Total extinction of desire and suffering, the state of liberation through full enlightenment.

**No-self**  Buddhism's central teaching that there is no independently existing entity that can be called the self; that the self is mental construct derived from the moment-to-moment stream of perceptual experience.

✦

**Paramitas**  Lit "perfections," or ways for transcendence to liberation. The six paramitas are the main practices of Mahayana bodhisattvas: giving (*dana*), morality (*sila*), patience (*ksanti*), diligence (*virya*), meditation (*dhyana*), and wisdom (*prajna*). The ten paramitas, practiced by bodhisattvas, consist of the six paramitas plus four others: expedient means (*upayakausalya*), vows (*pranidhana*), power (*bala*), and all-knowing wisdom (*jnana*).

*Platform Sutra*  A scripture attributed to the seventh century Chan master, Huineng (638-713), who was the sixth patriarch of Chan, and perhaps the most famous of the Chinese patriarchs. He was the founder of the Southern School of Chan, which emphasized sudden enlightenment.

**Pratyekabuddha**  A self-enlightened being who has attained liberation from all suffering by contemplating dependent origination.

**Precepts**  The five basic precepts, or guidelines for Buddhist behavior, are: 1) not to kill, 2) not to steal, 3) not to engage in sexual misconduct, 4) not to lie, and 5) not to take intoxicants. There are the eight precepts for laypersons and prospective monks or nuns, which are the Five Precepts plus 6) not wearing jewelry or perfumes, not singing and dancing, and not watching entertainment, 7) not sleeping on a raised bed, and 8) not eating after the noon meal. For those taking the bodhisattva precepts, there are ten major and forty-eight minor precepts, not listed here.

**Preta**  Lit. "departed one," one who exists in the realm of the hungry ghosts, one of the six realms of rebirth. Pretas are characterized as beings suffering from greed, jealousy, and envy. See **Deva.**

**Pure Land**  The Land of Supreme Bliss (Sanskrit: *sukhavati*), or the Western Paradise of Amitabha Buddha. It is a pure realm that came into existence due to the vows of Amitabha Buddha. Anyone who sincerely invokes his name and expresses the wish to be born there will be reborn in the Pure Land.

❧

**Sangha**  Lit. "crowd" or "host." There are three significant meanings to the word. First, the Sangha is one of the Three Jewels of Buddhism, along with the Buddha and the Dharma.

In this sense, Sangha refers to the abstract entity of all those who have devoted their lives to the teaching of the Dharma. Second, sangha can refer to a specific community of monks or nuns, such as in a monastery. Third, sangha can refer to the Buddhist community at large, including monks, nuns, and laypersons.

**Sastras**  Scriptures written by patriarchs of Buddhism usually consisting either of theoretical syntheses of other scriptures, or commentaries on sutras.

**Samadhi**  Like dhyana, samadhi refers to states of meditative absorption, but it is a broader and more generic term than dhyana. Although numerous specific samadhis are mentioned in Buddhist scriptures, the term samadhi itself is flexible and not as specific as dhyana. In Mahayana sutras, the term samadhi is inseparable from wisdom, or prajna.

**Samsara**  Lit. "journeying." The relentless cycle of birth and death and suffering in which ordinary, unenlightened sentient beings are deeply entangled. There are three realms within samsara: the desire realm, the form realm, and the formless realm.

**Samskrita**  Lit. "conditioned." The term refers to all dharmas (including our actions, words, and thoughts) that are subject to arising, subsiding, and passing away, in other words, conditioned, and producing karmic results, i.e., "with outflows."

**Sastra**  Generally, a commentary on a sutra, or a treatise based on existing sutras.

**Shakyamuni** Lit. "sage of the Shakya." The honorific given to Siddhartha (given name) Gautama (surname) of the Shakya (clan), as a tribute to his dedicated search for enlightenment. This name is also used to distinguish him among other buddhas as the historical Shakyamuni Buddha who lived and taught in India around 600 BCE. Shakyamuni is also distinguished from Maitreya Buddha, who is said to be the next buddha to appear in this world.

**Sravaka** One who has heard the teachings of the Buddha; also, a follower of the lesser vehicle (Hinayana).

**Sutra** Generally, scripture. Specifically, a recorded "open" teaching of the Buddha that can be practiced by anyone. The distinctive mark of a Buddhist sutra is the opening line, "Thus have I heard." This indicates that what follows are the direct teachings of Buddha, as remembered and recorded by his disciples. See **Sastra.**

❧

**Ten epithets of a Buddha** Thus-come, Worthy of Offering, Right and Universal Knowledge, Perfect Clarity and Conduct, Understanding the World, Unsurpassable Worthy One, Instructor of People, Teacher of Heavenly and Human Beings, Buddha, the World Honored One.

**Three Jewels (Sanskrit: *triratna*)** The Buddha, the Dharma, and the Sangha, collectively the "crown jewels" of Buddhism, so to speak. As such, fealty to the Three Jewels is the highest aspiration that Buddhists may undertake. In fact, to begin the Buddhist path, one ordinarily undergoes the ceremony of taking refuge in the Three Jewels. See **Three Refuges.**

**Three Refuges**  Buddhists customarily enter the path by taking the Three Refuges, a ceremony in which they declare themselves as taking refuge in the Three Jewels. The essence of the ceremony, conducted by qualified Buddhist teacher, is that the refuge taker pronounces three times, "I take refuge in the Buddha. I take refuge in the Dharma. I take refuge in the Sangha." See **Three Jewels.**

**Twelve Entrances**  The six sense faculties together with the six sense objects, or "dust." See **Eighteen Realms and Eight Consciousnesses.**

**Twelve Links of Conditioned Arising**  The Twelve Links of Conditioned Arising (*nidanas*) are stages of *samsara* connecting one cycle of birth and death to the next. They are: 1) fundamental ignorance, 2) action, 3) consciousness, 4) name and form, 5) the six entries or sense faculties, 6) contact, 7) sensation, 8) desire or craving, 9) grasping, 10) existence or becoming, 11) birth, and 12) old age and death. See **Samsara.**

❧

**Vexation**  Sk.: *klesa*. The innate mechanism to possess and to act, tainted by an attachment to self, which in turn continues the cycle of samsara. Vexations include all kinds of mental states such as joy and resentment, sadness and happiness, as well as greed, hatred, delusion, arrogance and doubt.

**Wisdom**   In Buddhism, wisdom or *prajna,* is the state of mind in which one directly perceives the true nature of phenomena and existence as impermanent and void of self-identity.

**Yogacara**   The Mahayana doctrine, referred to as Mind-Only, which posits that everything is a construction of the mind. Maitreya Bodhisattva is often regarded as the founder of this school. Asanga and his brother Vasubandhu developed the school in the first half of the fifth century.